For the Lost Sheep
(I)

For the Lost Sheep
(I)

PAUL C. JONG

Hephzibah Publishing House
A Ministry of THE NEW LIFE MISSION
SEOUL, KOREA

For the Lost Sheep (I)

Scripture quotations are from *the New King James Version.*

ISBN 89-8314-705-9
Cover Art by Min-soo Kim
Illustration by Young-ae Kim
Printed in Korea

Hephzibah Publishing House
A Ministry of THE NEW LIFE MISSION
P.O.Box 18 Yang-Cheon Post Office
Yang-Cheon Gu, Seoul, Korea

♠ Website: http://www.nlmission.com
http://www.bjnewlife.org
♠ E-mail: newlife@bjnewlife.org
♠ Phone: 82(Korea)-11-1788-2954

Table of Contents

The sin of the world

Preface

One must present the gospel of the water and the Spirit if told to present the Truth of salvation for sheep who have spiritually gone astray. The gospel of the water and the Spirit consists of Jesus' baptism and His death on the Cross, and it is the basic Truth that achieves salvation from sin. We must believe that Jesus eternally saved us from the sins of this world. He made us whole forever through the baptism He received and through His blood. Sinners must believe in the fact below in order to be saved from their sins: God's righteousness was fulfilled when Jesus was baptized by John the Baptist. Now, whosoever believes in the gospel of the water and the Spirit will be saved.

Do you have sin?

When a person confesses their sins, God then tells him that Jesus already took away all his sins through His baptism 2,000 years ago. So, this person confirms that he has no sins in his heart, even though he is insufficient. No one who believes in Jesus' baptism and blood has sins in his heart. Of people who believe in Jesus' baptism and His blood of the Cross, none of them has sin. I invite you who have spiritually lost your way to return to the gospel of the water and the Spirit.

Then, how can you resolve the problem of sins you will commit in the future?

In 1 John 2:1-2, it says, *"My little children, these things I write to you, so that you may not sin. And if anyone sins, we have an Advocate with the Father, Jesus Christ the righteous.*

And He Himself is the propitiation for our sins, and not for ours only but also for the whole world." I can clearly tell people who have spiritually lost their way that they will have no sins if they believe in the gospel of the water and the Spirit.

You would have probably discovered that you had unstable faith and emotions even if you offered prayers of repentance for your sins everyday. I ask you a question: "Are you a sinless Christian or a Christian sinner?" I do not wander anymore now that I have found the blessed gospel of the water and the Spirit. I am free now that I have been saved from all my sins. I can tell you that there is no need to offer prayers of repentance everyday because of original sin or personal sins.

You will now come in contact with the gospel of the water and the Spirit. I hope that you will meet with the Lord's righteousness by faith like I did.

Hallelujah! ⌧

Sermon

1

Must We Go and Wash In the Pool of Siloam?

< John 9:1-12 >

"Now as Jesus passed by, He saw a man who was blind from birth. And His disciples asked Him, saying, 'Rabbi, who sinned, this man or his parents, that he was born blind?' Jesus answered, 'Neither this man nor his parents sinned, but that the works of God should be revealed in him. I must work the works of Him who sent Me while it is day; the night is coming when no one can work. As long as I am in the world, I am the light of the world.' When He had said these things, He spat on the ground and made clay with the saliva; and He anointed the eyes of the blind man with the clay. And He said to him, 'Go, wash in the pool of Siloam' (which is translated, Sent). So he went and washed, and came back seeing. Therefore the neighbors and those who previously had seen that he was blind said, 'Is not this he who sat and begged?" Some said, "This is he.' Others said, 'He is like him.' He said, 'I am he.' Therefore they said to him, 'How were your eyes opened?' He answered and said, 'A Man called Jesus made clay and anointed my eyes and said to me, 'Go to the pool of Siloam and wash.' So I went and washed, and I received sight." Then they said to him, 'Where is He?' He said, 'I do not know.'"

These Scripture passages speak of Jesus, as He was passing by, coming across a man who was blind from birth and making his eyes open.

A blind person would feel immensely stifled and stuffy for not being able to see what is in front. This man mentioned in today's Scripture passage was blind from birth, so from a fleshly perspective, don't you think that his life was so very cursed? Being born blind from birth, it must have been very hard on him in itself. Yet, the disciples went so far as asking, "Rabbi, who sinned, this man or his parents, that he was born blind?" Then, how deeply was he hurt by such words? However, the disciples of Jesus and the people near by asked Jesus carelessly about the cause of his blindness as if that was none of his business. He didn't become blind because he wanted to, yet he has to live a stifling life for the rest of his life. And so, if has the understanding that he has to go on living as a blind all through his life because of his parent's sins, because of a certain person, or because of someone else, this blind man would perhaps go on living resenting that person all through his life. Anyway, the stifled feeling the blind person has to go through because of people's finger pointing must be so great that it cannot be put into words.

Why Are Human Beings Born as the Spiritual Blind?

The Lord said, *"Neither this man nor his parents sinned, but that the works of God should be revealed in him," (John 9:3)*. This means that he had become blind in order to reveal the works of God. Thus, all that the blind man has to do is to see what sort of work God wants to reveal, instead of resenting his parents or someone else.

Then, what does the passage that states this blind man had

to have been born as a blind from birth mean? This passage means that it was the will of God for everyone to be born fundamentally as a sinner when he or she is born onto this earth. The Bible says that everyone is born as a sinner from birth just as everyone has become a sinner because of the sin of one man, Adam (Romans 5:12). Therefore, what else could a sinner be except a spiritual blind fundamentally? How stifling is it to be spiritually blind? Even though the eyes of the flesh are open, because the spiritual eyes are closed, a person is blind; and even though the person reads the Bible, that person is unable to realize the genuine gospel of the water and the Spirit. Like so, such a person does not know the meaning and the intention of the Word of God, and so, how stifling could this be to the person? From birth, people are spiritually blind, and since the blind cannot know the Word of God on his or her own, they must truly be stifled to death.

Yet, to His curious disciples, our Lord answered, *"Neither this man nor his parents sinned, but that the works of God should be revealed in him."* What then do you think exactly is the work that God wants to reveal? If a person is to remain as a spiritually blind person, prior to knowing its reason clearly, all that the person can do is to lead a life filled with riddles.

Why did people have to be born as sinners into this world from birth? Why was it that they could not but be born as fundamental sinners? If we were to interpret this Word outspokenly, I cannot but say that the reason for people being born as sinners is to reveal the glory of God. It means that this was included in God's plan. If so, we must find out what sort of a plan toward us that plan of God was.

It Is Clearly God's Will That God Had Made Humans Be Born Fundamentally as the Spiritual Blind

That will lies in us becoming a sinless child of God by believing in the remission of sins, that is, our Lord having come down to this earth and having atoned for our sins by the water and the blood for us. If God had made people be born as the righteous from birth, what would have happened? God's plan would not have been realized. Also, God would not have been able to show His justice to us, His creation. If we had been born as the righteous, there would have been no need for us to know His justice.

The work that God wants to do is like this. In the beginning, God created all the creations. And on the sixth day, He created man in the image of God with the dusts of the ground. And with the Spirit of God blown into the man's nostrils, the man became a living being. God created the man in the likeness of His image because He wanted to live together with people in the beautiful Heaven by giving them a heart that yearns for eternity (Ecclesiastes 3:11). And, knowing that people will fall into sins, God made plans to clothe people with the blessing of becoming God's children by sending down His only begotten Son to the humankind and cleaning their sins by the water, the blood, and the Spirit. And so, that is why God had you and me be born as sinners onto this earth. And for the reason like this, Jesus said that people are born as the blind not because of their parent's sins or because of their own sins but solely because God wants to reveal the works that He wants to do in them. Therefore, inside the gospel of the water and the Spirit, we must become those who bring enormous glory to God by taking into our hearts the will of God and obeying it.

The Work God Wants to Realize upon Human Beings

The work God wants to do is to turn all sinners into God's children by making them be born again by the gospel of the water and the Spirit. People are all born from the mother's womb, but once people believe in the gospel of the water and the Spirit given by Jesus and receive the remission of sins, they get to be born again as God's children. It means that people's dead souls are brought back to life when their spiritual eyes are opened by the power of the gospel Truth. Just as a larva becomes a cicada, a person is also born again by believing in the gospel of the water and the Spirit of Jesus Christ at heart after having been born once as a human being. And, by being cleansed of all one's sins like white snow, one can becomes a righteous person, a child of God. In other words, by believing in the gospel of the water and the Spirit, a person becomes a child of God who is a partaker of divine nature. God said that this is being born again.

We can easily see in the natural environment that a larva in water turns into a dragonfly and that a maggot becomes a fly. Like so, even though people are born onto this earth wearing a flesh, there is a way of being born again. And that is to become the people of God by believing in the gospel of the water and the Spirit. Those who are born again as people of God can go and live eternally and happily in the Kingdom of God. This is why in the Gospel of John it is said that a person who is not born again cannot see the Kingdom of God.

People tend to think of both maggots and flies as being dirty and creepy, but a maggot would wish for a prompt transformation, as it watches flies flying in the sky. And by having gone through the transformation, it would want to freely fly in the sky. It's the same with a larva. For its life as a cicada which would last only for a few weeks, a larva lives underground for about six years. And even after having spent that time, it doesn't become a cicada right away. After having been underground for such a long period of time, it will have to climb up a tree arduously, and then, it has to remain as a pupa for a time. It painstakingly becomes a cicada, but then it only chirps briskly for a single season of summer and dies. Even a mere creation yearns to be born again like that.

God allowed us to be born again as His people. Regardless of whether one wants it or not, God gave the gospel of the water and the Spirit to the entire humankind and fairly provided the way of being born again in Jesus Christ. And God clearly said that the only way for a sinner to become the righteous is none other than the gospel of the water and the Spirit. Actually, a sinner being born again, us becoming God's children, and us going to Heaven belong in all to the sovereignty of God. That a larva becomes a cicada is something that is done fundamentally by the will of the Creator. Likewise, for you and me to be born on this earth is also due to God.

A person cannot receive the remission of sins even if he does not commit sins. Also, a person cannot become the righteous by abiding by the Law perfectly. As it is said in the Book of Ecclesiastes chapter 7, verse 20, *"For there is not a just man on earth who does good and does not sin,"* there is no one who does not commit sin. Therefore, we must be born again as the righteous by accepting the will of God. And that method is precisely in the gospel of the water and the Spirit that God has given to us. God makes us the righteous. You must understand clearly that we cannot become the righteous by not committing sins but rather, it is possible because God has made us the righteous by the gospel of the water and the Spirit. Let me reiterate again: we can become the righteous only by the God-given gospel of the water and Spirit.

What kind of work did God do onto us? Before we endeavor to become the righteous by our own efforts, we must know what kind of work God did onto us in order to have us sinners be born again. To do so, we must listen carefully to the gospel Word of the water and the Spirit that God has given us and also we must look into it with careful attention. Because God has saved us with the gospel of the water and the Spirit, we can be saved by believing in that Truth. Nevertheless, most Christians continue to lead a religious life fervently, unaware of God's Word. They tend to think that so long as they put on an effort into whatever they can do, whether it is the prayer and fasting, donations, missionary work, or volunteering, they will receive salvation. There also are numerous people who think that salvation can be explained with the following equation: Faith in Jesus Christ + One's own merits = Salvation. However, this is an incorrect function and an incorrect answer.

Regarding a sinner being born again, not even 0.1% of one's own deeds goes into it. A sinner being born again is entirely the work of redemption that belongs to God. Our becoming the people of God and the righteous is, in all, God's grace and nothing else. Should even just 0.1% of our merits be added, nothing will come of it.

Our Lord was born on this earth to make sinners be born again, and as He lived on this earth for 33 years, He completed such a mission through the gospel of the water and the Spirit. However, people cannot be born again because they neither know nor believe in the work carried out by Jesus. Because they are in a state of being the spiritually blind, they cannot understand the real meaning of God's Word even if they read the Bible with their eyes. God has already perfected the salvation and has clearly recorded it in the Bible. Therefore, we must open our spiritual eyes and perfectly see the gospel God has given us.

Today's Scripture passage shows the work that our God wants to perform on the sinners. To heal the blind man, our Lord spat on the ground, made clay with the saliva, and pasted it on the eyes of the blind man. Jesus is God and the Creator. All Jesus had to do was to speak out just a single phrase, "Be healed!" Yet, do you think Jesus healed the blind man by spitting on the dirt, kneading it, and pasting it on his eyes because He didn't have the power? No! In this passage, what the Lord wants to say to us through it is shown. The Lord kneaded dirt with His saliva and opened the eyes of the blind man so that not only those who was watching the blind man getting healed but also people of this current generation will be able to know the secret of the cleansing of sin shown in the passage and then receive the remission of sins.

As the Lord spat on the ground, made clay with the saliva, and anointed both eyes of the blind man, He said, *"Go, wash in the pool of Siloam," (John 9:7).* When translated, the word 'Siloam' means 'sent.' Let us consider for a moment that there a blind person among you right now. If I were to paste the eyes with some clay that I had kneaded with my saliva and then if the blind person were to go and wash in the pool of Siloam, would that blind person truly open his or her eyes? Such method is not the way for a blind person to open his or her eyes. Instead, we must find a spiritual meaning from this account. This passage tells us how cursed we human beings are starting from the time we were born on this earth, and it also tells us what sort of a curse we were born destined to receive. In other words, this passage is speaking to us about the sins of us human beings and the judgment for those sins.

We were born with sins from birth, and if we do have sins, then what is its price? It is precisely spiritual death. No matter how extravagantly one has lives in the world and how much one knows the Bible, if that person still has sins in his or her heart for not having been born again, then where would that person go in the future? The person will go to hell. The person cannot but be cast into the lake which burns with fire and brimstone. Such life is cursed. The Lord is telling us that if we, who are born as sinners, do not receive the remission of sins, our lives themselves will be cursed.

Would One Know One's Own Sin?

Through the Book of Leviticus chapter 13, I will explain what the sins of people are like. Leviticus chapter 13 shows how the priests should discern leprosy, and it is something peculiar. God said that if the leprous sore is on a person just a little, then that person is unclean, but if the leprosy is covered all over the skin, then that person is very clean.

Let's look at the Book of Leviticus chapter 13, verses 9 through 17.

"When the leprous sore is on a person, then he shall be brought to the priest. And the priest shall examine him; and indeed if the swelling on the skin is white, and it has turned the hair white, and there is a spot of raw flesh in the swelling, it is an old leprosy on the skin of his body. The priest shall pronounce him unclean, and shall not isolate him, for he is unclean. And if leprosy breaks out all over the skin, and the leprosy covers all the skin of the one who has the sore, from his head to his foot, wherever the priest looks, then the priest shall

consider; and indeed if the leprosy has covered all his body, he shall pronounce him clean who has the sore. It has all turned white. He is clean. But when raw flesh appears on him, he shall be unclean. And the priest shall examine the raw flesh and pronounce him to be unclean; for the raw flesh is unclean. It is leprosy. Or if the raw flesh changes and turns white again, he shall come to the priest. And the priest shall examine him; and indeed if the sore has turned white, then the priest shall pronounce him clean who has the sore. He is clean."

In the Old Testament times, the priests examined those who had leprosy. Because leprosy was contagious, once a priest confirmed that a person had leprosy, then that person had to be isolated from other people. Just as the priests of the Tabernacle had examined whether or not a person had leprosy like that, right now, the servants of God examine whether a person is a sinner or a righteous person. Only the righteous who has become one of God's people can discern a righteous person from sinners.

If a certain person's skin showed colored spots and turns red and as they spread and sink inward, that person was first said to be unclean, and then, that person was confined to his or her house. It was because the person was under the suspicion of having leprosy. After that, the person was confined for seven days, and once again, the person was examined. If the colored spots hadn't spread, then the person was said to be 'clean' for it was not leprosy. However, if the skin had sunk in with the outbreak and the spread of white spots, then the person was cast out from the town for it was leprosy.

Which Type of Leper Are You Spiritually?

Here in Leviticus 13:12-13, it is written, *"And if leprosy breaks out all over the skin, and the leprosy covers all the skin of the one who has the sore, from his head to his foot, wherever the priest looks, then the priest shall consider; and indeed if the leprosy has covered all his body, he shall pronounce him clean who has the sore. It has all turned white. He is clean."*

There is a difference between God's Word and what we normally think of as a common sense. God said that a small outbreak and spread of leprosy was unclean, but if that leprosy had broken out all over the skin and covered the patient from head to foot, then that patient was proclaimed to be clean. What do you think? Between a person with leprosy spread all over the body and a person with just a little bit of leprosy, which do you think is more unclean? We must think about the meaning of this criterion. In the passage, God told the priests to cast out those who had a little bit of leprosy on a single part of their body for they were unclean. Leper patients who weren't cast out were those that had leprosy all over their body from head to foot and thus had turned white.

At the incipient stage of leprosy, it is said that the skin becomes tremendously thin and fine. The initial symptom of leprosy is the skin turning so fine that not even applying high-quality makeup would make it like that. The skin turns milky-white like that, and then it starts to burst into sores. The cheeks of the face burst and the ears burst. And starting with oozing of discharge from sores, the body begins to rot. Starting off like that, all the joints of the body then start to fall off one by one. Without having felt pain, one would loose the eyebrows, the nose, the nails, the fingers and the toes. Yet, the priest of the Tabernacle judged the leper, whose entire body had been covered by leprosy bacilli spreading from head to foot, to be clean.

This is a part that cannot be understood by human thinking. One cannot but wonder how is it that someone who was covered with a little bit of leprosy got cast out yet someone who was covered entirely with leprosy got to be judged as being clean, but the Bible's secret of the remission of sins and the Truth of God are precisely contained here.

All Humans Were Sinners before God

Once leprosy breaks out all over the body, one can see that the person is a leper even if a doctor does not diagnose the person's illness as leprosy. And so, even if someone near doesn't speak about it, one can think on one's own, "Alas, I have leprosy! I must receive some treatment!" However, with just a small break out of leprosy, one does not think of it seriously, saying, "It can't be leprosy. I'll be fine. It's just a small sore. It probably is just a simple skin disease."

Here, we must reflect back on ourselves on the way we see sins. People who acknowledge themselves as small sinners think that it would be fine since they have committed just a few sins; such people do not wish to hear the gospel of the water and the Spirit and receive salvation hastily. Such people cannot receive the remission of sins. And this is why God says that someone like this is more unclean.

Then, what sort of people can receive the remission of sins? It is none other than those who admit themselves as being perfect sinners, from the top of their head to the soles of their feet. Those who get to receive salvation by the gospel of the water and the Spirit are those who say, "I am a perfect sinner. I cannot but go to hell. There isn't a single righteousness of mine, goodness of me, or anything of mine to boast. Please God, save me from all these sins."

The Bible is a book of the salvation of humankind. The Bible is a book about Jesus Christ; it is the Word of the remission of sins; it is the book of God's plans for our salvation. The Bible speaks about our remission of sins, and it shows us God's purpose for creating us humans and the truth about Heaven. In order to perfectly accept this Word, we must know what sort of a person we ourselves are before God.

There are many people on this earth who believe in Jesus. If one were to climb up to a high place late at night, one would be able to see that there are so many churches around us by looking at the countless red neon cross signs. However, among those who believe in Jesus like that, there are many people who think of themselves as 'small sinners.' These people try to receive the remission of sins by coming to God with what little sin they have committed and asking for forgiveness, "Dear God, I have committed such and such sins. That's all. Please, forgive me of these sins." Instead of trying to receive the remission of sins and be born again fundamentally by believing in the gospel of the water and the Spirit, they are just asking for the forgiveness of only those particular sins that they acknowledge themselves.

Would people like that get accepted before God? Are they those that believe in Jesus properly? God does not approve of such people as His children. In God's view, complete sinners are those who will be born again. If you continue to think that you are just a small sinner, try to think about a few things once more. You have committed that sin today, but then do you think that you will not commit it tomorrow? Also, do you think you can go to Heaven so long as you get a remission only for that sin you have committed today? You will be committing sins every day as you go on living into the future, can you say, "Dear God, please forgive just this sin"? God has atoned for our sins once and for all with the gospel of the water and the Spirit. Yet, if we are trying to receive the remission of sins every day, must Jesus be repeating daily the work of receiving the baptism from John the Baptist and dying vicariously on the Cross? I want you to think about this once again.

Our Lord did not atone for our sins just by His lips. He has forever atoned for our sins once and for all by completing the gospel of the water and the Spirit. If you believe in this, you do not need to beg for the remission of sins day after day. It is because you have already received the remission of all your sins. To say that you will go on living without committing sins from the moment when and if God were to forgive just one or two sins that we have committed. God has blotted out all our sins once and for all, yet why would you try to blot out the remaining sins with your own righteousness? God has blotted out all our sins 100% perfectly by the gospel of the water and the Spirit.

But people who are not very well aware of themselves being a complete sinner pray and cry out, saying, "Dear God, I've committed this much sin today. Please blot it out for me." As they do so, they go on claiming one must receive the remission of sins every day. However, even if such people do believe in Jesus, they cannot receive the remission of sins. Even if they have clear faith in the Cross on which Jesus has died, because they don't have faith in the baptism through which Jesus has taken on sins, they do not get to receive the remission. People get to receive salvation only by clearly believing that the Lord has come down to this earth and blotted all the sins of the world by the water and the blood. However, if people were to think that they are just small sinners, then they won't be able to receive the impeccable remission of sins because they haven't passed on all the sins to Jesus perfectly. When Jesus was taking on the sin of the world from John the Baptist through the baptism, did He take on just a little bit of it? Did He say, "You, John the Baptist, give Me just a little and tell people to blot out the remaining sins by themselves"? That was never so. At that time, Jesus took on all the sins of humankind without leaving behind any.

God saved the grave sinners who could not but go to hell 100% and receive curse, not those who can be saved with just a little bit of His help. A sinner can be saved by faith only if God atones for all his or her sins. In the name of Jesus Christ, I hope for all the sinners of this world who are listening to this sermon to know that they are 100% sinners and have all their sins be taken care of once and for all by believing in the water of the baptism received by the Lord and His blood.

Our God has perfectly blotted out the sins that had filled people who were 100% sinners from the top of their head to the soles of their feet. It is because God wants to send us to Heaven. We must search the heart of God through the Scriptures. And, we must understand each other's hearts. If we do not know each other's hearts, then it amounts to nothing. Having fellowship with each other is to exchange one's heart with others. It is not having conversations about the world and it isn't exchanging jests. It is speaking one's heart with sincerity. And, as one listens to the other's heart, both hearts are exchanged. Also, it is to know with the heart what one must do toward the other. This is the genuine fellowship, and this is the genuine love.

God said to us, "You cannot but go to hell. If I hadn't saved you from sins by the gospel of the water and the Spirit, you would have had no choice but to receive curse." It is said that people look at the outer appearance but God looks at the center of a person's heart. That is why He said, *"You have heard that it was said to those of old, 'You shall not commit adultery.' But I say to you that whoever looks at a woman to lust for her has already committed adultery with her in his heart" (Matthew 5:27-28).*

Are you or are you not a 100% sinner who has committed all sorts of sins in your heart as well as by actions? Are you still a 50% sinner? We are 100% sinners. But, if our God has completely atoned for our sins 100%, then are we a perfectly righteous person or not? Because the Lord has atoned for sins 100%, we now are the righteous. We have become perfect once and for all by believing in the gospel of the water and the Spirit.

If we were to think about what sort of people we ourselves were before God prior to having been born again by believing in the gospel of the water and the Spirit, we cannot but acknowledge that we had been those who were completely useless and destined to go to hell. In God's view, those who have sins in their heart, even just 0.1%, aren't God's children. And so, it is said that our Lord came down to this earth to save sinners. How sinful are those sinners? They are 100% sinners. Our Lord came to save 100% sinners. Whether or not we recognize the gospel of the water and the Spirit, in God's view, we were already sinners. In God's view, we were 100% sinners because we were born with sins inherited from our parents even if we don't commit sins. Dear fellow believers, do you understand this? In God's view, we are 100% sinners. For this reason, our Lord pasted the clay made with His saliva on the eyes of the blind man. And He told him to go and wash in the pool of Siloam.

Proper Faith

Why did the Lord say to the blind man to go and wash in the pool of Siloam? We know the Apostles appear in the New Testament. The word 'Apostle' means one sent by God. Siloam also means 'sent.' To receive the genuine remission of sins, one must go and wash in the water with which Jesus received the baptism. A person doesn't just get well by going and washing in the pool of Siloam not knowing anything about the Truth. Of course, the blind man was healed because he had obeyed the Lord's word, but in actuality, our Lord had given the sinner the remission of sin, which allowed the sinner to be healed from the sickness of sins, by spitting on the ground and making clay with the saliva. We have received the remission of sins by believing in this.

Only when people meet God's servants who have received the remission of sins, that is, those who have been sent by God, they can clearly find out that they are truly sinners and that if they die now, they will go to hell. After that, they must listen to the gospel of the water and the Spirit that God's servants tell them. Like so, only by listening to the gospel of the water and the blood with which our Lord has made us be born again, does one receive the remission of sins and has his eyes open up brightly. Just as the blind man had his eyes open up perfectly after being pasted with the clay made with Jesus' saliva and then washing his eyes in the pool of Siloam, we must also open our spiritual eyes by believing in the gospel of the water and the Spirit in which Jesus had received the baptism and died vicariously on the Cross for us. The Lord is telling us this. Can you understand it?

No matter how atrocious and wicked a sinner may be, if that person were to hear and believe in the gospel of the water and the Spirit told by those who have been born again by the gospel of the water and the Spirit, the person can receive the remission of sins. Just as the blind man cannot read the Bible even if he tried, a sinner can neither interpret the Word of God by himself or herself nor understand the Truth contained in the Bible. For this reason, such a person must listen to and believe in the Word of God told by those who have truly been born again by believing in the gospel of the water and the Spirit.

In the Second Book of Kings chapter 5, a commander named Naaman appears. He was the commander of the army of Syria, and he was a great and honorable man in the eyes of his master because he once had given victory to the king of Syria. He was also a mighty man of valor, but a leper. Although he had all the things necessary on this earth, he was in misery because of this sickness. And so, to heal his sickness, we went to find Elisha, a servant of God. According to Naaman's thinking, the leprosy would get healed only if Elisha were to come personally, place his hands on his head, and pray in tongues, saying, "La-di-la-di Lal-la." So he came riding a long way to Israel.

But Elisha not only did not meet the commander Naaman but instead, through his servant named Gehazi, told Naaman to go and wash in the Jordan seven times. At first when Naaman heard this, he got angry. From a human perspective, he had every reason to be angry, for Elisha had passed on only the necessary words by sending a mere servant instead of coming out to welcome him, a commander of the army of a big country. And so, he tried to return to his country.

But at that moment, one of the servants dissuaded him from doing so. The servants persuaded the commander Naaman by saying, *"My father, if the prophet had told you to do something great, would you not have done it? How much more then, when he says to you, 'Wash, and be clean'?"* The servant was telling Naaman to just try it once, for it would not be too late go back to Syria, bring the army, and then annihilate this country, should his words turn out to be nothing but lies. Hearing those words, the commander Naaman judged that they have some truth in them. Then, saying, "Well, I'll try it once," he went to the Jordan River, took off his clothes, and washed himself seven times. Just then, his leprosy was healed, and his flesh was restored like the flesh of a little child.

Like this, the sins of people can only be cleansed by the water and the blood, not by speaking in tongues or some wonders. Thus, the waters of the Jordan River through which one receives the cleansing of sin are written in the Old Testament. This gospel of the Jordan River is the secret of Jesus' baptism, being born again, and the remission of sins. What that can save sinners from all their sins is precisely the gospel of the water and the Spirit.

You Must Believe in the Gospel of the Water and the Spirit to Be Born Again.

Do you know and believe in the baptism of water that Jesus had received at the Jordan River? Jesus said that He has saved all the sinners by the water, the blood, and the Spirit. Jesus has perfectly saved you and me by the water and the Spirit. And He says that only those who are born again by believing in this Truth can enter the Kingdom of God.

Just like the commander Naaman, those who haven't yet been born again try to just go back instead of obeying the Word of God, thinking that the Word differs from their thoughts. They come to receive the remission of sins, but then they try to go back thinking that it doesn't adhere to their thoughts, saying, "I think of the remission of sins as something like the following: there has to be the fire coming inside my heart, and also, there has to be the laying on of the hands in a grand fashion, beating of drum, crying, and praying loudly." However, God did not save the humankind through their emotional fullness. If one tries to receive the salvation through an emotional fullness, then that is a false salvation.

If you want to receive the remission of sins, you must throw away your own thoughts. If you dare try to receive the remission of sins with your own thoughts, you will fail every time. If you don't throw away your thoughts and do not even believe in the gospel of the water and the Spirit with which Jesus has atoned for all your sins, you will go to hell infallibly. Knowing that Jesus was going to paste on his eyes clay made with His saliva, if the blind man had resisted by saying that he doesn't want it, he would not have been able to open his eyes. If he had thought, "Even without it, I have been treated contemptuously as someone born blind, yet You are going to paste on my eyes clay made with saliva! Really, do You think that a blind man doesn't have any self-esteem?" he would have said, with a hurt pride, "Even if I cannot open my eyes, let it be that way. I cannot be a part of such a dirty act. I won't do it." And then, if he had continued to be stubborn like that and refused to obey the Lord, he would have never been able to open up his eyes all throughout his life. But the blind man committed his everything to Jesus.

You must also throw away your self-esteem in order to receive the remission of sins. The ones who had the commander Naaman hear the gospel were a small girl and Gehazi. Servants of God who do God's work may seem like useless ones with a shabby appearance on the outside. But God works in a way that is different from human thinking. Our Lord also did not show off His majesty when He came to this earth. Truly, our Lord lowered Himself, lower than the common people, and by lowering Himself, He met and became friends with the poor, the sick, and the pitiful. And also, He saved them from all their sins. Also in this day and age, our Lord wants to remit people's sins. Just as He had been with the lowly when He was on earth about 2,000 years ago, He still wants to be together with those who have a humble heart, realizing that they themselves are complete sinners.

I want you to know this fact. I am speaking about the very fact that to receive the remission of sins, you must throw away your own thoughts. People, regardless of who they are, have their own thoughts and standards. Do you have a standard of your own that goes, "One will receive the remission of sins in such and such way"? You must throw that away. To be born again, you must throw away all the styles, standards and thoughts of your own. You must throw them all away and then receive the gospel of the water and the Spirit that God gives you.

The Lord said to the blind man, "Go and wash in the pool of Siloam." This means that we must meet the apostles sent by God, in other words, the people who were sent by God. Sinners must meet the righteous sent by God. This, in other words, means that you must meet those who have received the remission of sins by the gospel of the water and the Spirit ahead of you. When you meet a righteous person who has received the remission of sins by the gospel of the water and the Spirit, you can receive the definite remission of sins. 'Siloam' refers to the servants of God who are spreading the gospel of the righteousness of God. And the blind refers to sinners who have to receive the remission of sins. Every sinner must meet those who are spreading the gospel of the water and the Spirit without fail.

Today's Scripture passage in the Book of John chapter 9 is speaking about this. In the Book of John chapter 9, all that the blind man did was hearing Jesus' Word in which he was told to go and wash in the pool of Siloam, going and washing there, and then coming back with good eyesight. Just as it is said, *"So then faith comes by hearing, and hearing by the word of God" (Romans 10:17)*, if you go to the Church of the born-again, the sins in your heart are cleansed completely. By listening to and believing in the gospel of the water and the Spirit, you become like the Scripture passage in the Book of Isaiah that says, *"Though your sins are like scarlet, they shall be as white as snow; Though they are like crimson, they shall be as wool" (Isaiah 1:18)*. Like so, our Lord has completely cleansed all our sins through the gospel of the water and the Spirit.

The disciples of Jesus were all righteous people. Right now in this world, are there righteous people? Yes, there are. They are none other than those who have been born again by the gospel of the water and the Spirit. Jesus came to this earth in human flesh and took on all our sins through the baptism He had received from John the Baptist. Then, to reconcile us sinners with God, He gave Himself up as the propitiation. Our Lord has made us the righteous by the water and the blood. Therefore, we must know that human beings are sinners from birth. We must realize that Jesus has washed away all the sins clean by giving us, who have been born as sinners, the water and the blood and that by vicariously receiving all the judgment on our behalf, He has made those who believe in this Truth the born-again people of God.

What kind of sinners are we human beings? We are the

worst of sinners who commit innumerable sins by heart, retain sins inside the heart, and commit sins through acts until death. However, because the Lord loved such sinners like us so much, He cleansed all our sins by the gospel of the water and the Spirit. Through the account of a blind man coming back with good eyesight after having been told by the Lord to go and wash in the pool of Siloam, He spoke to us about the salvation given by the water and the Spirit. Like so, a sinner gets to receive the remission of sins by believe in Jesus through the gospel of the water and the Spirit. All you have to do is to go and wash in the pool of Siloam.

I would like to speak to you about how I had gone and washed my eyes in the pool of Siloam. It has now been about 30 years since I had started believing in Jesus. But, for the first 10 years of Christian life, I had lived as a Christian sinner. For those 10 years, as I was studying theology, I was in constant agony because of sins inside my heart. But the Lord met with me.

Before I was born again, when I read the Bible, I couldn't grasp the real meaning of the Word because I had been spiritually blind so severely that what was black were just letters and what was white was just paper. At times, I read it with full emotion, but that emotional fullness did not last long. And on most occasions, I was just idling by with the view, "What is black are just letters and what is white is just paper." There is a characteristic common to all those who believe in Jesus without having been born again: at the beginning of their faith in Jesus, believing in Jesus makes them feel really great, but as they believe more and more, they become weary because of those sins that still remain in their hearts. Someone being in agony due to the tormenting sins inside the heart despite having faith in Jesus is a clear proof that the person has not been born again. Back then, because I had believed just in the blood of the Cross without being aware of the gospel of the water and the Spirit, I also wasn't able to receive the remission of sins.

However, once you receive the remission of sins through the gospel of the water and the Spirit, you will no longer worry over problems of sin. It is because everything has been solved. In order to receive the remission of sins, you must carefully examine to see if you clearly acknowledge yourself as a sinner who truly cannot but go to hell. Only by doing so, you can receive the remission of sins by listening to the gospel. If you don't know how much of a sinner you are for the sins deep inside your heart haven't surfaced, you cannot become a righteous person 100% perfectly.

We human beings do not live every day in virtue, and then for some reason, by accident, commit sins. Rather, we commit sins because the 12 kinds of sins inside of us are revealed (Mark 7:21-23). Someone may seem so virtuous that the person might not commit any sin. But it is because the person hides the sin inside the heart with virtuous acts and righteous images. Human beings, regardless of who they are, are fundamentally those that commit sins until death. From a spiritual perspective, the sins that you haven't committed yet are actually the same sins as those you have already committed. They were also included in the sin of the world which John the Baptist had passed on to Jesus through the laying on of his hands.

And thus, our God has blotted out all our sins. And the Lord has shown us the secret of the remission of sins through the miracle of opening the blind man's eyes. If you want to receive the remission of sins, like this blind man, you must meet our Lord, and as He commands, go to those who have been sent by God and listen to the Word from them. The Lord has given us the account of the blind man to teach us about this.

Understanding God's Word properly isn't difficult. If you believe in the God-given keyword for being born again, the gospel of the water and the Spirit, you can be born again at once. And, as you hear God's Word more and more, you will be able to understand what this Word of the gospel, by which you have received the cleansing of sins, is saying.

Within Christianity of this day and age, there are many ministers who go on ministering without having been born again. Because they go on ministering without having been born again, they don't even know whether or not their followers have been born again. If we look at the Scriptures, false shepherds who cannot discern sheep from goats spiritually are referred to as hirelings. We the born-again servants are precisely the pool of Siloam mentioned in today's Scripture passage. No matter who he or she may be, any blind person can be washed clean by going and washing in the pool of Siloam, as instructed by the Lord. The place for the remission of sins is the pool of Siloam.

The gospel of the water and the Spirit, according to which Jesus received the baptism and died vicariously on the Cross, is the fountain of salvation. That is why our Lord said, *"Whoever drinks of the water that I shall give him will never thirst. But the water that I shall give him will become in him a fountain of water springing up into everlasting life" (John 4:14).* The fountain of water springing up into everlasting life is such that the more you draw from it, the more joyful it becomes for you, and the more delightful and beautiful water comes out. You will also understand this once you receive the remission of sins.

Dear fellow believers, go and wash in the pool of Siloam! Don't you want to open your eyes by going and washing in the pool of Siloam after having had the clay made with Jesus' saliva pasted on your eyes? As for you all, please be born again by opening your spiritual eyes by coming to God's Church right now, and hearing and believing in the gospel of the water and the Spirit. So long as you have the proper faith of accepting that you are a complete sinner, you will also be able to hear the Word of God and receive a complete remission of all so many sins that are like a thick cloud. To do so, you must go and cleanse your sins spiritually in the pool of Siloam.

Spiritually, the pool of Siloam means 'those who have been sent by God.' Right now, you must believe in the gospel of the water and the Spirit through those who believe in the righteousness of God ahead of you. It is because if you believe in the gospel of the water and the Spirit, your sins will be cleansed absolutely. ✉

Sermon

2

The Law

Those Who Have Truly Met Jesus Christ

< John 9:1-12 >

"Now as Jesus passed by, He saw a man who was blind from birth. And His disciples asked Him, saying, "Rabbi, who sinned, this man or his parents, that he was born blind?" Jesus answered, "Neither this man nor his parents sinned, but that the works of God should be revealed in him. I must work the works of Him who sent Me while it is day; the night is coming when no one can work. As long as I am in the world, I am the light of the world." When He had said these things, He spat on the ground and made clay with the saliva; and He anointed the eyes of the blind man with the clay. And He said to him, "Go, wash in the pool of Siloam" (which is translated, Sent). So he went and washed, and came back seeing. Therefore the neighbors and those who previously had seen that he was blind said, "Is not this he who sat and begged?" Some said, "This is he." Others said, "He is like him." He said, "I am he." Therefore they said to him, "How were your eyes opened?" He answered and said, "A Man called Jesus made clay and anointed my eyes and said to me, 'Go to the pool of Siloam and wash.' So I went and washed, and I received sight." Then they said to him, "Where is He?" He said, "I do not know."

God's Church is where the righteous who have received the remission of sins are gathered, and God is pleased with this

Church and cares deeply about it. With His eyes of grace, God always watches over His Church on this planet earth. The will of God and His heart are manifested in His Church. As we are abiding in this Church, God therefore hears our prayers and answers our requests. As you know, a mother's eyes are always set on her toddler, and the eyes of a groom are always set on his bride. Likewise, as the Father of the righteous people and our Groom, it is only a matter of course for God to also love us His children and devote His attention to His Church, which is His bride.

Therefore, it is in none other than in God's Church that we can see for ourselves how pleased God is when we preach the gospel of the water and the Spirit, and how He works in our lives. When seen through the eyes of man, it may seem as though the Church is difficult to run and it has little power to spread the gospel. However, despite this, God has blessed His Church to prosper, and by strengthening the souls that are gathered there, God continues to produce sturdy workers who can carry out His work. We should never forget the fact that God is always rejoiced by His Church and He blesses it all the time.

Why Are We Spiritually Blind?

Today's Scripture passage revolves around a visually disabled man. As you know, visually disabled people refer to the blind who can't see. For various causes, their eyes have no sight and they can't see anything. For those of us who have no vision problem, we can't even begin to imagine just how much suffering and hardship they go through.

But did you know that there actually are other visually

disabled people in this world who are even more miserable than them? They are none other than the spiritually blind. For those who are physically blind, the only problem is that they can't see physical objects, but for those who are spiritually blind, their problem is on a completely different dimension. Many people today are living as spiritually blind people. In the present world, there are far too many people whose lives are guided by their own conviction, rather than the faith that's approved by God. Although such people profess to believe in God through the "religionized" Christianity, since they are still sinners with a sinful heart and they follow their own plans rather than the will of God, they may be classified as spiritually blind people. We call them "Christian sinners." These people cannot see themselves straight before the Word of God. Even as they hear and read the Word of God, they are completely oblivious to the will of God manifested in the gospel of the water and the Spirit, and so they still remain sinners and continue to live in this sinful state.

No matter how often we warn them that they will go to hell if they have sin, it's all useless. On the contrary, they retort by saying, "I am not blind. Since I believe in Jesus, I've already been remitted from the original sin that I was born into, and now all that I need is to just give prayers of repentance to be remitted from my personal sins. So why will I ever end up in hell, when I am such a good Christian?" Like this, there are so many spiritually blind people on this earth who are completely ignorant of the righteousness of God and filled with spiritual arrogance instead.

In today's Scripture passage, Jesus met a man who was blind from birth. The disciples then asked Him, "Because of whose sin did this man become blind? Is it because of his sin, or his parents' sin?" Jesus then answered, "No, it's because of neither his parents' sin nor his, but to reveal God's work. He was born blind so that the work of God would be manifested."

God often reveals His will through parables and symbols in His Word of the Scriptures. The blind man in this passage also draws an analogy to the spiritually blind people rather than the physically blind. In other words, this passage explains why God allowed us humans to be born into spiritual blindness. Jesus said here that it's not because of our sins that we became blind. Why, then, did we have to be born on this earth with spiritual blindness? It was to make us be born again through the gospel of the water and the Spirit that God gave us. God wanted to bestow His grace of salvation on us. He allowed us to be born with spiritual blindness so that we would be born again through the gospel of the water and the Spirit; so that God may save us and open our spiritual eyes; and so that His righteousness may be revealed to us.

The spiritually blind are those who, trapped in sin, cannot realize the gospel Truth of the water and the Spirit even when they hear the Word of God. All of us humans were born as such blind people. God had allowed us to be born temporarily blind because He wanted to complete the amazing work of delivering such people from sin through the gospel of the water and the Spirit. In other words, God had permitted us to be born spiritually blind in order to fulfill His will to make us His sinless people. Do you grasp this will of God?

The Lord said, *"I must work the works of Him who sent Me while it is day; the night is coming when no one can work. As long as I am in the world, I am the light of the world."* As we have received the remission of sins by believing in the gospel of the water and the Spirit, our hearts are no longer in the darkness of the night but under the broad daylight. That's because the Spirit of the Lord dwells in our hearts. It's because once the Lord ascended to Heaven, He gave the Holy Sprit to the hearts of the believers in the gospel of the water and the Spirit. Therefore, we must carry out God's work until the day the Lord returns to this earth and lifts us up to the sky. Once we the believers in the gospel of the water and the Spirit are lifted up by the Lord, the night will come when we will not be able to work even if we wanted to work. Like this, the Lord wants us to preach the gospel while it is permitted by Him, while there still are those who will receive the remission of sins.

It's written, *"When He had said these things, He spat on the ground and made clay with the saliva; and He anointed the eyes of the blind man with the clay. And He said to him, 'Go, wash in the pool of Siloam' (which is translated, Sent). So he went and washed, and came back seeing" (John 9:6-7).* Referring to the blind man, our Lord had said, *"This man is blind so that the work of God would be revealed."* He then spat on the ground, made clay with the saliva, anointed the blind man's eyes, and said to him, *"Go, wash in the pool of Siloam."*

The Bible writes that when the blind man went to the pool of Siloam and washed his eyes as told, he returned with his eyes opened. When looked from man's perspective, it makes no sense at all to spit on the ground, make clay with the saliva, and put it on the blind man's eyes to open his eyes. If we had done this in this time and age, spitting on the ground, making clay with the saliva, putting it on some blind person's eyes, and telling him to go to the pool of Siloam and wash himself, not only would no one listen to us, but no one would return with his eyes opened either. Like this, there are many parts in the Word of God that do not make any sense at all when we consider it according to our own human logic.

However, the Word of God is always beyond the limits of what we humans can think. The Bible says that to open the blind man's eyes, our Lord spit on the ground, made clay with the saliva, and put it on his eyes. As the ground refers to the human heart in the Bible, that Jesus spat on the ground means that man's heart is spiritually accursed. We spit at someone so worthless and evil that we can't stand him, to show our spite. Like this, that Jesus spat on the ground means that we humans were cursed. Since everyone is born spiritually blind, everyone's spirit is in a sinful state, and none other than this is man's accursed state. This means that because everyone is born with sin, and because everyone is therefore cursed by God spiritually, unless the Lord does something for us, man cannot help but remain in his accursed state until his death.

To help your understanding, let us turn to Matthew 15:7-20 here: *"'Hypocrites! Well did Isaiah prophesy about you, saying: "These people draw near to Me with their mouth, And honor Me with their lips, But their heart is far from Me. And in vain they worship Me, Teaching as doctrines the commandments of men."' When He had called the multitude to Himself, He said to them, 'Hear and understand: Not what goes into the mouth defiles a man; but what comes out of the mouth, this defiles a man.' Then His disciples came and said to Him, 'Do You know that the Pharisees were offended when they heard this saying?' But He answered and said, 'Every plant which My heavenly Father has not planted will be uprooted. Let them alone. They are blind leaders of the blind. And if the blind leads the blind, both will fall into a ditch." Then Peter answered and said to Him, 'Explain this parable to us.' So Jesus said, 'Are you also still without understanding? Do you not yet understand that whatever enters the mouth goes into the stomach and is eliminated? But those things which proceed out of the mouth come from the heart, and they defile a man. For out of the heart proceed evil thoughts, murders, adulteries, fornications, thefts, false witness, blasphemies. These are the things which defile a man, but to eat with unwashed hands does not defile a man.'"*

Here the Lord is explaining what kinds of sins we have in our hearts, and with what kinds of sins everyone is born. Rooted in our hearts are evil thoughts, murders, adulteries, fornications, thefts, false witness, and blasphemies, and these things that proceed out of the human heart is what defiles mankind. The Lord is saying here that everyone is born with such sins, and this is precisely why man is born on this earth in an accursed state. The reason why Jesus Christ spat on the ground, made clay with the saliva, and put it on the eyes of the blind man was to make us realize that by our fundamental human nature, whatever is in our hearts is all sinful, and because of these sins we are destined to be spiritually cursed. It was to make the blind man realize his accursed sins in his heart that Jesus had put the clay made with the saliva on his eyes. This passage also points out none other than our own imperfect spiritual state.

By What Means Does the Lord Point out Our Sins?

It's the very Word of God that points out our sins through the Law. Unless we look at ourselves through the Word of the Law of God, we can never realize our basic nature that is full of sins. If it were not for the Law, we would remain completely oblivious to the fact that we are destined to be cursed for our sins, and that we will be destroyed in the end. If we were to evaluate ourselves based on the ethical standard of the world, many of us would say, "What's so evil about me? If there is anyone as virtuous as I am, let him step forward!" However, if we truly see ourselves as reflected by the righteous Word of God, then we would see that we are indeed evil all the time. All that the Lord wants from us is to recognize that nothing but "evil thoughts, murders, adulteries, fornications, thefts, false witness, and blasphemies" come out of our hearts. As such depraved sinners, we have nothing to say even if we were cursed and cast into hell for these sins. There is no one good in this world but only God. When we look into our hearts based on the written Word of the Law, we cannot help but admit that all of us truly deserve to be cast into hell.

That everyone is born in this world with sin means that everyone is born in the state of spiritual death. However, people are born without realizing this truth, and many of them live in this world ignoring it. A spiritually blind person does not realize that his heart is terminally ill. Such people are dying a slow death, not even realizing that they are blind, as the candle light flickers in the wind only to be extinguished in the end. Therefore, as all the people in this world are destined to be destroyed from the birth, and yet they do not actually realize it, they may be said to be spiritually blind walking on the way of death.

You Must Realize That Those Who Have Not Received the Remission of Sins Do Not Actually Realize That They Are Heading to Hell

Not realizing that they are doomed to destruction by God's just judgment, such people only try to do good deeds or rely on one of man-made religions while living on this earth. Before you and I received the remission of sins, we had also not known our fundamental selves and only tried to live virtuously under all kinds of religions. However, there is one big problem with all this effort that is made outside of God: Everyone's heart is fundamentally sinful, but no one actually realizes this. In other words, human beings live and die without even realizing that they themselves are a brood of sin born with a heart full of murderous, decadent, jealous, foolish, and lying desires.

To such ignorant and foolish people like us, God is saying through the account of the blind man in today's Scripture passage, "You are destined to hell and destruction." Given the fact that everyone has such a sinful heart, it's nothing more than a lie to claim that anyone can go to Heaven if he does good deeds. God made it clear that "the wages of sin is death" (Romans 6:23). What about us then? How were we before we were born again? Did we know that we were destined to be destroyed? No, we had no idea! In those days, we didn't even know that we were sinful, nor did we know that we would be destroyed for these sins, and that's why we only tried to live virtuously on ethical grounds. Not knowing the Truth, we were doomed to expend our time and effort in a useless endeavor only to be cast into hell in the end. Like a bruised reed, we were accursed beings destined to die without even realizing it.

However, God said, *"A bruised reed He will not break,*
And smoking flax He will not quench,
He will bring forth justice for truth" (Isaiah 42:3). Our Lord did not want man's life and soul to die; far from it, He was the God of love who wanted to light up the smoking flax of life for everyone. Therefore, realizing that we ourselves are destined to be destroyed, we must look at the Word of God through the eyes of faith. We must be freed from our spiritual blindness and open our eyes of faith. Only then can God's

brilliant flame of life be set ablaze in our hearts that are dripping in sin by nature.

The Lord said in Isaiah 42:7-8, *"To open blind eyes, To bring out prisoners from the prison, Those who sit in darkness from the prison house. I am the LORD, that is My name; And My glory I will not give to another, Nor My praise to carved images."*

And the deaf who have ears." Referring to us humans, the Lord is saying here that we are blind even though we have eyes, and we are deaf even though we have ears. The blind, the deaf, the smoking flax, and the bruised reed mentioned in the Bible all refer to sinners. In other words, the Lord is saying in these passages that every human being is fundamentally born with accursed sins. And just as He said, each and every one of us was indeed born with a sinful heart. Unless we received the remission of sins from God by faith, we were all destined to end up in hell. However, the Lord blessed sinners to realize their true selves. By spitting on the ground, making clay out of the saliva, and putting it on the eyes of the blind, He opened their eyes.

My fellow believers, take a look at your own heart and see how it is reflected on the Word of Truth. You will then realize your fundamental nature that constantly stirs up filthy and depraved desires in your heart. As human beings, our hearts sometimes harbor lustful desires, and other times murderous thoughts, arrogant minds, and foolish desires as well. If we were to be judged for all these things, it's unmistakably clear that we would all deserve to be cast into hell. If our God were to intervene and judge us for all the sins that arise in our hearts, would we go to hell or enter Heaven? We can't help but admit our helpless condition inevitably destined to hell.

However, to Us Who Were Bo
Heart, God Has Given the Lig

As the Lord came to this earth
gospel of the water and the Spir
wholeheartedly, then we will not go
by faith. What would have happened
saved us from sin out of His compas
just to think about it. The Lord spat
with the saliva; and He anointed the
the clay. And He told him to was
Siloam. Like this, it is by realizing ou
Lord's gospel of the water and the S
spiritual eyes.

My fellow believers, had God
once and for all with His Word, then
be cast into hell. Yet our Lord ca
people like us, saved us through the
Spirit, and opened our eyes of faith.
for this. If we have received the rem
from our fate that had destined us t
this means that our Lord has led us t
We must therefore believe in the g
Spirit that has led us to the Truth o
delivered us through the gospel of th
though we all deserved to be conder
sins, all of us ought to thank Him si
the right guidance of the Lord.

It is not out of luck that tho
Church have received the remissio
has blessed us with the gospel of th
because we wholeheartedly believe

believing in the gospel of the water and
s blind man. When our Lord came to this
ıe flesh of man, He bore all our sins by
His own body. By thus taking away all
ucified to death, He has saved us. In this
abled all of us who believe in the gospel
e Spirit to be born again. Through His
way all our sins, including all the sins that
d all the sins that we commit with our
ereby opened the eyes of every spiritually

e were all inevitably destined to be
our inherent sins, our Lord has made it
be destroyed for these sins, for He loves
as saved us from all our sins through the
and the Spirit, and in doing so He has
Kingdom of God. He has delivered us the
spel of the water and the Spirit from
ower of the darkness, and moved us to the
is by thus believing in the gospel of the
given by Jesus Christ that our spiritual
we could become God's true children.
today's Scripture passage, *"Some said,*
aid, 'He is like him.' He said, 'I am he.'
him, 'How were your eyes opened?' He
'A Man called Jesus made clay and
d said to me, "Go to the pool of Siloam
and washed, and I received sight'" (John
an had probably been a beggar, surviving
thers. His clothes would no doubt have
ever, once his eyes were opened by the
ould have thrown away his filthy rags and

changed into new, clean clothes. So those who didn't recognize him as a changed man came to him and asked him, "Are you that man who used to be blind?" And the blind man said yes. The people then said to him, "Then tell us how your eyes were really opened," to which the man said, "A Man called Jesus spat on the ground, made clay out of saliva, put it on my eyes, and told me to go to the pool of Siloam and wash in there. So I did as I was told, and my eyes were opened." When the people asked him where Jesus was, he said that he didn't know. The reason why they asked him for the whereabouts of Jesus is because the day when the blind man's eyes were opened was none other than the Sabbath Day. As the man who had been blind said that he didn't know where Jesus was, the people took him to the Pharisees.

The Pharisees in those days were strict adherents of the tradition of the Law. To keep the Sabbath Day of the Old Testament, they prepared all their food on Friday, the day before the Sabbath. They even fed their livestock beforehand on Friday rather than on the Sabbath. They lived in strict adherence to the statutes of the Law, not even traveling too far on the Sabbath Day.

It's written in today's Scripture passage, *"Now it was a Sabbath when Jesus made the clay and opened his eyes. Then the Pharisees also asked him again how he had received his sight. He said to them, 'He put clay on my eyes, and I washed, and I see.' Therefore some of the Pharisees said, 'This Man is not from God, because He does not keep the Sabbath.' Others said, 'How can a man who is a sinner do such signs?' And there was a division among them. They said to the blind man again, 'What do you say about Him because He opened your eyes?' He said, 'He is a prophet'" (John 9:14-17).*

This passage depicts the scene where the man who had

been blind was interrogated by the Pharisees after receiving the remission of sins from Jesus. The Pharisees thought that since Jesus didn't keep the Sabbath, a day when no one was supposed to do anything, He was not from God, and since such a Man performed a miracle, He should be arrested. That's why they were asking the blind man where Jesus was. Today, in this age and time, some religionists also denounce the righteous in a similar fashion, saying, "The Bible says that there is no one just, not even one. So how can you be a righteous person? You are a heretic!" Like these religionists, the Pharisees who insisted only on the Law were interrogating the formerly blind man who had now received the remission of sins.

My fellow believers, was it wrong for Jesus to open the eyes of the blind man on the Sabbath, when no one was supposed to do anything? No, that's not true. Although Jesus was born on this earth, He was the only One who was fundamentally sinless. Therefore, regardless of whether or not it was the Sabbath Day when the Lord opened the eyes of the blind man, this was still a good work and there was absolutely nothing wrong with it. Is it right to impose rules even on good deeds, saying, "You can't do that since today is Saturday, but you can do it tomorrow as it is the Lord's Day"? If someone is drowning, is it right to say, "I can't save you now since today is the Sabbath Day, but if you are still alive tomorrow, I'll save you then"? That's why our Jesus said, "If one of your own herd falls into a ditch, wouldn't you try to save it? This man was blind, and so isn't it more important to open his eyes than keeping the Sabbath Day? Isn't is more imperative to enable people to receive the spiritual remission of sins?" Regardless of whether it was the Sabbath Day or not, it was right to open the blind man's eyes. Yet despite this, the Pharisees had failed to realize the love of God hidden in the Law, and they were instead leading their lives of faith foolishly bound by the letters of the Law.

My fellow believers, just as the formerly blind man was persecuted by the Pharisees, so is it inevitable for us to also face persecution after we receive the remission of sins. Some people say to us, "How dare you claim to have received the remission of sins? Tell me about this gospel of the water and the Spirit. The Book of Romans says that there is no one just, not even one. So how can you say that you are a righteous person whose sins have disappeared by believing in the gospel of the water and the Spirit? You surely are a heretic. Those who preach the gospel of the water and the Spirit are not orthodox Christians, but they are heterodox. They are heretics. What kind of church is this?"

Nowadays, there are many Christians throughout the world who have received the remission of sins by believing in the gospel of the water and the Spirit through our books. But I've heard that after receiving the remission of sins, they are often summoned by their pastors and interrogated as though they were facing a religious trial.

Do you know by whom Peter and the other disciples of Jesus were arrested for preaching the gospel of the water and the Spirit? They were dragged to and interrogated by none other than the chief priests, who can be described as the leaders of Christianity in today's term. Do you then know to whom you'll be dragged when you receive the remission of sins by believing in the gospel of the water and the Spirit? You will be dragged to the very pastors and elders who had been guiding your religious life and interrogated by them as though you were put on a religious trial. This will happen inevitably once you receive the remission of sins by believing in the gospel of the water and the Spirit. However, just as the formerly blind man who was blessed by the Lord to open his spiritual eyes was wiser than the Pharisees who were adhering only to the Law, you should realize that those of us who have received the remission of sins through the gospel of the water and the Spirit are also wiser than our persecutors.

My fellow believers, before we received the remission of sins, we had to live as sinners always even though we believed in Jesus. It was not uncommon for you and I to come to church and offer prayers of repentance in tears to try to be remitted from our sins. At first, we felt good after praying in tears thinking of the blood that Jesus shed on the Cross, as we felt like our hearts were refreshed and cleansed, but when we kept offering such prayers of repentance repeatedly, our tears soon dried up. So when we couldn't shed any more tears, we even tried to think of all kinds of tragic things to wring out false tears. We did this because, in those days, we had foolishly thought that only then those around us would approve us as good Christians. However, my fellow believers, this was a religious trap set by Satan to drag our souls to hell. You must realize that such false tears and false prayers of repentance are nothing more than Satan's deception, designed to lead the unredeemed to have false faith and ultimately drag them to hell.

To help your understanding, let's turn to the Bible here. It's written in John 9:18-23: *"But the Jews did not believe concerning him, that he had been blind and received his sight, until they called the parents of him who had received his sight. And they asked them, saying, 'Is this your son, who you say was born blind? How then does he now see?' His parents answered them and said, 'We know that this is our son, and that he was born blind; but by what means he now sees we do not know, or who opened his eyes we do not know. He is of age; ask him. He will speak for himself.' His parents said these things because they feared the Jews, for the Jews had agreed already that if anyone confessed that He was Christ, he would be put out of the synagogue. Therefore his parents said, 'He is of age; ask him.'"*

My fellow believers, you and I have opened our eyes of faith by believing in the gospel of the water and the Spirit. Although we had been spiritually blind before, our eyes of faith have now been opened wide. In other words, we have now become righteous people, even though we had been sinners ignorant of the gospel of the water and the Spirit. However, if you say in the Christian community where you belong, "I am a righteous person, for I have received the remission of sins by believing in the gospel of the water and the Spirit," then you will be excommunicated by those who still have not received the remission of sins.

It is for this very reason that the parents of the blind man said, "He is indeed our son. It's true that he was a beggar, and it's also true that he was blind. And it's also true that our son can now see. While all these are true, we do not know Jesus." These parents knew already that if they admitted to know Jesus Christ, they would be excommunicated from Judaism. As they had not received the remission of sins yet, they were afraid of being excommunicated, and that's why they said that they didn't know Jesus.

Let's turn to today's Scripture passage again and see John 9:23-35: *"Therefore his parents said, 'He is of age; ask him.' So they again called the man who was blind, and said to him, 'Give God the glory! We know that this Man is a sinner.' He answered and said, 'Whether He is a sinner or not I do not know. One thing I know: that though I was blind, now I see.'"*

The Pharisees at that time were trying to paint Jesus as a

sinner based on their own doctrines. Gripped by their own legalistic conventional understanding, they interrogated the formerly blind man, saying, "How could Jesus Christ have taken away all the sins that we commit every day?" Such acts of the Pharisees were blaspheming the glory of Jesus. It was akin to a sinner blaspheming the glory of the redeemed. Without even realizing it themselves, they were challenge the very God in whom they believed.

Like these Pharisees, many Christian sinners in the world try to suppress those who have received the remission of sins by believing in the gospel of the water and the Spirit. If this Church that God blessed were not here, then you and I would have been oppressed inevitably, and we would have to once again lead a torturous religious life among sinners. However, you must realize that there is no truth that can bring salvation to you other than to believe that Jesus Christ took upon all your sins through His baptism and blotted them all out with the blood of the Cross. Jesus has blotted out all our sins once and for all with the gospel of the water and the Spirit, and so if we deny this Savior, where would we attain salvation? To repeat, there is no other way to be saved from sin but to believe in Jesus Christ's gospel of the water and the Spirit.

Therefore, my fellow believers, as those who have received the remission of sins, we must fight the spiritual battle of faith against the modern version of the Pharisees. Is it wrong to receive the remission of sins by believing in Jesus who came by the gospel of the water and the Spirit? Was it wrong for Jesus to open the eyes of the blind man on the Sabbath? Whether that day was the Sabbath Day or not is not what's important. Is it more important for you to keep the Sabbath or to receive the remission of sins by believing in the gospel of the water and the Spirit? The Lord said that the Sabbath was established for man. Our Lord said that He is the Master of the Sabbath. He made it clear that it's not the Sabbath Day that's important, but what's important is to believe that Jesus Christ is the Savior who has blotted out all our sins.

Like the Pharisees in today's Scripture passage, those who do not recognize Jesus' gospel of the water and the Spirit in this age and time are blaspheming the love of our Lord and His salvation, and they are challenging Him. On the day when everyone's sins are judged, the Lord will infallibly condemn such people who don't believe in the gospel of the water and the Spirit even as they know it. How can we say that we are still sinful when we believe that Jesus Christ, who has come by the gospel of the water and the Spirit, is our Savior? If your tab is all paid off, can you still say that you still owe money? If so, then you are still a sinner.

However, the formerly blind man said, *"Whether He is a sinner or not I do not know. One thing I know: that though I was blind, now I see" (John 9:25).* Put differently, he was testifying here, "I may not know much about Jesus, but I know that I've met Him and my eyes were opened." Even so, the Pharisees continued to taint Jesus as a sinner and interrogated the blind man, and so he said to them, *"I told you already, and you did not listen. Why do you want to hear it again? Do you also want to become His disciples?"* Then the Pharisees got angry and cursed the man, saying, *"You are His disciple, but we are Moses' disciples" (John 9:28).*

As a man blessed by God, Moses symbolizes the Law. So if your faith is still under Moses, then it means that you are still under the condemnation of sin. However, the Pharisees said, *"We know that God spoke to Moses; as for this fellow, we do not know where He is from."* Then the blind man said, *"Why, this is a marvelous thing, that you do not know where He is from; yet He has opened my eyes! Now we know that God does not hear sinners; but if anyone is a worshiper of God and does His will, He hears him" (John 9:30-31)*. The man who had been blind could not understand what the Pharisees were saying. For those who have received the remission of sins by believing in the gospel of the water and the Spirit, it's all weird to hear what's uttered by those who have not received the remission of sins. The formerly blind man who just received the remission of sins now won the spiritual battle against the Pharisees, who used to be his colleagues of faith. Like this, let me assure you that we the redeemed will also infallibly win our battle against those who do not believe in the gospel of the water and the Spirit, for we believe in this true gospel.

Those Who Believe in the Gospel of the Water and the Spirit Will Be Driven out of Worldly Religions

My fellow believers, as those who believe in the gospel of the water and the Spirit, you and I are righteous people. As we are sinless, we will enter the Kingdom of Heaven for sure. However, when people believe in the gospel of the water and the Spirit, they are often excommunicated by those who don't believe in this gospel. So those who fail to win their spiritual battle against these people end up intentionally denying their faith that had brought them the remission of sins, and they revert back to the spiritual blindness of the past that had kept them sinful, saying, "My heart is also sinful, so please don't drive me out." They do this because it would allow them to avoid excommunication.

However, in God's sight it's an unrighteous act for the righteous who have received the remission of sins to return to their false faith of the past, and to thus avoid excommunication. Even if you are excommunicated, if you follow the Lord together with the righteous, you will be happy. This means that since you have become a child of God, you do not have to revert back to become the Devil's child again. If anyone says to you, "You are still sinful, and it is right for you to revert back to your former self as a blind person," then you should clearly testify the gospel of the water and the Spirit, saying, "I don't know about anything else, but one thing clear is that even though I was a sinner, I've now become a righteous person." It is the unambiguous truth that we have become righteous people and opened our spiritual eyes by believing in the gospel of the water and the Spirit. Like the man who had been blind in today's Scripture passage, I ask you to testify to your former colleagues of false faith that you have been saved through the gospel of the water and the Spirit. And if they excommunicate you, then I admonish you to embrace it boldly.

The blind man in today's Scripture passage was also driven out by the Jews. It's said here in verse 34, *"They answered and said to him, 'You were completely born in sins, and are you teaching us?' And they cast him out."* In the Pharisees' eyes, this man who did not follow their Law was a great sinner.

However, the man who had been blind but opened his eyes by the Lord's blessing was no longer blind. Hearing that he had been cast out, Jesus found the formerly blind man and said to him, *"Do you believe in the Son of Man?"* The man answered, *"Who is He, Lord, that I may believe in Him?"* Jesus then said, *"You have seen Him, and it is He who is talking with you."* Then the man said, *"Lord, I believe!"* and he followed Him.

Like this man who had been blind, do you also believe in

Jesus as your Savior who came by the gospel of the water and the Spirit? Amen! I want you to grasp here clearly that when the formerly blind man was driven out by the Pharisees, the Lord found him and met with him. Like this, when you are cast out of false Christianity, Jesus Christ will receive you and God's Church will embrace you into its arms. In other words, when you are driven out by the false believers, you will not wander forever, but instead, Jesus the King of kings and the fountain of all blessings will welcome you into His arms and bless you, waiting for you in God's true Church. Therefore, all who have received the remission of sins must escape from their old relationships marked by falsehoods. You should turn around and leave the gatherings of false believers before you are cast out.

So, my fellow believes, if you have really received the remission of sins by believing in the gospel of the water and the Spirit, and if you don't want to be forced out by the false believers, then I admonish you to leave yourself. Get out of there and say, "I can't possibly continue to associate myself with sinners who don't believe in the gospel of the water and the Spirit. How can a righteous person be with sinners? How can you preach to me when you can't even blot out your own sins? How can you call yourself my leader when you can't even bring the remission of sins to me?" Our Jesus will then find you and meet with you, just as He had found the blind man.

The Lord said, *"For judgment I have come into this world, that those who do not see may see, and that those who see may be made blind."* For those who are spiritually blind, their sight is like trying to see through thick smoke—while they do see some spiritual things, they only see vaguely and cannot discern them properly. Although they hear that Jesus has blotted out the sins of this world once and for all with the gospel of the water and the Spirit, they continue to have doubts, wondering, "You say that Jesus has blotted out all the sins of this world, but I am not sure if He has really blotted them out." And those who can't open their spiritual yes, and believe in and follow false doctrines until the end, conclude by saying, "Jesus took away original sin, but He didn't take away my personal sins." It is these people that our Lord says are spiritually blind. The Lord said that those who do not see will see, and those who see will be made blind.

Was it then the Lord's intention to condemn such spiritually blind people and cast them all into hell? No, that was not His intention. Let's turn to John 9:41 here: *"If you were blind, you would have no sin; but now you say, 'We see.' Therefore your sin remains."* Even though everyone is born spiritually blind, if anyone admits himself and acknowledges that he is completely blind, then he can find Jesus, believe in the gospel of the water and the Spirit, and thus receive the remission of sins. However, if one does not realize himself, and seek after fleshly blessings only, then such people will not be able to receive the remission of sins. Therefore, those who do not believe in the gospel of the water and the Spirit properly, and instead say that although Jesus took away their original sin He did not take away their personal sins, cannot help but remain spiritually blind until the last day. Even though they profess to believe in Jesus on their own, in God's sight, they have not been able to wash away their hearts' sins nor receive the remission of sins. We must remember that although those who know that they are blind can come out to Jesus and received the remission of sins by believing in the gospel of the water and the Spirit, for those who think that they are neither completely blind nor have opened their eyes spiritually—that is, those who think that they are neither righteous people nor sinners—it is difficult to receive the everlasting remission of sins. I admonish you to take this to your heart, remembering that those who don't believe in the gospel of the water and the Spirit are forever doomed to live with their sins and to be judged for these sins.

My fellow believers, not just anyone can receive the remission of sins. Those who think that they have opened their eyes; those who do not believe in the gospel of the water and the Spirit and have not received the remission of sins from Jesus even as they claim to know the Word of God like the Pharisees; the arrogant who do not realize their true selves and just shout out to Jesus, "I believe! I believe!"; and the prideful who think that their faith is good enough even though their hearts still remain sinful—all these people cannot receive the everlasting remission of sins, and they will instead be condemned for their sins. They are the spiritually blind people who have not been remitted from their personal sins, even though they may say that they've been remitted from their original sin. If a spiritually blind man leads another blind man, both will fall into a pit. Likewise, these people themselves are not only destined to fall into hell while shouldering their sins, but they are also destined to drag others with them. All of us must realize this clearly.

My fellow believers, as you and I believe in the gospel of the water and the Spirit, we are no longer spiritually blind. Although we were all born spiritually blind, now that we have found Jesus Christ who has come by the gospel of the water and the Spirit, and now that we believe in Him, we have opened our spiritual eyes. The Lord looked for us and came to us, who had been blind by nature, and said to us, *"Go, wash in the pool of Siloam."* In obedience to this we believed in the gospel of the water and the Spirit given by the Lord, that the Lord washed away our sins once and for all with the gospel of the water and the Sprit, and we have thereby opened our eyes of faith and returned to God with full eyesight. Our Lord has opened our eyes both spiritually and physically as those who believe in the gospel of the water and the Spirit.

However, there still are many people who have not opened their eyes. Those who stand against Jesus—that is, those who say that their eyes of the flesh are open—still cannot recognize the Lord, their spiritual eyes are still blind, and they still cannot see the Kingdom of God properly. Their sins still remain in their hearts. Although many people in this age and time claim to have opened their spiritual eyes on their own, these people still remain sinners as they have not washed away their hearts' sins. You have now heard the gospel of the water and the Spirit and perhaps even started to believe in it, but if your reputation in the church you are attending now and your loyalty to it are obstructing you from walking on the way of the righteous, then you should boldly throw away this reputation and turn your steps to the way of believing in the gospel of the water and the Spirit. Otherwise you will never receive the remission of sins from the Lord.

Have you really received the perfect remission of sins by wholeheartedly believing in the gospel of the water and the Spirit? If this is indeed true for you, then just like the blind man recorded in today's Scripture passage, you will also be persecuted by the worldly church and even be driven out from it. But you shouldn't fear this. If you believe in the gospel of the water and the Spirit, then it is only normal for you to be cast out from where you had belonged until now. Better yet, it's actually a blessing for you to leave your old church before you are driven out. When the blind man in today's Scripture passage was excommunicated, Jesus found him and blessed him. I hope this will also happen to you. I admonish you all to truly have faith in the gospel of the water and the Spirit.

Again I admonish you to cast aside the glory and fame of the church to which you had belonged, become one with the believers in the gospel of the water and the Spirit, and lead your life of faith anew. It is my sincerest hope and prayer that you would all become one with God's Church by placing your faith in the gospel of the water and the Spirit, unite with your new Church, give your testimony of salvation for the sake of those who still have not found Jesus who has come by the gospel of the water and the Spirit, and embark on this blessed road to proclaim the gospel together with the born-again saints. ✉

SERMON

3

The Mystery behind The Blind Man Whose Eyes were Healed

< John 9:8-41 >

"Therefore the neighbors and those who previously had seen that he was blind said, 'Is not this he who sat and begged?' Some said, 'This is he.' Others said, 'He is like him.' He said, 'I am he.' Therefore they said to him, 'How were your eyes opened?' He answered and said, 'A Man called Jesus made clay and anointed my eyes and said to me, 'Go to the pool of Siloam and wash.' So I went and washed, and I received sight.' Then they said to him, 'Where is He?' He said, 'I do not know.' They brought him who formerly was blind to the Pharisees. Now it was a Sabbath when Jesus made the clay and opened his eyes. Then the Pharisees also asked him again how he had received his sight. He said to them, 'He put clay on my eyes, and I washed, and I see.' Therefore some of the Pharisees said, 'This Man is not from God, because He does not keep the Sabbath.' Others said, 'How can a man who is a sinner do such signs?' And there was a division among them. They said to the blind man again, 'What do you say about Him because He opened your eyes?' He said, 'He is a prophet.' But the Jews did not believe concerning him, that he had been blind and received his sight, until they called the parents of him who had received his sight. And they asked

them, saying, 'Is this your son, who you say was born blind? How then does he now see?' His parents answered them and said, 'We know that this is our son, and that he was born blind; but by what means he now sees we do not know, or who opened his eyes we do not know. He is of age; ask him. He will speak for himself.' His parents said these things because they feared the Jews, for the Jews had agreed already that if anyone confessed that He was Christ, he would be put out of the synagogue. Therefore his parents said, 'He is of age; ask him.' So they again called the man who was blind, and said to him, 'Give God the glory! We know that this Man is a sinner.' He answered and said, 'Whether He is a sinner or not, I do not know. One thing I know: that though I was blind, now I see.' Then they said to him again, 'What did He do to you? How did He open your eyes?' He answered them, 'I told you already, and you did not listen. Why do you want to hear it again? Do you also want to become His disciples?' Then they reviled him and said, 'You are His disciple, but we are Moses' disciples. We know that God spoke to Moses; as for this fellow, we do not know where He is from.' The man answered and said to them, 'Why, this is a marvelous thing, that you do not know where He is from; yet He has opened my eyes! Now we know that God does not hear sinners; but if anyone is a worshiper of God and does His will, He hears him. Since the world began it has been unheard of that anyone opened the eyes of one who was born blind. If this Man were not from God, He could do nothing.' They answered and said to him, 'You were completely born in sins, and are you teaching us?' And they cast him out. Jesus heard that they had cast him out; and when He had found him, He said to him, 'Do you believe in the Son of God?"

He answered and said, 'Who is He Lord that I may believe in Him?' And Jesus said to him, 'You have both seen Him and it is He who is talking with you.' Then he said, 'Lord, I believe!' And he worshiped Him. And Jesus said, 'For judgment I have come into this world, that those who do not see may see, and that those who see may be made blind.' Then some of the Pharisees who were with Him heard these words, and said to Him, 'Are we blind also?' Jesus said to them, 'If you were blind, you would have no sin; but now you say, 'we see.' Therefore your sin remains.'"

John chapter 9 tells the story of a blind man whose eyes were opened. Today I would like all of us to meditate on this passage. That the blind man's eyes were restored is really true, and there is a mystery behind it. We need to meditate on this account with spiritual discernment. It is indispensable for us to have such eye-opening experiences, and we must as a necessity, try to understand the mystery behind this incredible story where Jesus Christ healed this blind man's eyes. That the blind man's eyes were opened is a great mystery. The Bible says that this blind man eyes were immediately opened when he went to the pool of Siloam and washed his eyes as instructed by the Lord. A great mystery is hidden in this story.

What Do the Spiritually Blind People Need to Do to Have Their Eyes Opened?

The Apostle Paul said in Romans 7:22-25, *"For I delight in the law of God according to the inward man. But I see another law in my members, warring against the law of my mind, and bringing me into captivity to the law of sin which is in my members. O wretched man that I am! Who will deliver me from this body of death? I thank God—through Jesus Christ our Lord! So then, with the mind I myself serve the law of God, but with the flesh the law of sin."* If spiritually blind people come to understand this passage and realize the God given gospel Truth of the water and the Spirit, they then will have their blind eyes restored. Firstly we need to grasp the fact that we serve the law of God with our hearts, but with the flesh we serve the law of sin. We need to realize what this passage really means. Those who do not understand the mystery in this passage are 'the blind,' even though they may claim to be able to see.

The Lord said in the last verse of John chapter 9, *"If you were blind, you would have no sin; but now that you say, 'We see.' Therefore your sin remains."* Jesus said that if the Pharisees were really blind, they could have become sinless, but because they claimed to see, they remained as sinners. This passage means that those who claim to see the Truth even as it is proved that they do not understand it, they profess to know Jesus even as they do not really know Him, profess to be saved by believing in Jesus and being ignorant of His gospel Truth of the water and the Spirit, are all Christian sinners. The Bible has been translated into practically every vernacular language, and so it may seem as though we can understand it just by reading the black words on the white paper, but actually it is not so easy to understand. That is because the Lord spoke of spiritual things.

Paul said that his flesh served the law of sin, but with his mind he served the law of God (Romans 7:25). Every Christian serves the law of God, at least in his heart. All of us fear God.

We know that He is the Absolute Creator, the Almighty and our Perfect Savior; and we believe in His salvation. So we can all approach God in gratefulness and with respect. But to those who do not fear God, and do not know who He really is, and do not understand who Jesus Christ really is, and who do not realize the gravity of His wrath —should as a matter of importance first try and understand what the Apostle Paul said.

Paul said that he served the law of God with his heart and the law of sin with his flesh. This is true for everyone, irrespective of whether one is born again or not. It is everyone's heartfelt desire to live virtuously and uprightly. Yet despite this, everyone serves sin with his body. That is why the Bible says that in order to follow the Lord, we must cast aside our carnal thoughts and submit ourselves to Him. Nevertheless everyone serves the law of sin with his flesh. This means that everyone follows what the flesh desires. But in the heart, people really desire to serve the law of God. To receive the remission of sins in this condition—that is, while serving the law of God with the mind and the law of sin with the flesh— you should first fear God from the heart. You should respect God and realize just how majestic He is, and fear and honor Him. And you should realize His Truth of salvation He which was given to you.

This is why the Bible is so very difficult to understand even though it may appear easy. When the Bible is interpreted according to ethical and moral understandings, it may seem to make sense to fleshly minds, but the Bible is not about ethics and morals. Unlike the classical texts of Confucianism, which are essentially ethical writings, the Bible is certainly not a book of moral teachings as some make it out to be. The philosophical ideas of Socrates or Plato are man's own thoughts and claims, but the Bible is the perfect Word of God that is spoken to all mankind. Sometimes it will speak to the born-again and other times it will be addressed directly to those who have as yet not been born again. That is why it is so complicated.

Many Christians profess that it is very easy to believe in Jesus. They say that one can become a child of God just by praying to Him and accepting Jesus as his Savior. But not everyone can become God's own child just by accepting Jesus in his prayer. This is such a foolish claim. Just because one says with his mouth that he accepts the Holy Spirit or Jesus, this does not mean that Jesus or the Holy Spirit actually comes into that person's heart. God does not do our bidding. God is fundamentally different from us. He is holy and perfect, and we are no match for Him. Referring to Jesus, John the Baptist said, *"He who is coming after me, is preferred before me, whose sandal strap I am not worthy to loosen."* So just because anyone says, "Jesus, please come into my heart. I believe in you. I accept you," He will not actually enter into that person's heart. He lives in a wholly different dimension, whose majesty and scale far surpasses ours. We need to fully understand that not just anyone can receive God and talk with Him.

If you really want to know God, then you must first meet Jesus Christ, and your heart should fear Him. In other words, you must first realize just how lowly and insufficient you are before His presence, and how exalted, great, majestic and perfect Jesus really is. Only then will you come to respect Him from the depth of your heart.

Before turning to today's passage from the Gospel of John, we should ascertain if we really love the law of God and really desire to follow it with our whole hearts, or if we are serving and following the law of sin with our flesh. And we should know who this God really is, and we must also know who we really are, this is important. Also we must know who Jesus Christ is and what the God given gospel of the water and the Spirit really is. The Lord spoke to us in various ways about the real condition of man, a good example of this is Paul's admission where he served the law of God with his mind and the law of sin with his flesh. This means that in the flesh, everyone keeps following only after his own greed. It therefore does not matter how much we pray or how determined we might be. With our hearts we follow what we think is right, while with the flesh, we follow the law of sin.

Those who are able to follow the law of God with their hearts are the ones who have received the remission of sins, but those who have not received the remission of sins follow the law and even commit more wicked sins with their hearts. Seeking after evil with the heart is a sin greater than a sin of following evil with the flesh. The Lord said to the Pharisees, *"You strain out a gnat and swallow a camel."* This means that people swallow huge transgressions as big as a camel, but they strain out tiny offenses and ask the Lord to forgive them. People like this are hypocrites. There are also many who say that while they have been remitted from their original sin, their personal sins remain intact, and these daily sins are remitted away just by offering prayers of repentance.

All this is because they do not know God. And also because they do not know the gospel Truth of the water and the Spirit that God the Father has given to us through His Son. People generally are ignorant and live a faulty and ignorant standard of life, and do not even realize their own sins. When measured by the Lord's barometer, we steal with our hearts everyday, we get angry, and we murder dozens of people in just single day. Yet we walk around as though we are pious and not sinners.

A Korean poet, Dongju Yun once wrote a famous poem titled "Prelude." It goes like this:

Let me have no shame
Under the heaven
Till I die.
Even winds among the foliage
Pained my heart.
With a heart that sings of the stars,
I'll love all dying things.
And I must fare the path
That's been allotted to me.
Tonight also
The winds sweep over the stars.

Those who have set a high standard to live without any shame before God, know just how many sins they commit in any given day. That is why Christians and non-Christians alike should have a 'high spiritual standard of life.' Because people possess a 'hypocritical standard' they think they are not sinners before God and therefore their hearts are not troubled at all. And because of this carnal standard, they think that they are not going to hell. It is also because their standard is so low that they say, "I am good enough. And if someone like me goes to hell, then everyone else will go to hell." If the standard is high then one is compelled to admit to God that he deserves to be cast into hell a dozen times, and realizes that he really needs to be saved by God and asks for His help. Therefore we must have a high standard.

God gave 613 statutes of the Law commanding us that no one should have any other gods before Him. He summed up these 613 statutes of the Law into ten major commandments for us. Although we were born through our earthly parents, we need to understand that we were born because of God. But while living in this world we will serve all kinds of idols. So, calling us a brood of sin God gave us the Law so that we would realize this sin. Yet despite this people worship idols rather than God. God tells us that we are evildoers, neither knowing nor believing in the peace and salvation that God has given into our hearts, nor keeping them.

Those Who Are Blind Will See, but Those Who Already Claim to See Will Be Blind Forever

Jesus said, *"If you were blind, you would have no sin; but now that you say, 'We see." Therefore your sin remains."* A real blind man met Jesus and He opened up his eyes. John chapter 9 says that this blind mans eyes were opened, but for the Pharisees whose eyes were wide open, their sins remained intact. This blind man did not know himself, but once he met Jesus Christ he became aware who he really was, and because of this he received the remission of his sins. We also have received the remission of sins, because our spiritual eyes have been opened. Our spiritual eyes were opened when we came to believe in the gospel of the water and the Spirit, and realized just what terrible sinners we were, we received the remission of our sins by knowing and believing that the Lord accepted our sins through His baptism, was condemned for all these sins, rose from the dead and saved all of us. We were once blind, but our eyes have been opened and we have of the heart received the remission of sins. In contrast, those who see themselves only with their eyes of the flesh but not with the eyes of the heart still have sins remaining, and that is why they are still blind. Therefore we must try to understand exactly what Jesus said here.

We need to know that Jesus Christ made man together with His Father and the Holy Spirit. Jesus was very much involved when you and I were made, and including our ancestors. This very Jesus whom we believe in now was fully engaged in our creation. That is why we call Jesus, God. We call Him the Son of God. We say that He is the Creator, the Savior and the Judge.

In John chapter 9, when Jesus met a blind man, He spat on the ground, made clay with His saliva and put this clay over the blind man's eyes. He then told him to go and wash himself in the pool of Siloam. This means that even though we were all cursed, Jesus came as our Savior and washed away all our sins. The word Siloam means "sent." Jesus Christ was 'sent' by God the Father. He was 'sent' to save you and me from sin.

That Jesus spat on the ground to make clay and put it on the eyes of the blind man implies human beings are the accursed. In other words, you and I were destined for hell, but God the Father sent the Lord to us by coming down to this earth as our Savior, and He has saved us completely. Coming to this earth incarnated in the flesh of man, Jesus received the baptism with His body to bear all our sins, was condemned on the Cross while shouldering all those sins, and has thereby saved us. Just as the water in the pool of Siloam washed away all the clay, spit and filth that was on the eyes of the blind man, and he received his sight, the Lord likewise has cleansed away all our sins with His baptism and His blood on the Cross. If our Lord had not come to this earth to take upon your sins and mine by being baptized, He could not have borne the condemnation of sin, no matter how many times He suffered death on that Cross.

Leviticus chapter four and Matthew chapter three depict the relationship between the 'laying on of hands' in the Old

Testament and Jesus' water baptism in the Jordan River. The laying on of hands means that a sinner has to pass his sins over onto a sacrificial animal. You should pay particular attention to the fact that Jesus was baptized by John the Baptist in a form of 'laying on of hands' to take upon all the sins of the world once and for all. If Jesus Christ had not been baptized for us, then our sins would have still remained intact in our hearts, and we would still have all our accursed sins with us. Jesus died on the Cross because He had taken upon all our sins by being baptized by John the Baptist who was the representative of all mankind. By bearing all the condemnation of our sins, He has saved us, and become our Savior.

For 400 years, from the death of Malachi to the coming of Jesus, there was no true servant of God in Israel. Because God did not send His servants to Israel for this long period, the world became corrupt. When we turn to the Book of Malachi, we will read that mankind had become corrupted and filthy, and due to the fact that no one was looking for God, the Lord did not send any servants to His people for 400 years.

But at the beginning of the New Testament era we find a man named Zacharias, who was a righteous man in the sight of God. He truly believed in the sacrificial system of the Old Testament and offered sacrifices by faith. Zacharias' wife, Elizabeth was an old woman by now. She was way past menopause and could not bear any children. But it was the work of God that John the Baptist was conceived in her. God spoke to Zacharias as well through an angel. While Zacharias was serving in the Temple, an angel appeared before him and said, "Your wife will bear a son, and you shall call his name John."

Some six months later, an angel appeared before the Virgin Mary as well and said, "Mary you have found favor with God. You will bear a Son, and you shall name Him Jesus." When Mary said, "How can this be, since I do not know a man?" the angel said, "Elizabeth your relative has also conceived. God has done this."

To save you and me from sin, God sent both John the Baptist and Jesus to this earth. When the two turned 30, John the Baptist baptized Jesus as the representative of mankind, Jesus went to him and was baptized as the Savior of mankind. This is God's work. It was not done according to any man's plans. After baptizing Jesus, John the Baptist declared publicly, *"Behold! The Lamb of God who takes away the sin of the world!" (John 1:29)*

Because of our sins, we were destined to be sent to hell and to be enslaved by the Devil. But despite this Jesus came to this earth to save us by bearing all our sins and condemnation. Jesus came here to do this work, He first sought to be baptized by John the Baptist, and when John baptized Jesus, all the sins of mankind were passed onto Him. It was for 'this work' that John the Baptist had come into this earth. And he was also sent by God the Father. Jesus Christ the Son of God and John the Baptist were both sent by the Father according to His will. This was to fulfill the promise God had made in the Old Testament. In other words, by being baptized by John the Baptist, Jesus shouldered all our since once for all, and He was crucified and shed His blood to bear the condemnation of sin. And by rising from the dead, He has saved us completely. This is the providence of God and His work. Jesus said that there was no one in the world who was greater than John the Baptist.

Elijah was one of the greatest prophets in the Old Testament who fought against 850 prophets of Baal and Asherah all by himself, so that he could lead the children of Israel back to God. To settle who really was the true God, Baal or Jehovah, Elijah and these prophets had decided to offer sacrifices. The prophets of Baal and Asherah prayed all day from sunrise to sunset, but they could not get their sacrifices on the altar to burn. But when Elijah prayed to God, fire came down from heaven and consumed all the flesh sacrifices, firewood, and even licked up the water that filled the trenches surrounding the altar. When the people of Israel witnessed this incredible thing they admitted that only Jehovah was the real living God and they returned back to Him. There was no prophet as amazing as Elijah.

Just as Elijah had led the people of Israel back to God, it was none other than John the Baptist who was to lead everyone back to God. Matthew 3:16-17 says, *"When He had been baptized, Jesus came up immediately from the water; and behold, the heavens were opened to Him, and He saw the Spirit of God descending like a dove and alighting upon Him. And suddenly a voice came from heaven, saying, 'This is my beloved Son, in whom I am well pleased.'"* Baptism also means to be covered with something.

By being baptized by John the Baptist, Jesus was covered with our sins. He had accepted them all leaving not one behind. Jesus Christ thus took upon our sins through His baptism, and by bearing the condemnation of our sin, He could saved us completely. This is the will of God the Father. No one can change this.

We must know this Truth of salvation that God had fulfilled for us. Even before the foundation of this world, God had planned to wash away all our sins with the gospel of the water and the Spirit and make us His children through His Son Jesus Christ. And according to God's plan, we have received the remission of our sins and come to praise God and enjoy the glory of Heaven. In this plan we find Jesus and John the

Baptist; we also find God's servants of the Old Testament, today's servants of God, and you and me as well.

Just as you have a plan and purpose when you make something, likewise God also had a plan and purpose when He made you and me and created this universe and all things in it. God's plan and purpose is none other than the remission of your sins and mine. Having cleansed away our sins and made us the brides of Jesus Christ, we will be taken to His Kingdom to enjoy everlasting life and live forever in power and glory. That is why we must know this wonderful plan of God.

Those who profess that they can see and do not at the same time know anything about the gospel of the water and the Spirit are all blind. It is those who have received the remission of sins into their hearts that have had their spiritual eyes opened. Jesus told the blind man to go to the pool of Siloam and wash his eyes. When the Lord came to this earth as our Savior, He took upon all our sins by being baptized by John the Baptist. You should also go to that place and pass your sins onto Him by faith. You and I must pass our sins onto Jesus. We must believe and acknowledge wholeheartedly that God has set our salvation in this way, and that He has blotted out all our sins and saved us in this way. That is how we are saved, and there is no other way. Because you believe in God and the Truth that was established by Him, and because Jesus Christ took upon all your sins by being baptized, He is telling you to go to the pool of Siloam and wash yourself.

Condemnation for our sins must be borne on the Cross. Our sins were passed over onto Jesus by faith through the baptism He received, and Jesus bore the condemnation of all our sins on that Cross. When Jesus Christ was crucified, your old self and my old self were also crucified. Therefore it is no longer I who live, but Jesus Christ lives in me and you. Jesus

Christ came to this earth to save you and me from sin, shouldered all our sins by being baptized by John the Baptist, carried the sins of the world to the Cross, and was crucified, whipped and brutally killed to bear the condemnation of our sin. By His own body He washed away all our sins and was condemned for them. The Bible tells us that, *"The wages of sin is death."* The body of Jesus perished while shouldering all our sins. But in three days after he died, He rose from the dead just as He had promised. He has thus saved us.

So rather than being drawn into man's own fleshly thoughts and the lies brought in by the Devil, we must grasp God's great plan and believe in it accordingly. We must say, "In the name of the Lord Jesus I command you, be gone Satan!" It is written, *"You shall know the truth, and the truth shall make you free."* It is therefore absolutely critical to have the right knowledge about our salvation. If you really desire to wash away all your sins, you must go to the pool of Siloam and wash it there. This means that underneath the Cross is not the place where you should be asking God to wash away your sins. Jesus was crucified to bear the condemnation of our sins because He had already taken upon them by being baptized by John the Baptist. He was condemned for the sins of the world. And the sins of the world include none other than your sins and mine, and all the sins of both our ancestors and their many descendants.

The Lord bore all our sins by being baptized, blotted them all out by being condemned on that Cross, and has through this become our Savior. He has saved us perfectly from sin. The reason why people still have sin in their hearts despite all this is because they do not believe in what the Lord had accomplished for them. It is because they have not united their hearts with Christ at each and every Righteous Act of His ministry. You should unite your heart with Jesus Christ when He was baptized. When Jesus was baptized, He commanded John the Baptist, *"Permit it to be so now, for thus it is fitting for us to fulfill all righteousness."* That Jesus was baptized means that He accepted all the sins of mankind. Your sins were also passed onto Him at that time. That is why Jesus is the Lamb of God. Just like the sacrificial animals of the Old Testament, Christ accepted all our sins onto His sinless body by being baptized. You should therefore unite your heart with this Righteous Act. Since all the sins of the world were passed onto Jesus when He was baptized, you must realize and grasp that your sins were also passed onto Him.

People nowadays say that John the Baptist is insignificant. Even among biblical scholars and pastors, there are those who say that John the Baptist was a complete failure. But we need to know this is what ignorant people say. Regarding the role of John the Baptist, the Bible testifies as the following:

"As it is written in the Prophets:
'Behold, I send my messenger before your face,
Who will prepare your way before You.'
'The voice of one crying in the wilderness:
'Prepare the way of the LORD;
Make His paths straight''" (Mark 1:2-3).

Because John the Baptist passed sin onto Jesus, it was possible for all the wretched people in this world to be washed from their sins. This is because Jesus Christ shouldered all our sins and was condemned for them on the Cross. John the Baptist is not the one who saved us, but his duty was to pass all the sins of mankind onto Jesus in obedience to the will of God. He was one of the most precious servants of God. In the whole land of Judea only John the Baptist could say to the Jews, the Pharisees and the chief priests that they were a brood of vipers.

He could say such things because he had the God-given authority as His servant.

You should therefore let your heart be united with this Truth that your sins were all passed onto Jesus. And you must unite with the Truth that Jesus shouldered the sins of the world and was crucified. He was wounded for our transgressions, He was bruised for our iniquities, and He shouldered all the sins of the world, each and every sin that we have ever committed which we inherited from our parents. He bore all our sins and was condemned in our place with His crucifixion. To become our Savior He was baptized by John the Baptist and was condemned on that Cross. If He had not received this baptism, there would have been no need for Him to go to that terrible Cross.

If you read the Bible carefully, you will see just how important the role of John the Baptist really was. His role was to prepare the way for the Lord (Luke 3:4-6; Isaiah 40:4). Therefore God will send all those whose hearts are arrogant to hell, but for those who truly acknowledge God and fear Him, He has given to them the remission of sins and made them His very own children. This is the righteous will of God and His just work.

Words cannot express just how thankful I am that the Lord took upon all our sins and opened up our blind eyes. Are you also grateful? ⌧

SERMON

4

Believers in the Divinity of Jesus Receive Salvation by Believing in the Gospel

< John 9:8-41 >

"Therefore the neighbors and those who previously had seen that he was blind said, 'Is not this he who sat and begged?' Some said, 'This is he.' Others said, 'He is like him.' He said, 'I am he.' Therefore they said to him, 'How were your eyes opened?' He answered and said, 'A Man called Jesus made clay and anointed my eyes and said to me, 'Go to the pool of Siloam and wash.' So I went and washed, and I received sight.' Then they said to him, 'Where is He?' He said, 'I do not know.' They brought him who formerly was blind to the Pharisees. Now it was a Sabbath when Jesus made the clay and opened his eyes. Then the Pharisees also asked him again how he had received his sight. He said to them, 'He put clay on my eyes, and I washed, and I see.' Therefore some of the Pharisees said, 'This Man is not from God, because He does not keep the Sabbath.' Others said, 'How can a man who is a sinner do such signs?' And there was a division among them. They said to the blind man again, 'What do you say about Him because He opened your eyes?' He said, 'He is a prophet.' But the Jews did not believe concerning him, that he had been blind and received his sight, until they called the parents of him who had received his sight. And they asked

them, saying, 'Is this your son, who you say was born blind? How then does he now see?' His parents answered them and said, 'We know that this is our son, and that he was born blind; but by what means he now sees we do not know, or who opened his eyes we do not know. He is of age; ask him. He will speak for himself.' His parents said these things because they feared the Jews, for the Jews had agreed already that if anyone confessed that He was Christ, he would be put out of the synagogue. Therefore his parents said, 'He is of age; ask him.' So they again called the man who was blind, and said to him, 'Give God the glory! We know that this Man is a sinner.' He answered and said, 'Whether He is a sinner or not I do not know. One thing I know: that though I was blind, now I see.' Then they said to him again, 'What did He do to you? How did He open your eyes?' He answered them, 'I told you already, and you did not listen. Why do you want to hear it again? Do you also want to become His disciples?' Then they reviled him and said, 'You are His disciple, but we are Moses' disciples. We know that God spoke to Moses; as for this fellow, we do not know where He is from.' The man answered and said to them, 'Why, this is a marvelous thing, that you do not know where He is from; yet He has opened my eyes! Now we know that God does not hear sinners; but if anyone is a worshiper of God and does His will, He hears him. Since the world began it has been unheard of that anyone opened the eyes of one who was born blind. If this Man were not from God, He could do nothing.' They answered and said to him, 'You were completely born in sins, and are you teaching us?' And they cast him out. Jesus heard that they had cast him out; and when He had found him, He said to him, 'Do you believe in the Son of God?"

He answered and said, 'Who is He, Lord, that I may believe in Him?' And Jesus said to him, 'You have both seen Him and it is He who is talking with you.' Then he said, 'Lord, I believe!' And he worshiped Him. And Jesus said, 'For judgment I have come into this world, that those who do not see may see, and that those who see may be made blind.' Then some of the Pharisees who were with Him heard these words, and said to Him, 'Are we blind also?' Jesus said to them, 'If you were blind, you would have no sin; but now you say, 'We see.' Therefore your sin remains.'"

All of us are working very hard to the best of our abilities in order to support the gospel ministry. As our brothers and sisters are supporting the gospel ministry with their financial help along with all the servants of God, I hope and pray that they would all prosper. As we continue to work diligently, I believe that the Lord is blessing our ministry, but I am also praying for even more blessings. We've made many preparations, because whether we can carry out the work of God successfully or not depends on how well prepared we are. We desire to supply the things that people need, and to thus give them joy and be loved by God. So we want to support the gospel ministry.

We believe that God's work will prosper, and we know that we must prepare ourselves, ask God for His help, rise up to the challenge, and knock on the door for His help. I believe that the Lord will then sooner or later complete all the work that He has entrusted to us. The Bible says, *"Faith is the substance of things hoped for, the evidence of things not seen."* I am sure that if we believe, the Lord's work will also succeed. If we work by faith, then everything will go well, but if we don't have faith, then we will end up giving up our work half way. But I believe that the Lord's work will succeed for sure.

No matter what, we must live with hope. The gospel should also be preached with hope. Whether we are preaching the gospel to the world or working to raise financial means, we must do both with hope. Everyone should have a dream. Only when one has a dream can the person prepare for the future. Anyone who has no dream is as good as dead. It's already April, but soon the summer discipleship training camp will come and go, followed by the winter discipleship training camp, and the next year will then be right around the corner. Unless one has a worthy goal, he will end up wasting his time and destroying himself. To spread the gospel of the water and the Spirit, all of us should rise up to the challenge with hope and faith.

I am sure that if we continue to carry out what we can do and ask for God's help, He will bless us and make us prosper. Sooner or later, we will cover the entire world with the gospel of the water and the Spirit and make it known to everyone. We work with a dream that all the 65 billion people on the planet will come across the gospel of the water and the Spirit. As long as we ready ourselves and seek God's help, I am sure that this dream will come true in little time. My mind is also busy thinking about how we can preach the gospel all over the world. To spread the gospel successfully, we also need to succeed in our businesses; if we instead go about carelessly, it will be more difficult to preach the gospel. So it's my belief that we all need to work more diligently.

When the Prophet Nehemiah was rebuilding the city of Jerusalem, there were many detractors around him. So he prayed to God, and God instructed him to guard every construction site of the city with armed forces and to equip every worker with a sword or a spear. God helped the people of Israel to rebuild Jerusalem in this way. None other than this is how God's work is achieved. It's not wrong for God's servants to try hard to make money in order to support the gospel ministry. On the contrary, just praying while remaining idle is wrong. Rather than blindly and rashly jumping into the mission field abroad as missionaries expecting that God would take care of us, it is far better for us to do what is feasible for us. All our forefathers of faith also followed God while raising cattle or tilting the ground.

It is totally biblical and normal for us to serve the gospel of the water and the Spirit while running businesses and working like this. This is much better than what's happening in ordinary churches, where pastors and evangelists sit around doing nothing more than just preaching a few times a week, visiting the homes of the believers, and collecting offerings from them. Even if these people were to work to death, all that they can achieve in a hundred years is just building a church building.

I've heard that some Evangelicals ridicule our mission strategy. If the servants of God were not to work and stay idle, trying to evangelize with your offerings, then nothing will be accomplished. I will just tell you to keep making donations. But in this way, it's simply impossible to publish our books and distribute them throughout the whole world. If we want to prosper and help others as well, then we must work. Haven't you read in the Bible how the Apostle Paul served the gospel himself? He also had a job to make money for his living and ministry, and we call his ministry "tent-making mission" (Acts 18:3). We must work by faith. Let us then prepare for our work by faith to see how much God would bless us this summer.

Why Is It Wrong for the Blind Man to Open His Eyes on the Sabbath Day?

We just read John 9:8-41 for today's Scripture passage. It was on the Sabbath Day that the blind man opened his eyes. That his eyes were opened on the Sabbath became an issue. People took the blind man to the Pharisees, and they asked him, "How were your eyes opened?" The blind man then said, "Jesus put some clay on my eyes and told me to go to the pool of Siloam and wash there. So I did as I was told, and my eyes were opened." In the Pharisees' eyes, Jesus was clearly a sinner for having healed the sick on the Sabbath. So arguing that it was impossible for a sinner to perform a miracle, they accused Jesus of wrongdoing and tainted him as a heretic.

John 9:35 says, *"Jesus heard that they had cast him out; and when He had found him, He said to him, 'Do you believe in the Son of God?'"* The Son of God here refers to Jesus Himself. The man then asked the Lord who the Son of God was, and when the Lord told him it was He, the man said that he believed in Him. By believing in Jesus and the gospel of the water and the Spirit, we have received the remission of sins and opened our spiritual eyes. For us to live out our faith also, we need to be ready to answer the following important questions: "Do you believe in the Son of Man? Do you believe in the Son of God? Do you believe in Jesus Christ the Son of God as your Savior?"

Jesus is the Son of God the Father. This fact is extremely important. To God the Father, Jesus is His Son, and to us, Jesus is God Himself. That's why when Jesus asked the man if he believed that Jesus was the Son of God, he said he did, and by his faith he was spiritually saved. Whoever believes in the Son of God can be saved, but whoever does not believe cannot be saved. The implication here in this question—"Do you believe in the Son of God?"—is whether we believe not only that Jesus is the Son of God, but also God Himself. In other words, the question is whether we believe that Jesus is God Himself who healed the sick, performed miracles, and remitted away people's sins. Jesus is the Son of God, the true God and our Savior, and it is only if we believe in this that our faith is made pure and perfect.

If you just recognize and believe in Jesus only as the Son of God, rather than believing that He is also the very God who created the universe, then your beliefs would constitute only a religion of your own making. When human beings give birth, they give birth to human beings. Likewise, God the Father bore Jesus Christ as His Son. Just as God the Father is divine, so is His Son divine. And this only begotten Son of God made the universe and everything in it, including you and me. This is an extremely important knowledge.

The core question raised in the Gospel of John is this: "Do you believe in the Son of Man? Do you believe that Jesus is the Son of God the Father, and that He is also God Himself and your Savior?" The overall theme of the Gospel of John is that Jesus is the very God who made the universe. In other words, it is Jesus who created the heavens and the earth and made us, just as it is written, *"In the beginning God created the heavens and the earth. God said, 'Let there be light'; and there was light."* Jesus Christ is the Creator who made you and me, and He is the Savior who has saved us from sin. Jesus Christ is the Savior who has delivered us from sin to make us God's children, and He is also the Judge. It's absolutely critical to understand this Jesus properly and believe in Him properly.

As the blind man opened his eyes on the Sabbath, people took him to the Pharisees. The Pharisees then accused Jesus of being a sinner, saying, "Since He opened the eyes of this blind man on the Sabbath, He must be a sinner." And they said that although they knew that God had sent Moses, they didn't know who Jesus Christ was. Simply put, they didn't believe in Jesus. Because they did not believe that Jesus was the Creator of man and our Savior, and that He was God Himself, they made an issue out of what Jesus did and stood against Him.

Today also, there are many people who are like these Pharisees. Even among Christians, there are plenty of people who don't even realize that Jesus is God Himself and the Creator. We celebrated Easter Sunday just recently. A certain church in our city put up a banner saying, "Rejoice! Let Us Dance in Joy!" However, did the members of this church really believe that Jesus was resurrected? The sad reality is that most Christians do not believe that Jesus was resurrected literally. Although many Christians profess to believe that Jesus Christ was resurrected back to life, they take this only figuratively and don't believe that He actually rose from the dead again. Because they don't really believe that Jesus is God Himself, they can't quite bring themselves to believe unwaveringly that Jesus rose from the dead again literally.

The Bible says, *"All things were made through Him, and without Him nothing was made that was made."* It also says, *"In the beginning God created the heavens and the earth. God said, 'Let there be light'; and there was light."* The One who said these things is none other than Jesus Christ who came to save us. It is through the written Word that we are able to know who Jesus is, and it is by believing in this Word that we are able to realize and believe that Jesus is indeed our God, our Creator, and our Savior. No one comes to know and believe in Jesus by his natural human instincts. Anyone who doesn't believe in who Jesus is by believing in this Word is someone who doesn't actually believe that Jesus is God Himself. This is an extremely important issue.

Although many people today profess to believe in Jesus, in reality, there are more Christians who don't actually believe that Jesus is God. Some religious groups do not believe that Jesus is God Himself and the Creator. They argue that only Jehovah is God, and that Jesus is merely one of His creatures, just like you and me and all the angels. So because they think like that, even when we tell them that Jesus has saved all humankind through the gospel of the water and the Spirit, they say that it's completely irrelevant to them.

If Jesus were not God, we could not have been saved from sin. He created us and made the universe and all its hosts. And when we fell into sin and destruction deceived by Satan, He came in the flesh of man to save us His creatures from sin. Jesus, God Incarnate, bore our sins on His body by being baptized, was crucified to shed His blood to death, rose from the dead again, and has thereby saved us. It's all thanks to His righteous act that we were saved from sin. We have reached our salvation all because the Lord our Maker came to this earth, took our sins upon His body, bore our condemnation, and has thereby saved all of us from sin. It's because He is God Himself that we were saved; if He were just a creature rather than God Himself, then He could not have saved us. Like this, faith in the divinity of Christ is absolutely indispensable to us. For Jesus to be our Savior, He must be God Himself and our Creator. Only then could He save us from sin, and only then is our salvation made perfect.

Anyone born of a human being is another human being; no human being can give birth to a dog. Some people may act like a dog though born as human beings, but no one gives birth to a dog. So, if Jesus Christ is the only begotten Son of God the

Father, then Jesus is also divine. We must believe without any doubt that just as Jesus' Father is divine, so is Jesus also divine.

It's Foolish to Believe in God According to Our Fleshly Thoughts

Some people think in their fleshly minds that if Jesus had a Father, then He must also have a mother. For example, Catholics think that if Jesus is the Son of God, then God must have a wife, and they call Mary the Queen of Heaven. Since Mary is Jesus' mother, they pray to her, saying, "Hail, holy Queen, Mother of Mercy! Our life, our sweetness, and our hope!" What nonsense this is! Jesus is the Son of God and our Creator. If He is your Creator and mine, then He is the Creator of the universe and all its hosts. That's why He is God. If someone claims to be divine even without having created the universe and all things in it, he is a fraud. So religion is different from faith.

There is no gender in the Kingdom of Heaven, and so there is no distinction between men and women. Jesus was once asked by someone who was curious about the first resurrection: "Lord, we are curious about the first resurrection. In our Jewish tradition, if the older brother passes away and leaves his wife behind as a widow, then she must live with her bother-in-law. But let's say that the first brother-in-law died, and so the widow lived with her second brother-in-law. When the second brother-in-law also died, she lived with the third brother-in-law. Let's say that this family had eight brothers, and that as they all died, the woman ended up living with all eight brothers before passing away. Then whose wife would this woman be when the first resurrection occurs on the last day?" Jesus then said to him, "You have misunderstood. When the Kingdom comes, every righteous person will go through the first resurrection, but in that Kingdom there will be neither men nor women, just as angels have no gender."

As Jesus opened the eyes of the blind man, he was cast out by the Pharisees. Jesus then sought him out and met with him. And He said to him, *"Do you believe in the Son of Man?"* The man then said, *"Who is He, Lord, that I may believe in Him?"* Believing that Jesus is God Himself, all of us must trust that Jesus is the Creator and our Savior, and we must also lead our lives of faith trusting that He has blotted out all our sins with the gospel of the water and the Spirit.

The Pharisees persecuted Jesus and stood against Him precisely because they didn't recognize who He was. They would have never done so if they had known who Jesus was. In this present world as well, if people would really grasp who Jesus is, they would all believe in Him. For those who know and believe that Jesus is God Himself, when we tell them that Jesus has blotted out all our sins with the gospel of the water and the Spirit, they would receive the remission of sins by believing in this Truth. The most important faith is to believe that Jesus is God, our Creator, and our Savior. It is from this rock-solid belief in the divinity of Jesus that all faith begins.

Without this belief, your faith is nothing. If Jesus were not divine, then the fact that He has saved us through the gospel of the water and the Spirit would also be nothing more than a hypothetical notion and a complete illusion. Even if some religious leader took upon your sins and died in your place, it would still be completely useless. This leader is still just a sinner before God like everyone else, and so no sinner can save another sinner.

Jesus Christ, in contrast, is righteous and holy. He is not a sinner. He became man for a short while only to save us from sin. It's to save us that He became man temporarily and bore our sins on His body. It's not into His heart that Jesus accepted all our sins, but He bore them on His body. As Jesus took upon our sins on His body by receiving His baptism, died on the Cross, and rose from the dead again, He could become our everlasting Savior completely and perfectly. If our sins were passed onto Jesus' heart, and Jesus also had sin in His heart, then our salvation could never have been made perfect. No sinner can save another sinner. Because a sinner must be condemned without fail, God rendered His judgment on Jesus by crucifying His body. He allowed Jesus' body to reach death once, and then He resurrected Him again. Like this, God passed our sins to Jesus' body, not to His soul.

As we live out our faith, the very first faith that all of us must have is that Jesus is our God. This faith, that Jesus is our Creator and our Savior, is absolutely indispensable for all of us to have. It's written in the Gospel of John, *"In the beginning was the Word, and the Word was with God, and the Word was God" (John 1:1).* Where it says, *"In the beginning was the Word,"* it means that when the universe was first created, there was the Word of God saying, *"Let there be light."* And where it says, *"The Word was with God,"* the Word here refers to Jesus Christ. Since it's Jesus our God and our Creator who spoke this Word, this means that He has existed from the beginning. It's also written, *"The Word was God."* That's why we say that Jesus is the "God of the Word." In other words, it is with His Word that Jesus created the universe, and it is with His Word that He worked.

John 1:2-3 says, *"He was in the beginning with God. All things were made through Him, and without Him nothing was made that was made."* The pronoun "He" here refers to Jesus

Christ. It refers to the one and only Jesus Christ. It's Jesus who spoke the Word in Genesis chapter one that created the universe. So referring to Jesus, the Gospel of John continues on to say: *"All things were made through Him, and without Him nothing was made that was made. In Him was life, and the life was the light of men" (John 1:3-4)*; *"He was in the world, and the world was made through Him, and the world did not know Him. He came to His own, and His own did not receive Him. But as many as received Him, to them He gave the right to become children of God, to those who believe in His name" (John 1:10-12)*; and, *"The Word became flesh and dwelt among us, and we beheld His glory, the glory as of the only begotten of the Father, full of grace and truth" (John 1:14).*

Thus the Bible makes it clear that the Word that created the universe came to us incarnated in the flesh of man, full of grace and truth. In short, Christ is indeed God Himself; He has fulfilled everything according to His Word; He has brought true salvation to us; He is the real Creator who made the universe; and He is the Savior who has delivered His people from all their sins. The world was made through Him.

The Gospel of John was written by the Apostle John. It tells us clearly that Jesus is the One who made this world. He not only made the world, but He also came to this earth to save us from sin, and He has indeed saved us according to His will. It's Jesus Christ who gives life to the universe and all things in it, and it's also Jesus Christ who, even though you and I were destined to be condemned for our sins, has given us new life. Those of us who believe that Jesus is our Creator and Savior can also believe that He has saved us from sin through the gospel of the water and the Spirit, but those who don't believe in this are not real believers no matter what else they might believe in. We believe that Jesus is God Himself, and we believe in the God-spoken gospel of the water and the Spirit.

I trust that you also believe like this. I give all my thanks to God. ⌧

SERMON

5

The Law

The Lord Has Saved Us Who Were to Be Cursed

< John 9:1-7 >

"Now as Jesus passed by, He saw a man who was blind from birth. And His disciples asked Him, saying, 'Rabbi, who sinned, this man or his parents, that he was born blind?' Jesus answered, 'Neither this man nor his parents sinned, but that the works of God should be revealed in him. I must work the works of Him who sent me while it is day; the night is coming when no one can work. As long as I am in the world, I am the light of the world.' When He had said these things, He spat on the ground and made clay with the saliva; and He anointed the eyes of the blind man with the clay. And He said to him, 'Go, wash in the pool of Siloam' (which is translated, Sent). So he went and washed, and came back seeing."

How have you all been?

One of the beautiful works of the church of God is when various people work together in unity. Whenever I conceive a plan of action, I often experience the weaknesses of my flesh especially towards the end of that task. But even though I get tired, I am challenged by it and strive to finish the work, for I enjoy seeing the completion of this precious work. But it seems that some people have a tendency of shying away from doing challenging 'righteous works.'

Whenever I go on a subway or when passing by a busy

street, every now and then I see people wearing a banner, walking about and shouting, "Disbelief is hell, but Jesus is Heaven." When considering this, I believe that this gospel of the water and the Spirit will become more effective than shouting and wearing banners like this. The reason for this is because the words they speak are not the gospel of the water and the Spirit which says that Jesus had died having taken on all the sins of the world through His baptism which He received from John the Baptist. For this reason they find it is easy to shout and go crazy, "Jesus, Heaven! Disbelief, hell!" in an open public place these days, and the result of this is that the world treats them as the crazy's and with contempt.

The Lord told us clearly, *"Make friends for yourselves by unrighteous mammon" (Luke 16:9)*. Therefore our pastors and missionary workers, as well as our lay believers, are earning money by running various businesses to support the spreading of the gospel of the water and the Spirit. If we just shout out, "Jesus is Heaven! Disbelief is hell!" without the gospel of the water and the Spirit, then people will not come to know the gospel of the water and the Spirit, and will not be able to go to Heaven with these few empty words. Therefore, we must have the desire to persistently carry out works that are useful to the evangelization of this gospel, and we should possess endurance to finish that work we had started.

More than anything else, I would like to inform you that it is a blessing for the church of God to support the evangelization of the gospel by constantly raising up workers of God who will spread the gospel of the water and the Spirit. If God's Church was not here and if the forerunners of faith had not provided you with work to do, we would not have been able to spread the gospel so energetically.

If this were the case we would have carried out the work

of serving the Lord's gospel of the water and the Spirit all on our own without the guidance from God's Church. As a result of this we would have stopped preaching the gospel within a year. For certain people it would have been just a month or two. Nevertheless, if our hearts were not standing firm on this gospel of the water and the Spirit it would lead to a rapid cooling off of our hearts love towards God. And the result of this it will incite the desires of the flesh to rise up and seek and follow after things that rot away. Therefore even if we did become a worker of God for having received the remission of our sins by believing in the gospel of the water and the Spirit, and did not continue steadfastly serving the gospel by knowing the will of God, then our hearts would die a spiritual death. For this reason, when the church of God entrusts a certain duty to you, you must carry out that duty diligently and be thankful that you have been entrusted with that precious duty.

Once in a while, certain workers in the ministry think that it would be good to do the work of God independently by leaving God's Church. It would be fortunate if they were to laboriously serve the gospel of the water and the Spirit all by themselves, but most of them are unable to do this. At first it seems as though they are coping well doing the work of God. But soon the desires of the flesh begin rising up in their hearts, resulting in them throwing in the towel. When people start to serve their own fleshly desires, it would only mean certain death. Therefore, I speak to all pastors, missionary workers, and all those who are faithfully carrying out the work of God inside the Church, please remain inside the Church that serves the gospel of the water and the Spirit to the end, by thanking God.

Naturally, if they really desire their independence, I will allow them to leave at any time. Anyone who does not want to work with me, I will allow them to leave and serve the gospel of the water and the Spirit all by themselves. If you desire your independence, then all you have to do is leave God's Church and serve the gospel of the water and the Spirit. But before you do this, please think seriously about it? Try to visualize whether or not it will be easy for you to serve the gospel of the water and the Spirit all by yourself and at the same time to keep your heart secure. Only then will you begin to realize just how blessed and how joyous it is to be working together in union with the fellow workers in God's Church. Would there be anyone amongst the students of the Mission School who wishes to start an independent ministry, if so please raise your hands. I will support you. As for those narrow minded satisfaction seekers, who seek after not having to worry about putting food on the table, and getting welcomed as pastors, having luxurious cars, and receiving a large amount of money as honorariums, it would be better for the ministry if we were to send them in that direction.

We need to know that the Apostles, the Fathers of our faith of the Early Church, and those of us who truly love the Lord desire to spread the gospel throughout the world, and they do not chase after their own carnal desires. They only work for the benefit of the gospel of the water and the Spirit. The Lord said in the Book of Proverbs, *"Take away the dross from silver, And it will go to the silversmith for jewelry" (Proverbs 25:4).* Like these Words, if you don't refine silver, you won't be getting useful jewelry. Also should you are to leave silver in its original form, it will just be a lump of some silver, having no particular use. Silver spoons, silver hairpins, silver crowns, and so on are all things created by melting and refining it into pure silver. Likewise, after having been born again by believing in the gospel of the water and the Spirit, we must go through a sufficient amount of spiritual training, by dwelling in the gospel of the water and the Spirit so that the dross and impurities can be removed from our hearts. No one is capable of removing this dross from his heart all on his own. By giving up oneself wholeheartedly to the Lord, you become a useful tool through the Lord. Therefore, only after the removal of our fleshly greed, we can through the Church be disciplined by doing the entrusted works of God.

I must be honest there are times when I get exasperated when I see workers inside the Church. Amongst the people especially amongst the younger ones, they look so fragile like lambs, they seem as though they will die if left alone. But if they are given some guidance, they will survive and live. There are also people who do not realize just how important and how thankful they should be by doing this precious work of God inside the Church, by doing this they do not realize the fact that they are dying due to having fallen into the desires of the flesh. It is spiritually frustrating for me, but they will not realize anything by my teaching. Therefore I will leave them alone until they realize that fact by themselves.

There Was a Man Who Was Born Blind

We read the Word in the Gospel of John chapter 9. It tells us that as Jesus was passing by with His disciples, He saw a man who was blind from birth. Jesus' disciples asked whether it was the man's own sin or that of his parents that had caused this mans blindness. To this question, Jesus answered, it was neither this man nor his parents who sinned which causes his blindness, but rather that the works of God should be revealed in him. Actually, this Scripture passage is very simple. Jesus and the disciples saw a blind man, and the disciples asked Jesus for its reason. Jesus answered, "That the man was born blind was not due to him having sinned nor his parents having sinned, but rather, that the work of God should be revealed in him." This Word spoken by Jesus means, everyone who was born as sinners can be truly born again by receiving the gospel of the water and the Spirit from Him.

Actually, in order to understand this account properly, we must realize why the Lord had given us all the gospel of the water and the Spirit. In other words, we must know the Lord's intention that was shown to us in the gospel of the water and the Spirit. So, in order for you to understand the meaning of today's Scripture passage, you must first be born again by believing in the gospel of the water and the Spirit, otherwise its truth will always be hidden away from you.

In the Book of Romans it is written, *"Therefore, as through one man's offense judgment came to all men, resulting in condemnation, even so through one Man's righteous act the free gift came to all men, resulting in justification of life. For as by one man's disobedience many were made sinners, so also by one Man's obedience many will be made righteous" (Romans 5:18-19).* According to this truth written in the Bible, we are the descendants of Adam and Eve who had committed sin, therefore because of this we are born 'as sinners,' having inherited that sin. We became sinners because we were born with sin, and our descendants after us will also become sinners. It is saying to us that sins are hereditary; therefore everyone without question becomes a sinner.

But what is the Lord trying telling us today? He is telling us that it is not because this man or his parents had committed sin, but rather God wanted to show His works through him. So, we can see that the Word, which says that the offense of one man Adam had caused many people to become sinners, is true. The Bible says that just as through one man's offense had led many people to become sinners, everyone is born with sin. But the Bible also says, *"Therefore, as through one man's offense judgment came to all men, resulting in condemnation, even so through one Man's righteous act the free gift came to all men, resulting in justification of life" (Romans 5:18).* So we can see that God had desired to show His glory through that blind sinner. The Word the Lord is saying to us is, "that the works of God should be revealed in him."

Even before the birth of Adam and Eve, God had planned to blot out the sins of mankind by the gospel of the water and the Spirit in Jesus Christ, His Son. Originally it was the will of God to make mankind, Gods children. This is why even before anyone was born and even before Adam and Eve had committed any sin due to Satan's temptation, God had planned the gospel of the water and the Spirit for the purpose of saving us from sins and then adopting us as His children. Through John the Baptist the representative of mankind, God had all the sins of mankind transferred onto Jesus when He was baptized, and had Jesus pay the price for all the sins of mankind.

Everyone is born with sin: all people are born 'sinners' not because they themselves or their parents had committed sin, but because God the Father had them be born as sinners for the purpose of making us His people in His Son Jesus Christ. Therefore like this blind man God had us born as the 'spiritually blind.' Of course, there are those who are physically blind from birth. But when we look at ourselves in a spiritual sense, we are blind from birth and cannot see the gospel of the water and the Spirit. This is so not because of anyone's mistake. It is for the sole purpose of God the Father wanting to show the work that He had carried out; this plan for the salvation in His Son Jesus Christ.

Let us read the Gospel of John chapter 9 verse 6 and 7 together. *"When He had said these things, He spat on the ground and made clay with the saliva; and He anointed the eyes of the blind man with the clay. And He said to him, "Go, wash in the pool of Siloam" (which is translated, Sent). So he went and washed, and came back seeing."*

After announcing that He was the light of this world, He spat on the ground and made clay with His saliva; and with this clay He anointed the eyes of the blind man and told him to go wash it off in the pool of Siloam. Then the blind washed his eyes with this water and came back 'seeing.' What does this mean? It means that through the Law of God, the Lord made sinners realize their sin, and through this they received salvation by returning to the Lord through the God given gospel of the water and the Spirit.

When Jesus was going about healing this blind man, He spat on the ground and with this mixture made clay. And then he anointed the eyes of the blind with this wet clay. From a human perspective this would be an insulting and demeaning action. But being blind is demeaning enough, yet Jesus made clay from the dust of the earth and anointed his eyes with it. He then told the blind to go and wash himself in the pool of Siloam.

The miracle is this that those who have met and obeyed the Lord were all healed of their sicknesses, regardless of what it was. Rather than grumbling about how Jesus anointing the eyes with the clay mixed with saliva, the blind man went to the pool of Siloam and washed his eyes quietly and obediently according to the Lord's command. Then this blind man eyesight was restored and he was able to have very good eyesight.

I am stressing something here; this Scripture passage is not telling us that if we obey well, we will receive blessings. Leaders inside Christianity tell their followers that if they obey and offer their tithes well, they will receive many blessings, and should they offer large sums of money by taking out a loan with faith, their businesses will prosper beyond their wildest dreams. We need to know, they are all liars. The Lord told us clearly here that our 'spiritual eyes' would be opened if we would listen and understand and believe in the gospel of the water and the Spirit well. He definitely did not say that our 'spiritual eyes' would be opened if we offer our money.

The meaning of Jesus spitting on the ground and making clay with His saliva, and anointing the eyes of the blind man, means that we are the accursed ones before God. We would spit on people who are really vicious and loathsome. We hardly ever spit on common people, in fact we never think of spitting. But sinners are those who are destined to be cursed due to these loathsome sins. Therefore through this we can see God spitting on those destined to receive the curse from Him. This shows us clearly that all of mankind are 'the accursed.' Those in this world who have sins before God are not 'just sinners.' They are much more than this; they are these 'accused people.'

The Lord said, *"For the wages of sin is death, but the gift of God is eternal life in Christ Jesus our Lord" (Romans 6:23).* It is therefore only right that if people have sins, they ought to go to hell, having been cursed by God. They have to pay the price for their sins. But because we are so precious in God's sight, He does not want us to suffer destruction due to our sins. This is because He did not create us so that He could send us to hell. That is why God the Father sent His only begotten Son to us as the propitiation for all our sins. And Jesus Christ had accomplished His mission of atoning for all the sins of the world, through the gospel of the water and the Spirit. Therefore we must believe in Jesus Christ, who is the Savior of all of mankind, through the gospel of the water and the Spirit. To truly believe in Him, we should realize what the God given gospel of the water and the Spirit really is, and only through this gospel, can we receive the cleansing of our sins.

There is one important thing we must realize prior to being cleansed from our sins by the gospel of the water and the Spirit. And that is, realizing the fact that we are doomed to hell because of our sins, we are those who must gain everlasting life by receiving salvation from all our sins without fail. Not only do we have to receive the cleansing from our sins with the gospel of the water and the Spirit, we should also realize, by believing in this genuine gospel, we are really 'grave sinners' who cannot avoid the penalty of being cast into hell unless we receive the cleansing of all our sins. In other words, prior to believing in the gospel of the water and the Spirit and receiving salvation, we must know and confess the fact that we are those destined to be cursed by God due to our sins when we measure ourselves before the criteria set up by God's Law.

Why did the Lord spit on the ground, using His saliva to make clay to anoint the eyes of the blind man? He did this to show us publicly just how filthy we really are before God, and the fact that we are the seeds of sin destined to be accursed. We must bear in mind that it is only fitting for us to be cursed and destroyed before God due to our sins, and that it is only fitting for us to be sent into that terrible fire that will never die. Because of this we must go before God and confess that we are destined to receive 'such a judgment and the everlasting destruction' due to our sins. When we do this the Lord will then say to us, "You go now and wash yourselves in the pool of Siloam," and when we quietly and obediently do this, you will be cleansed from all of your sins 'once and for all' by washing your hearts which is completely scarred due to sins, and according to that Word, you will be perfectly healed. So in order for us to receive the cleansing of our sins before God and become His holy people, we must 'first know' and acknowledge what sort of a sinner we really are, and the fact that we are the ones who would be suffering the wrath of God.

And then only do we go to Jesus Christ by believing in the God given gospel of the water and the Spirit, and receive the cleansing of our sins through that Word of Truth. Jesus Christ is the Lamb of God sent by God the Father for the atonement of our sins. Jesus Christ did not come to us to carry out the work of salvation all by Himself at His discretion. He came down to this earth in accordance to the will of His Father, and as He lived out His life on this earth for those 33 years, He carried out this plan of His Father by taking on our sins through His baptism and vicariously dying on that Cross by shedding His precious blood according to that plan. The word 'Siloam,' when translated means, to be 'sent.' Jesus Christ is the Savior who had come to us having been 'sent' by His Father.

If we look at the Scripture passage in John chapter 9:4 we will read, *"I must work the works of Him who sent me while it is day; the night is coming when no one can work."* Jesus Christ was thus compelled to carry out the work according to the will of His Father. Only if we go to Jesus Christ can our filthy sins be cleansed and be gone forever. To do so, we should first realize that we are indeed 'the dirty ones' and have sins. And when we go before Jesus Christ, we must receive the cleansing of our sins by believing in the God given gospel of the water and the Spirit.

What is this 'water' mentioned in 'the gospel of the water and the Spirit'? It is Jesus' baptism. We should realize the

Biblical truth that God the Father had called upon John the Baptist as the High Priest and the representative of mankind, where he was instructed to place all the sins of mankind onto Jesus Christ through His baptism that was performed in the form of 'laying on of hands.' In this way John the Baptist baptized Jesus Christ, the Savior who had vicariously received 'the judgment' for all our sins by being crucified. By believing in Jesus Christ who had come by the gospel of the water and the Spirit, we can be cleansed from all our sins and look towards the love of God with restored eyesight. This means that we by faith receive the remission of our sins, and only then will be allowed to call God *"Abba, Father" (Romans 8:15)*.

By realizing the fact that God had allowed us to be born into this world and the fact that we are doomed to be put to death because of our sins, we must accept His love. Having come down to this earth to save all of mankind; the very first work that Jesus Christ did during this short period of His public ministry, was to be baptized by John the Baptist. We must know and believe in this truth that Jesus come down to this earth and received His baptism in order to take on the sins of the entire human race. Jesus came into this world through the body of a virgin, and when He was thirty years of age, He received His baptism from John the Baptist. Only then did He start His public ministry to save all of mankind.

The Very First Work Jesus Did in His Public Ministry Was to Receive Baptism from John the Baptist

By having received His baptism from John the Baptist, Jesus took on all the sins of the human race starting from Adam onto His body all at once. And by being crucified as the result of all those sins and dying on our behalf, He had thus saved us from all these sins and its destruction. If you do not or refuse to know and believe in this fact, then you cannot become a true Christian. When people claim to be regular church members while professing that they believe in Jesus just by lips without even knowing about the gospel of the water and the Spirit, then they are considered by God to be mere worldly religionists, likened to Buddhists who ceaselessly chant sutras without even knowing its literal meaning. This is so because sins still remain inside their hearts.

It is therefore very important to know how Jesus had taken onto Himself all of our sins and how He had perfectly solved 'the problem of sin.' We must clearly understand why He had to receive His baptism and what the exact meaning of this baptism really is, and then we must truly believe in the gospel of the water and the Spirit. Only then will we at once be perfectly cleansed from our sins, obtain everlasting life and the remission of our sins and become the children of God. When we are truly born again like this, we will go on witnessing on our own that the gospel of the water and the Spirit is the real Truth, even though we are not compelled to spread this genuine gospel. This is why it is important to have faith of knowing and believing in Jesus Christ who had come by the gospel of the water and the Spirit. We should also know ourselves well as well. We must know that even though we had been loathsome sinners, the Lord had saved us from our sins by the gospel of the water and the Spirit.

I really trust that you would not underestimate this Truth of salvation that being, the gospel of the water and the Spirit. The Lord told us clearly, *"Assuredly, I say to you, you will by no means get out of there till you have paid the last penny"*

(Matthew 5:26). Because sins still remain, despite them hearing this precious gospel, they will therefore not be able to get out of prison, that being hell. The price of sin is a terrible thing. It is so agonizing and painful that one would wish never to have been born at all.

We must realize just how disgraceful we really are and the fact that we are the accursed due to our sins, and then, we must believe in Jesus Christ who was sent by His Father. Through today's Scripture passage, we must clearly know that Jesus had taken on 'at once' all the sins of the world by receiving His baptism from John the Baptist. The Bible records the gospel Word of the water and the Spirit which was fulfilled by Jesus Christ and its relevancy and its foreshadowing of the Old Testament.

We should therefore know that we cannot cleanse away our sins without the gospel of the water and the Spirit. Our sins do not get washed away just by us 'knowing our sins' and asking for forgiveness. Rather we should realize the Biblical truth of this cleansing by knowing and believing in the gospel of the water and the Spirit. You should know how the Lord had blotted out all our sins in order for our hearts to be freed from 'all sins.' Our sins are not cleansed by our asking for forgiveness every time we sin. But despite this Biblical truth many Christians are praying to Jesus mistakenly. They continually offer their prayers of repentance sobbing and asking for forgiveness, and saying that they have done wrong.

The truth is we do not receive the remission of sins in this way we are wasting our time. We should rather believe in the fact that Jesus has blotted out all our sins by having received His baptism from John the Baptist and having shed His blood on that Cross. The Lord did not blot out our sins just by just shedding His blood on the Cross. The Biblical truth is that because Jesus had taken on our sins by receiving His baptism from John the Baptist, He thus received the judgment for all our sins vicariously. Jesus 'had' truly taken on all our sins People are nevertheless still 'spiritually blind' because they still go on with there fasting, offering prayers of repentance, and begging regardless without even knowing about how to be completely remitted from their sins. That is why the Lord says they are 'the blind from birth'.

We obtain our salvation when we believe in Jesus who came by the gospel of the water and the Spirit; this is the foundation of our faith. But this 'foundation of faith' is not obtained so easily. You really do not know how difficult it is to establish the foundation of faith. Jesus came to this earth, and in order to save you and me from the sins of the world, He had to work tirelessly for 33 long years. What I am trying to say is that 'this work' is not something 'so simple' as many make it out to be. In order to give us the gospel of the water and the Spirit, Jesus had to take on all the sins of mankind through John the Baptist who was its representative and was nailed to that Cross and died there instead of us, where He paid the full with His life. In this way He saved us from all our sins, curses and destruction.

If we were able to condense all the righteous acts of Jesus into one single sentence, we could say this; "Jesus saved us from the sin of the world by the gospel of the water and the Spirit." Therefore we should know fully what the 'water' mentioned in the Bible really is, who the Holy Spirit really is, and what the Truth that saved us from our sins really is, and then we must believe with this knowledge. Put differently, we must know and believe in the work the Lord had fulfilled for us with the gospel of the water and the Spirit.

After the Lord fulfilled all those works perfectly, He was

resurrected and ascended to the everlasting Kingdom. But the disciples remained behind on the earth. They were none other than the Apostles and their followers of the Early Church. The word 'apostle' means the 'sent ones.' When all the original Apostles had passed away, the Church Fathers became the church leaders, but unfortunately the gospel of the water and the Spirit gradually disappeared with the passage of time. Actually it will not be an exaggeration to say that the gospel of the water and the Spirit was totally exterminated from this earth with the declaration of the Edict of Milan in 313 A.D.

But Praise God in this age and time, He has established another faithful group of people who have inherited this very faith of the original Apostles. These people of God are none other than you and me. We together are currently preaching the gospel of the water and the Spirit throughout the entire world. We are right now spreading this gospel of the water and the Spirit to 6.5 billion people of this world. We are the defenders of the gospel of the water and the Spirit, and are carrying out the works of God to all of the world's peoples. Because the Lord sent us, we are obediently and faithfully doing His work.

And so, for all those who have as yet not truly met the Lord and as a result still have sins, should as soon as possible seek out and meet one of the truly born-again people who know the gospel Truth of the water and the Spirit. Because 'these people' are the ones who have been sent by God, when you meet them, hear the gospel of the water and the Spirit and believe in it, you will be cleansed of all your sins and gain everlasting life. To do this, you should deny your thoughts, learn the whole Truth step by step, and obtain answers to your questions. Only then will the problem of our sins be resolved. This is what this Scripture passage is telling us. It is saying we, who have met the Lord and have through it received the blessing of the remission of sins, are those who have come to see the world and God having had their eyesight's restored, and are also those who have come to receive the blessing which was accomplished by the Lord.

Dear fellow believers, the blind man went right away to the pool of Siloam, where he washed and then returned with his eyesight having been restored. Washing is an act of cleaning away filth. People say that death is the end of everything, but this is not true. For the righteous, there awaits the eternal Heaven, but for sinners, there awaits the judgment for sins in the everlasting fire of hell. For this reason you should without delay receive the cleansing of your sins by believing in the gospel of the water and the Spirit. You should receive the remission of your sins and be washed clean as snow and receive the Holy Spirit as a free gift from God.

To obtain salvation for our souls, we should meet up with those who have already met the gospel Truth of the water and the Spirit, and then with an open learning heart listen carefully to what they tell us about this truth. And then believe in it with all of our hearts. God has given us the Truth of the water and the Spirit. He has allowed us, who had been spiritually blind before to know our Lord Jesus Christ who had come by the water and the Spirit, and not only did He allow us to know the gospel Truth, He also allowed us to believe in it and to be truly born again. Therefore, by looking at today's Scripture passage, I hope for you to realize and understand the reason why God made us to follow and serve Him, and give thanks to God.

Also, for those who are still spiritually blind, I hope and pray that you would soon learn the gospel Word of the water and the Spirit from God's workers, pastors, missionaries and brothers and sisters in His Church. To perfectly learn the Word you should cast away everything you have heard and learned up to now. These thoughts are the yeasts of human thought. You should therefore not know this admonition in a doctrinally manner, but rather to throw away the yeasts of human thought before you meet the Lord. So go ahead and throw away the yeasts of human thought that you have so far accumulated and accept the gospel of the water and the Spirit. If you will do this, you will then receive all the blessings of Heaven from God. ⊠

Sermon

6

The Kingdom
of Heaven

Stand Firm in the Faith of Believing in Jesus Christ As Your Savior

< John 10:1-6 >

"Most assuredly, I say to you, he who does not enter the sheepfold by the door, but climbs up some other way, the same is a thief and a robber. But he who enters by the door is the shepherd of the sheep. To him the doorkeeper opens, and the sheep hear his voice; and he calls his own sheep by name and leads them out. And when he brings out his own sheep, he goes before them; and the sheep follow him, for they know his voice. Yet they will by no means follow a stranger, but will flee from him, for they do not know the voice of strangers." Jesus used this illustration, but they did not understand the things which He spoke to them."

Jesus Who Performed the Righteous Act

In the Gospel of John chapter 9, Jesus opened the eyes of a blind man and there arose much religious discussion owing to this affair. The blind man who met Jesus and obtained good eyesight told the Pharisees that it was rather strange that they did not know where He came from. The Gospel of John chapter 9 verse 30 says, *"The man answered and said to them, 'Why, this is a marvelous thing, that you do not know where He is from; yet He has opened my eyes!'"* We must all know where Jesus Christ came from. We were born from our physical parents; our parents were born from Adam and Eve who are the ancestors of humans; and Adam and Eve were born of the Triune God.

Then where did Jesus come from? Jesus Christ came to this world from the Heaven according to the will of God the Father as the Son of God the Father to save the sinners from sin. But after this blind man's eyes were opened, the Pharisees started dispute and asked this blind man how his eyes were opened. The blind man told them that his eyes became opened after he met Jesus and washed his eyes in the Pool of Siloam. The Pharisees who heard this tried to find fault from Jesus by asking why He did this on the Sabbath if He was truly an upright person. That's because the day the blind man's eyes were opened was the Sabbath and the Scriptures recorded that the Jews must not work on the Sabbath. Jews had a resolution to excommunicate anyone who worked on that day. It means that according to the Jewish Law, they ostracized and excommunicated anyone who violated the Law by working on the Sabbath. That's why the Pharisees were saying that Jesus would not have told the blind man to go wash in the Pool of Siloam during the Sabbath if He had been a godly person.

Pharisees even went to the blind man's parents and asked them how their son opened his eyes and how he could now see. They said that it was wrong if he opened his eyes on the Sabbath and that the parents who had left such a son alone on the Sabbath were wrong as well. Furthermore, they insisted that Jesus who opened the blind man's eyes on the Sabbath was also guilty of violating the Jewish Law. The blind man's parents were in a difficult situation because they also were

Jews and it was a significant violation according to the Law for their son to be pasted with clay on the Sabbath. Therefore, his parents just said, "We do not know anything except that our son was born blind and now he can see," because they did not want to become people who violated the Law. And he said, *"But by what means he now sees we do not know, or who opened his eyes we do not know. He is of age; ask him. He will speak for himself."*

Then, the Pharisees asked their son again. They asked him how his eyes were made open on the Sabbath. The Pharisees said that Jesus was surely a sinner who clearly does not follow God's will, because He opened the blind man's eyes on the Sabbath.

Spiritual Consideration of the Sabbath

This incident is such a laughable affair from the perspective of our times, but it was a serious incident from the Jewish perspective of the time that Jesus and the blind man and the Pharisees lived 2000 years ago. Jews absolutely do not work from the sunset on Friday till the sunset on Saturday evening because they believe the Law that commands them to keep the Sabbath holy. From the oral tradition, they say, "Even walking a few meters with the needle attached on the clothes on the Sabbath is a violation of the Law."

In any case, the Jews believed that the people who kept the Law well were the people who followed after God's will faithfully. Jesus healing the person from his sickness on the Sabbath became a great problem because it was a violation of the religious law at the time. Jesus spat on the ground and made clay with the saliva and put it on the blind man's eyes and commanded him to go wash in the Pool of Siloam. Then his eyes were healed as he washed his eyes in the Pool of Siloam according to Jesus' command. Jesus clearly did a good job, but that was a wrong thing that violated the Law when seen from the Jews standpoint. Unfortunately, it's because the day was the Sabbath.

The Sabbath begins at the sunset of Friday and ends at the sunset of Saturday. Today is the Sunday, therefore the period before the sunset yesterday is the Sabbath. Seventh-Day Adventist Church is representative of the denominations that keep the Sabbath literally. There are still many Seventh-Day Adventist Churches in Kangwon Province, Korea. They had worship service for God yesterday that is the Sabbath. They do not have worship service for God Sunday, which is the Lord's Day. And they have much feeling of pride and superiority in the fact that they are worshipping God on the Sabbath. They say, "Don't you know that God said He would bestow much blessing upon you if you kept the Sabbath according to the Old Testament and that you will go to the Kingdom of Heaven if you believe in Jesus and keep the Sabbath strictly?"

But that is actually wrong. We must look at the statute of the Sabbath spiritually. The word Sabbath means to rest in comfort. Looking at it spiritually, this word means that the Lord has blotted out all our sins. It means that the Lord blotted out our sins all at once with the Truth of the gospel of the water and the Spirit and gave us the true rest in our hearts. In other words, it means that God blotted out all our sins and made us able to go the Kingdom of God. That is the true meaning of the true Sabbath that God has given to us.

Literally, the Sabbath is from Friday evening till the Saturday evening. Those who claim that we should observe Sabbath punctually are wrong in this respect: There is a difference in time between nations according to their longitudinal locations. For example, today is the Sabbath, but the difference of hours between Korea and the United States makes it so that it may not be Sabbath there right now. That's why the Sabbath cannot be kept literally. To insist on the Sabbath literally even still can be described as the faith of a big frog in a small pond. They can make such claim because they live in Korea. But once they view this matter from an objective point of view, they also can understand that God did not give the Sabbath with such meaning and its true meaning is the remission of our sins.

In any case, the man who now can see after being blind all his life told the Pharisees that it was very strange. He said that it was strange that they did not know where He came from even though He opened his eyes. Let's talk about this for a minute. From common sense from your understanding, has there been any miraculous work in this world that a physically blind man's eyes were opened? Some people testify that they saw a blind person's eyes open when revival preachers or pastors laid hands on a blind person's eyes. Strictly speaking, however, did the eyes of the blind person really open? Or, did the person's weak sight become good enough to read the Scriptures after the laying on of hands and prayer? I am asking whether there was still some sight left and it became just a little better.

There are some ministers who say during the worship service that the Holy Spirit is entering through the window from the west. And such ministers tell the people to clap their hands and so forth to welcome the Holy Spirit because He is coming into the chapel at the moment and they do so. They also say that the Holy Spirit has healed many people now. There are many people in the world who follow the

Charismatic leaders and their claim is like that.

When we read the Book of Acts chapter 2, it records that on the 50th day after Jesus died on the Cross, the Holy Spirit descended upon Jesus' disciples as if the tongues of fire were separated while they were praying, and they became filled with the Holy Spirit from that point on and started preaching the gospel to the people vigorously. That's why the Day of the Pentecost implies the Holy Spirit to most Christians. And pastors of the Pentecostal Church sometimes say during the worship service that the Holy Spirit is coming in through the window on the west and ask their congregation to clap their hands toward Him, and they sometimes also say that they have the power to bring a dead person back to life. I don't know if you have ever seen a pastor who does such a thing. Though you may not know much, you may have heard of this or seen a poster. Maybe you have seen a poster that shows those people healing the sick people.

Then, did they really open the eyes of the blind person? I believe the mighty works and the miracles performed by Jesus who is God. But I don't believe the so-called miracles of the Christian sinners who have not even been born again. And I see people falling backwards when the charismatic pastors lay their hands on the sick and they speak in tongues. Interesting thing is that the person that fell backwards speaks the same tongues as the pastor does. And the person gets up and says that he can see the Bible even without the glasses. I also know this because I saw the videotape that shows such a weird thing. The person was not totally blind from the beginning, but he wore the glasses because he had bad eyesight. But now he says that he can see after the Holy Spirit healed him. Some person says that his lame legs have become normal after receiving the laying on of hands and prayer. Then he suddenly gets up and runs around praising God. Are such things true? Korean Christians believe such things because they are emotional, not intellectual.

There was a minister from abroad that came to Choonchun City to hold a revival meeting. And the poster for the meeting said that even the leg that became short by accident could become long if the minister laid his hands on the leg. To put it simply, they are claiming that in the instance where one leg has become shorter than the other leg, the shorter leg can become long again if the pastor laid his hands on the leg. Could that really happen? There is such a thing as the psychotherapy. Of course, for milder depressions, certain forms of psychotherapy do work well. But, spiritual swindlers deceive people using a kind of psychotherapy. Let's say, for example, I put on a show here and claim that the Lord says that He will heal many sick people now in this place. And then I say, "Fire! Fire! The Fire of the Holy Spirit!" and cause all kinds of commotion, and the feelings of expectation of the crowd is triggered. That's because people have such a thing called the crowd psychology. Once the crowd psychology is active, I say, "I want you to put your hands on the place that is hurting." And you feel as if the sickness is healed when you believe that your sickness will be healed when I pray to God. Like this, people with headache, stomachache, and the people with spinal cord injury perform the self-hypnosis according to the crowd psychology and feel that they are healed when such healing ministers pray for them. And when they ask the people who have been healed of their sicknesses from God to get up, many people here and there get up and clap their hands. And the people who haven't experienced the healing miracle take all the responsibility for nothing happening and say that the sickness was not healed because they did not have faith. This is so hilarious.

The person whose eyes had been opened from blindness asked the Pharisees whether they knew from where Jesus came. Jesus was the true Savior and God who came from Heaven as the Son of God the Father. But the Pharisees did not know where Jesus came from. That's why the blind man was harassed by the Pharisees as soon as his eyes were opened. The blind man said to the Pharisees, "I believe in Him. Do you also believe Him?" And the Pharisees emphasized the fact they were the disciples of Moses, saying, "You may be His disciple. But we are the disciples of Moses."

You will go to hell if you are disciples of Moses. Moses had to just look at the Land of Canaan but he could not cross the Jordan River. That's all Moses could do. Moses can only take us to Jesus Christ but he cannot take us to Heaven. Only Jesus can take us to Heaven. And the blind man was eventually excommunicated because he said that he was a disciple of Jesus. To be excommunicated means that he was cast out from the Jewish society.

Jesus heard the rumor that the Blind man was excommunicated and asked the man, *"Do you believe in the Son of God?"* And the blind man answered that he believed in Him and asked who Jesus was. And Jesus said to him, *"You have both seen Him and it is He who is talking with you."* Then the blind man said, "Lord, I believe," and bowed to Jesus.

The important thing is whether we believe in God's Son and whether we believe that He is the Savior who came to this world as God's Son. The faith that understands such things is very important. Where did Jesus Christ come from? He came from God the Father. The person who had his eyes opened after being blind from birth believed Jesus as the Savior. And Jesus said in conclusion, *"If you were blind, you would have no sin; but now you say, 'We see.' Therefore your sin remains" (John*

9:41). This means that many people who say they see are blind because they do not believe in Jesus, but those who know themselves as sinners will be able to see and receive salvation by believing in Him. Jesus ended His Word like this and gave us "the Parable of the Shepherd" from John chapter 10.

Jesus Is the Door of the Sheep

Jesus said in John 10:1, *"Most assuredly, I say to you, he who does not enter the sheepfold by the door, but climbs up some other way, the same is a thief and a robber."* This is the parable that illustrates Him. Jesus said that those who go into the place where the sheep are gathered together by climbing over the wall instead of going through the door are thieves and robbers; and the one who goes through the door is the Shepherd of the sheep. John 10:3 states, *"To him the doorkeeper opens, and the sheep hear his voice; and he calls his own sheep by name and leads them out."*

Jesus says that He is the door and the doorkeeper of the sheep. It means Jesus is the door to the Kingdom of Heaven. Jesus also said, "I am the way, the truth, and the life," and, therefore, no one can enter the Kingdom of Heaven without going through Him because He is the door to the Kingdom of God. No one can become a child of God except through Jesus. And anyone can enter the Kingdom of God after being cleansed from sin through Jesus and becoming a child of God.

Jesus is the door and the doorkeeper of the sheep. Anyone who has nothing to with Jesus cannot enter through that door. No matter what religion a person has believed or what good deeds he has done, he cannot enter the Kingdom of Heaven without believing in Jesus. The doorkeeper of Heaven is Jesus and how can we go in without going through Jesus? That's why we need to have a deep relationship with Jesus. That relationship means that we need to have the experience of receiving the remission of sins through Jesus Christ. Only those who have relationship with Jesus by understanding and believing that Jesus really took all our sins upon Him, that He died in our place, that He kept us alive, and that Jesus saved us, can enter the door of the Kingdom of Heaven.

John 10:16 from today's Scripture passage says, *"Jesus used this illustration, but they did not understand the things which He spoke to them."* Pharisees do not understand. They do not understand the things Jesus is talking about, the work He did to open the eyes of the blind, the reason Jesus said that He also does not judge the woman that was caught in the act of adultery. They do not understand because they are carnally minded. It's really easy when we look at the Word from the Gospel of John chapter 10 verses 1 to 6.

The A sheepfold is usually made by implanting posts in the plains and there is a door. They put fence around the place with the posts so the wolves or any other wild animals could not enter it and the owner used the door to bring the sheep in and out of the ranch. Sheep cannot live with any other wild beast. The sheep are put together only by themselves because sheep do not have the strength or physical means to fight against wolves, foxes, or wild dogs and therefore will be eaten up by them. They sometimes put a few shepherd dogs inside sheep pen but they do not harm the sheep because they are trained. The sheep must be protected because of such characteristics. This is what this Word is saying. How plain is that?

John 10:1 says, *"Most assuredly, I say to you, he who does not enter the sheepfold by the door, but climbs up some other way, the same is a thief and a robber."* The Lord spoke gently but also spoke with strong emphasis by illustrating the false leaders with words "a thief and a robber." Isn't this obvious? And the Lord says the one who goes through the door is the Shepherd of the sheep. The Lord came to this world for us and He was nailed to the Cross and died on the Cross after taking all our sins by His baptism received from John the Baptist and entered through the door of the Kingdom of Heaven by resurrecting from the death. Jesus came to this world and took all our sins upon Himself through the baptism He received from John the Baptist, preached the gospel Word for three years, was nailed to the Cross at the top of the Hills of Golgotha, and He said, "It is finished!" as he died on the Cross. At the very moment, the curtain in God's Temple was torn down into two from top to bottom. The curtain embroidered with Cherubim was woven of the blue, red, purple thread and the white fine linen, and it was weaved together so thick that even four horses could not rip it apart by pulling its four corners. But the curtain of the Temple was torn apart into two when Jesus died on the Cross.

As the Lord came to this world and said, *"I am the way, the truth, and the life. No one comes to the Father except through Me,"* Jesus was born to this world to take our sins upon Him. Jesus took all the sins of the world through the baptism He received from John the Baptist, died on the Cross, and was resurrected from death to save us from all our sins. Jesus Christ entered the Kingdom of Heaven where God the Father is by receiving the baptism from John the Baptist, dying on the Cross and being resurrected in three days. Therefore, now, whoever believes in Jesus as the Savior who blotted out all his sin can enter the place God the Father dwells as Jesus did.

The doorkeeper of the Kingdom of Heaven is also Jesus. Jesus personally became the door of Heaven and made it so that we could receive the remission of sins and enter Heaven if we believe in the gospel of the water and the Spirit. And He said, *"And when he brings out his own sheep, he goes before them; and the sheep follow him, for they know his voice. Yet they will by no means follow a stranger, but will flee from him, for they do not know the voice of strangers."*

Every sheep recognizes its master well. There are many among Israelites that are devoted to the stock farming, and the livestock follow the shepherd when he goes ahead of the herd. A really interesting thing is that all the animals, whether they are horses, goats, or sheep, follow after the owner when he goes ahead of the pack playing the pipe. We wonder whether the animals would really follow after the owner well or whether some of them will go astray to the side. But I saw it with my eyes and the animals really do follow after their shepherd because they will die if they don't. So the tourist put on the same hat and the clothes and plays the pipe and go ahead of the pack like he was the owner, but the animals do not follow him.

Jesus said this from this perspective because He already knew the characteristics of the sheep. Those who really know Jesus follow after Him. Those who know that Jesus is their Savior, that He is the Son of God from Heaven, that He is our Savior, that He has completed the gospel of the water and the Spirit, follow after Jesus.

But those who do not know Jesus do not follow Him because He is not their Savior. Here, the Word from John chapter 10, verses 4 and 5 says that we believe in Jesus with out hearts and follow Him if we really believe in the Lord as the Son of God from Heaven, if we believe that He is our

Savior, and if we believe that He blotted out all our sins through the gospel of the water and the Spirit. That's why those people are in God's Church listening to God's Word, doing the work that pleases Him, and rejoicing in His Word. But the people who are not, the people who do not understand Jesus correctly do not follow Jesus.

In the first half of today's sermon, I preached about receiving salvation by believing in Jesus and that Jesus is the Son of God from Heaven. From this point, I will end the sermon with the word about how we can really follow the Lord with faith.

How Should Our Faith Be in Order to Follow Jesus?

If our faith is going to follow the Lord, we can only follow Him through the gospel of the water and the Spirit and by nothing else. We need to have the faith of believing in the gospel of the water and the Spirit if we want to receive salvation from the Lord and go to Heaven. It is possible for all of us to go to Heaven only by believing in the gospel of the water and the Spirit.

Romans 7:4-6 says, *"Therefore, my brethren, you also have become dead to the law through the body of Christ, that you may be married to another—to Him who was raised from the dead, that we should bear fruit to God. For when we were in the flesh, the sinful passions which were aroused by the law were at work in our members to bear fruit to death. But now we have been delivered from the law, having died to what we were held by, so that we should serve in the newness of the Spirit and not in the oldness of the letter."*

If you and I want to receive salvation from sin by believing in the Lord, then we need to believe in the gospel of the water and the Spirit, and if we want to follow after the Lord, then we need to follow Him just by faith. When you look at only your physical state, you could never follow after the Lord. It's because you are constantly tripped up by yourselves and stumble. You could never follow the Lord in that physical state. And when we just look at ourselves, it is hard to say that we are people who have received salvation because we are weak and we have so many shortcomings. It's because we constantly are ensnared by sin and our shortcomings.

If you want to receive salvation from all our sins and we hope to have the faith of the righteous before God, then you must have the faith of believing that the Lord came to this world and blotted out all your sins through the baptism He received from John the Baptist and His blood on the Cross. You need the absolute faith in the gospel of the water and the Spirit if you wish to say that you will enter the Kingdom of God because you do not have any sin conscientiously even though your flesh is lacking. As such, you also need the gospel of the water and the Spirit even in following the Lord. You can never follow the Lord if you just look at your flesh. You cannot follow the Lord even if you wanted to because you are too weak and you give up too easily being bound by your shortcomings. Therefore, you need to follow the Lord by faith that believes in Him thoroughly.

The Romans 7:4 says, *"To Him who was raised from the dead,"* and it means that we can do God's work by going to Jesus Christ and receiving salvation and believing in Him. Though we have shortcomings, we can do God's work by going to Him through the faith of believing in the gospel of the water and the Spirit. We cannot follow Him no matter how much Jesus guides us and tells us to follow Him if we do not have faith. Can we follow Jesus without faith? No. We believe that Jesus Christ has blotted out all our sins by receiving the baptism even though our flesh is weak, that Jesus Christ entrusted the righteous work to us and gave us the ability and the faith to do the righteous work even though our flesh is weak. Even though we are not qualified to do the righteous work by ourselves, Jesus blotted out all our sins through the gospel of the water and the Spirit so that we can bear fruit for God. We can do this by believing in the righteousness of God. This is possible only through faith. Even after receiving salvation from sin, the only way we can follow the Lord is through faith. We cannot follow Him without the faith of believing in God. Also, no one can receive salvation without faith. Therefore, faith is more essential than any condition of your circumstance.

The Scriptures say, *"Believe on the Lord Jesus Christ, and you will be saved, you and your household." (Acts 16:31).* Believe in God's Word. God spoke so much of faith, saying "Do you believe in the Son of Man? Do you believe in the Son of God? Do you believe that the Son of God came to this world in flesh? It shall be done according to your faith." The faith makes us receive salvation, follow God, make us do God's work, and bear fruit. Do you believe? Therefore, we must follow the Lord with faith. When we follow the Lord without faith, we look at our weaknesses and shortcomings and the self that is less adequate than others and begin to question whether we can do God's work when we can't even take care of ourselves. If we look only at ourselves, we are prone to shrink back to destruction. It means that we fall into the deep mire spiritually. Do you understand? That's how it is.

The Romans 8:6 says, *"For to be carnally minded is*

death, but to be spiritually minded is life and peace." There are many times when we become a hostage of our own fleshly thinking. What happens when people who are not bom again are consumed with the fleshly thinking? From fleshly thinking, they can only wonder how can there be no sin when they commit sin every day. So they say, "We do have sin in us, don't we?" That's because they only look at themselves. Because they do not look up the will of God and because they do not know what the Lord from Heaven has done, they say, "How can there not be sin in us? All those who say there is no sin are heretics. There is none righteous, not one. How can you say there is a righteous person before God?" They are like this because they have fallen into their own thinking.

The Bible clearly says, *"For to be carnally minded is death, but to be spiritually minded is life and peace."* To be spiritually minded is to think of the things God has done. Although we are people who cannot help but go to hell because we are so lacking like this, the Son of God came to this world and took all our sins over to Himself at once by receiving the baptism from John the Baptist. And then He carried the sins of this world to the Cross and died on the Cross and resurrected from death in three days. Jesus went up to Heaven in this manner and consequently wiped away all our sins.

We often fall into fleshly thinking even after receiving salvation from sin by believing in the gospel of the water and the Spirit. And we do such things as we are carnally minded and become discouraged. And our perspectives become narrow and we begin to be shriveled up. We will eventually die when we become entrapped into our own weaknesses. To be carnally minded is death. When we become carnally minded, we fall into the weakness and begin to have a question whether the gospel of the water and the Spirit is correct, whether my work is more important than God's work now, and whether I can just ignore the reality when I am like this and the situation is like this, whether the Lord actually did save me or not considering the fact that I am so weak and lacking and my reality is drowning in misery. This will lead us to destruction in the end.

But turn around and be spiritually minded. The spiritually minded like to think of the things that God has done. What did God the Father and Jesus do for you and me? John 3:16 says, *"For God so loved the world that He gave His only begotten Son, that whoever believes in Him should not perish but have everlasting life."* The Son of God saved us by coming to this world and taking all our sins over to Him by receiving the baptism and resurrecting from the death after carrying the sin to the Cross and shedding blood and dying on the Cross. He took all our sins over to Himself through the baptism. That He received the baptism means that the sins of the humanity were transferred over to Him. Then it means that sins of you and I were also transferred over to Him. And He shed blood on the Cross and died. He took our sins over to Him by receiving the baptism on His body and brought us back to life from the spiritual and physical death by shedding His blood on the Cross as He said; and it means that and made us able to do the righteous work of God by believing in Him who gave up His body according to the Law.

Now, we must do the spiritual work by faith. To do so, we must be spiritually minded by faith. We have received the remission of sins by believing in the gospel of the water and the Spirit, but we must not become stagnant in that faith. The spiritual thoughts and fleshly thoughts always visit you and me. Such thoughts come to us every hour and every second each day one after another in turns. We think of fleshly things one moment and the spiritual things the next moment. In other words, we think of God's work one moment and then the fleshly work the next moment. Even the person who believes in the gospel of the water and the Spirit does not think of the spiritual things all the time or think of the God's work all the time. Even while doing God's work, the righteous also can be addicted to watching TV dramas; some sisters also may look at some good-looking guys on television and think they are fine. Some ministers even drool at the sight of pretty actresses on television. When I ask one of them if he really likes the pretty woman that much, then he says that he's just looking. But he has already fallen into the fleshly thought.

But, then, is the person who is asking that question not fallen into the carnal thought? No, that's not the case either. Everyone is prone to fall into fleshly thought. We are just comparing ourselves with one another trying to figure out whose faith is stronger and whose is not. There is only one absolutely righteous Being, and He is God, but humans are comparing each other even though they are all alike in God's eyes. While the spiritual thought and the fleshly thought take turns coming up in our thinking, we are comparing one another and saying this person is better than the other. We are beings who are carnally minded soon after being spiritually minded. That's why we can do the God's work only through the faith by confirming our salvation from sin through the faith of believing in the gospel of the water and the Spirit. We do the righteous work of God through the faith of believing in the gospel of the water and the Spirit that God has given. We can enjoy the spiritual and physical blessing only by faith. We must become strong and firm people through the faith even though we are always lacking.

Although we live in this world and we have both the spiritual thought and the fleshly thought in our weak flesh, we must always think of God's work more than the fleshly thought and live with the spiritual thought by making it our signpost in our lives. Otherwise, if we go astray too far with the fleshly thought, it will be difficult to follow God even though we have received salvation. Those who have received the remission of sins must look up to the spiritual work more often. They must look toward God's work. We must always look at the salvation God has given to us and live with faith. We can be steadfast by doing so. We can become the strong people even though we are weak. We can be freed from ourselves through faith even though we are weak. Romans 7:6 says, *"But now we have been delivered from the law, having died to what we were held by, so that we should serve in the newness of the Spirit and not in the oldness of the letter."* That we should not serve in the oldness of the letter means that we should not understand and believe the Word literally.

We must be freed from the curse of the Law and our weakness by believing in the righteousness of God. We can be freed from God's curse only through the faith. We have become free from our weakness and Law and the judgment of God by believing in the gospel of the water and the Spirit and by believing in the Lord. Therefore, we who believe in the righteousness of God are able to live a new life. The Scriptures say, *"Therefore, if anyone is in Christ, he is a new creation; old things have passed away; behold, all things have become new."* We just have to think of the spiritual work, that is, God's work, and look toward the things God has done for us. Therefore, we can always follow the Lord continuously without having the thread of the spiritual thought being broken.

The Lord said in John 10:4, *"And when he brings out his own sheep, he goes before them; and the sheep follow him, for they know his voice."* Didn't our Lord go before us? He blotted out all our sins by coming to this world and receiving the baptism and dying on the Cross. Then, didn't the Lord come to this world and has completed our salvation perfectly? The Lord came to this world and received the baptism and shed blood to blot out the sins of all the souls and give us the salvation. Then, didn't He save us from all our sins? That's why we could follow the Lord only through the faith in our Lord. You can follow through the faith of believing in the gospel of the water and the Spirit even though you have shortcomings personally. We have received salvation by believing in our Savior Jesus Christ and we have become the follower only by believing in God's love and the salvation He has given to us.

We must listen to this gospel even though we have received the remission of sins by hearing and believing in the gospel of the water and the Spirit because we are prone to fall into the fleshly thinking. That's why you must always think and believe in the gospel of the water and the Spirit. We must confirm and believe the gospel of the water and the Spirit and do such things. Our hearts become clean when we come to God's Church and listen and believe in the gospel of the water and the Spirit through God's Word. It is true that the sin is blotted away once we have received the remission of sins, but we must always face the gospel of the water and the Spirit if we want to keep our hearts clean.

Mind becomes filthy when it falls into the fleshly thought. That's why we need the gospel of the water and the Spirit even more. In conclusion, you and I can stand firm by looking toward the Lord and believing in Him even though we are weak. For this, we must always ruminate over the gospel of the water and the Spirit. We can always follow the Lord through the faith of believing in the gospel of the water and the Spirit and God's Word. God blessed us the born again who are so weak like this. Our God blessed you and me as the blessed people before the presence of God. We must be the people who look toward the righteousness of the Lord as often as we can with the understanding that we are weak. We have sought after the fleshly things and followed after the fleshly things more often until now, but we must be the people who think of God's work more often and follow it. Do you understand?

And the people who have much fleshly thinking also must not do God's work too much. God's work must be entrusted to people who are spiritually minded for it to be accomplished effectively and be blessed. Not just anyone can do God's work. Not just anyone can do the work of preaching the gospel of the water and the Spirit throughout the world. We must look toward the Lord and follow the Lord even more by believing the Lord's Word.

We often fall into our own weaknesses, but that's why we need to think of spiritual things even more. We must stand firm by believing in Jesus Christ through the gospel of the water and the Spirit. I want you to look toward the Lord who has become our Shepherd and follow Him. ✉

SERMON

7

Sin

Jesus Is
The Door of Salvation

< John 10:1-19 >

"'Most assuredly, I say to you, he who does not enter the sheepfold by the door, but climbs up some other way, the same is a thief and a robber. But he who enters by the door is the shepherd of the sheep. To him the doorkeeper opens, and the sheep hear his voice; and he calls his own sheep by name and leads them out. And when he brings out his own sheep, he goes before them; and the sheep follow him, for they know his voice. Yet they will by no means follow a stranger, but will flee from him, for they do not know the voice of strangers.' Jesus used this illustration, but they did not understand the things which He spoke to them. Then Jesus said to them again, 'Most assuredly, I say to you, I am the door of the sheep. All who ever came before Me are thieves and robbers, but the sheep did not hear them. I am the door. If anyone enters by Me, he will be saved, and will go in and out and find pasture. The thief does not come except to steal, and to kill, and to destroy. I have come that they may have life, and that they may have it more abundantly. I am the good shepherd. The good shepherd gives His life for the sheep. But a hireling, he who is not the shepherd, one who does not own the sheep, sees the wolf coming and leaves the sheep and flees; and the wolf catches the sheep and scatters them. The hireling flees because he is a hireling and does not care about the sheep. I am the good shepherd; and I know My sheep, and am

known by My own. As the Father knows Me, even so I know the Father; and I lay down My life for the sheep. And other sheep I have which are not of this fold; them also I must bring, and they will hear My voice; and there will be one flock and one shepherd. Therefore My Father loves Me, because I lay down My life that I may take it again. No one takes it from Me, but I lay it down of Myself. I have power to lay it down, and I have power to take it again. This command I have received from My Father.' Therefore there was a division again among the Jews because of these sayings."

Referring to Himself, Jesus said, *"I am the way, the truth, and the life" (John 14:6).* Who could dare to make such a claim? Only Jesus is the true God who can describe Himself like this. Those who believe in the Word of the remission of sins that Jesus has given us can be delivered from all their sins and receive new life. Even as we could not avoid but be destroyed and accursed for our sins, the Lord has become our true Savior, and so we have no choice but to thank Him. Everyone was set to suffer the terrifying wrath of God for his sins. But, what about you? Have you met the Savior who has freed you from all your sins? Those who have met the Savior are those who have received the remission of sins by knowing and believing in the gospel power of the water and the Spirit.

Through the Door of the Tabernacle Also, God Showed the Baptism and Blood of Jesus

We must remember the truth manifested in the door of the

Tabernacle and believe in it. In the outer court of the Tabernacle, there were 60 pillars, and to its east stood its gate, measuring 9 m in length and 2.25 m in height. And the fence of the court was all surrounded by white linen, measuring 22.5 m in its east and west sides, and 45 m in its north and south sides. But only the gate of the court of the Tabernacle was woven with blue, purple, and scarlet thread and fine woven linen. Of the total width of the court measuring 22.5 m, its gate took up 9 m, and so anyone could easily recognize this gate.

The white linen that was used for the fence of the court of the Tabernacle manifests our remission of sins and God's holiness. When we look at this white linen, we naturally think of cleanness, and when we connect this to people's souls, we are reminded of someone whose heart has become sinless by believing in the gospel of the water and the Spirit. Those who have received the remission of sins from God are pleased to meet and have fellowship with others who have also received the same remission of sins. But the sinful are not only are reluctant to have fellowship with the righteous, but they are also reluctant to come before the holy God. Because of their sins, the sinful are surrounded by darkness that prevents them from nearing the light of the gospel of the water and the Spirit, and so it is only natural that they would dislike the light itself at first. So if you are uneasy about the light, then you must realize that because of your sins, a wall has sprung up to separate you from God, and when you recognize this, you must find the Truth and get the problem of your sins resolved.

If you realize that you are suffering from the deadly illness of your sins that will send you straight to hell, then more than anything else, you now need the gospel of the water and the Spirit absolutely. If one knows that that he is bound to go to hell for his sins, then it is only a matter of course that he should be looking for a Savior who would deliver him. Yet many in this world are not looking for the remission of sins that Jesus has given them through the gospel of the water and the Spirit, even as they are sinners and they must look for this Jesus who is their Savior. They are like the man in Psalm 49:12 who, though in honor, does not realize this and perishes like beasts.

Coming to the sinners of this earth, the Lord wanted to deliver them from all their sins with the gospel of the water and the Spirit. So not only was our Lord baptized by John the Baptist to blot out all the iniquities of sinners, but He also washed away all their sins once for all by shedding His blood on the Cross. Having done these things, He is now waiting for us. Like this, for the gate of the court of the Tabernacle also, our Lord made all the preparations for the remission of sins by weaving it with blue, purple, and scarlet thread and thereby became the door of salvation for us so that we may be saved from our sins. Herein lies the reason why all sinners must now believe in Jesus as their Savior. To become the door of salvation for us the sinners, Jesus Himself came to us with the gospel of the water and the Spirit to remit away all our sins.

When Jesus turned 30 on this earth, He bore all our sins by being baptized by John the Baptist (Matthew 3:13-17), and He fulfilled all righteousness by being crucified and shedding His blood (John 19:30). And by rising from the dead again in three days (Matthew 28), He completed the salvation of all sinners from their iniquities. Therefore, He has now made it possible for anyone who wants to be saved to receive the remission of sins by believing in the baptism He received and the blood He shed on the Cross. We must believe that all these things were done for us, for the remission of our sins. As God has determined that anyone who does not believe in Jesus as the Savior cannot receive the remission of sins, all who now want to receive this remission of sins and enter Heaven must believe in the washing of sins and the condemnation of sins that Jesus fulfilled through the baptism He received and the death He suffered on the Cross when He came to this earth, and they must thereby become God's people who have cleansed away all their sins.

Those who are trying today to wash away their sins by believing only in the blood of the Cross must now learn the gospel Truth of the water and the Spirit. If you had not known the gospel of the water and the Spirit and therefore had believed only in the Jesus' blood on the Cross, then you must realize that your knowledge of the true gospel is only half-filled. The fact that those who believe only in this blood of Jesus continue to find out time after time that they have not been perfectly remitted from their sins is the proof that they still remain sinful even after having believed in Jesus for a long time.

The faith of those who believe that they are saved even as they believe only in the blood that Jesus shed on the Cross is clearly problematic. So rebuking their faith, Jesus says to them, "Did I only die for you? Was I not also baptized by John the Baptist, and did I not bear the sins of the world as well, all for you?" Every sinner must realize just how boundless and righteous the work of the baptism and blood of Jesus is, the work that has saved mankind from all its sins and punishment, and they must believe in this work of salvation with thanksgiving. If one realizes just how terrifying the punishment of sin reserved for the sinful is, then he has no choice but be infinitely grateful for this salvation of Jesus.

Receive the Salvation of the True Remission of Sins by Faith!

As you live on this earth, do you want to receive the remission of sins and live happily? Or do you want to live an accursed life for eternity by rejecting the gospel of the water and the Spirit that brings the remission of sins to you? Everyone wants to receive the eternal remission of sins, for everything to work out well, and to be happy, if not for others than at least for himself. But belying this desire to live a blessed life, sinners are simply incapable of receiving God's love and blessings, no matter how hard they try. There are some people for whom everything that they do is cursed, so much so that we feel sorry for them. But they do not know the reason why they are living such an accursed life. The reason is actually quite simple—it is because they have not been washed from all their sins by faith.

There are some people for whom, although they profess to believe in Jesus, everything that they do ends up in failure. This is because there is a wall of sin separating them from God. It is because the sinful are not at peace with God that they are cursed. When we profess to believe in Jesus, then, we must examine ourselves to see whether we really understand and believe in the gospel of the water and the Spirit, or we just believe in Jesus as our Savior blindly even as we have no idea what this gospel of the water and the Spirit is. We must believe correctly, and only when we believe in the gospel of the water and the Spirit can we be said to believe in Jesus correctly.

There are some people who consider themselves as good Christians, even as they remain sinful from not believing in the gospel of the water and the Spirit. We need to realize that anyone who has sin before the holy God is bound to live an accursed life because of this sin, and that in order to be entirely freed from this life of sin, he must be born again by believing in the gospel of the water and the Spirit. Therefore, even if people believe in Jesus as their Savior, if they do so without knowing the gospel of the water and the Spirit, then their faith is all in vain. All of us must thus realize the gravity of sin, and we must also realize that we can be blessed by God only when we learn the gospel Truth of the water and the Spirit and receive the remission of sins by faith.

We need to grasp this profound seriousness of sin, for no other reason than the fact that Jesus Himself told us in Romans 6:23 that "the wages of sin is death." If Jesus said that the wages of sin is death, then this can only mean that all those who have sin must either receive the remission of sins or otherwise be destroyed for their sins. It is more than likely for sinners to fail at everything that they do, as if a series of misfortune befalls on them. But they need to pause for a moment and consider the possibility that the reason for this is because of their sins. We must remember God's commandments, and if we now realize that the endless stream of all such unhappiness and curses is due to the fact that there is sin in our hearts, then we must believe in the gospel of the water and the Spirit, for the time has come for us to believe in this gospel.

God gave us His Law so that we would realize that death awaits anyone who has sin (Romans 3:20). And as each and every sin that all sinners have committed are written in their hearts, God wants them to wash away all these sins by believing in the gospel of the water and the Spirit. All the sins that people commit by breaking God's commandments are written in their hearts. By God's Law, therefore, they become sinners, live accursed lives, and ultimately end up facing their destruction. As soon as possible, even at this very moment, every sinner must now believe in the baptism Jesus received from John the Baptist and the blood He shed on the Cross, and they must be completely washed from their sins by this faith.

Everyone is bound to live this world in futility, only to turn into a handful of dust, and, after this, to face God's judgment that awaits him. But if you think that it was set by God for our lives to end in such purposeless hollowness, then you are gravely mistaken. On the contrary, the God-given gospel of the remission of sins is available to everyone, and all the blessing of God will be bestowed on whoever believes in this gospel. Now that all can wash away their sins by faith, thanks to the gospel of the water and the Spirit that brings the remission of sins permitted by God, it is my sincerest hope and prayer that you would all indeed wash away all your sins and become God's children by faith. By believing in the gospel of the water and the Spirit, everyone can cleanse away his sins and enter the Kingdom of God. This is why the gospel of the water and the Spirit is such an absolute necessity for all of us.

Describing our lives, God said, *"The days of our lives are seventy years; And if by reason of strength they are eighty years, Yet their boast is only labor and sorrow; For it is soon cut off, and we fly away" (Psalm 90:10).* Whether we live for 80 years or 120 years on this earth, what is imperative is that we know and believe in the gospel of the water and the Spirit. It would be not be such a problem if our lives were to end with our physical death, but for each and every one of us, there awaits an afterlife. This is why it is absolutely important for everyone to encounter and believe in the real Truth, for we can become God's children and live happily forever in His Kingdom only if we wash away all the sins of our souls by believing in the gospel of the water and the Spirit.

This is why Jesus has become the gate of the Kingdom of Heaven. To save us from our sins and welcome us to Heaven, Jesus Himself took upon our sins by being baptized, bore the condemnation of everyone's sins by shedding His precious blood on the Cross, and has thereby become our perfect Savior. By becoming the gate of Heaven Himself, Jesus has permitted anyone who has received the remission of sins to enter Heaven. As John 10:2 says, *"He who enters by the door is the shepherd of the sheep,"* Jesus is indeed the Shepherd of the sheep that have received the remission of sins, the gate of Heaven, the true Shepherd, and God Himself who leads us to the everlasting Kingdom of Heaven. Our Lord came to this earth as our Savior and gave Himself up for us. To those who believe in the gospel of the water and the Spirit, our Lord has opened the door of salvation wide and permitted the Kingdom of Heaven.

Receiving Jesus Is Not Just Saying, "I Believe in Jesus"

To receive Jesus into the heart is to believe that Jesus is God Himself and the Savior for all who believe in the gospel of the water and the Spirit. In our hearts we have faith in the baptism of Jesus and His blood on the Cross. We also believe that Jesus is the Son of God. This is our faith. Those who believe in the gospel of the water and the Spirit believe that Jesus is their Savior, and take the gospel of the water and the Spirit as the witness of faith.

Brothers and sisters, do you believe that Jesus is your Savior? Do you admit in your hearts that Jesus is the true Savior? Jesus is the Son of God. But at the same time, He is our Savior. Jesus is the Son of God and our Savior, and to wash us from all our sins, He accepted them once for all by being baptized by John the Baptist, went to the Cross, and was crucified to shed His blood to death. You must all infallibly believe in this. You must not allow yourself to be destroyed for not believing. You must believe that the baptism of Jesus and His precious blood were all for you.

Those who are yet to believe in this gospel Truth must now believe in the baptism and blood of Jesus with their hearts. We must wholeheartedly believe in this baptism of Jesus and His blood on the Cross, the Truth of the remission of sins, and we must thank God. We must believe in this Truth right at this moment without fail, for there is no other way to be saved but to believe in the gospel of the water and the Spirit and become God's children. Those who do not believe in the gospel of the water and the Spirit with their hearts have not yet become God's children. Therefore, it is my sincerest hope and prayer that you would all believe in this gospel, for there is no more time to delay. Believe now! You will then become God's child, be washed from all your sins, and enjoy all His glory and splendor.

Jesus is the gate of Heaven, and He is also its gatekeeper. By becoming our own God and our own Savior, Jesus has saved us from our sins, and He has given us the sure and clear faith that enables us to reach salvation and enter Heaven. We can only thank our Lord for His merciful love.

We Must Believe That Jesus Is the Only Good Shepherd and Perfect Savior

Our Lord said, *"I am the good shepherd. The good shepherd gives His life for the sheep. But a hireling, he who is not the shepherd, one who does not own the sheep, sees the wolf coming and leaves the sheep and flees; and the wolf catches the sheep and scatters them. The hireling flees because he is a hireling and does not care about the sheep" (John 10:11-13).* The *"hireling"* here refers to those who work only to feed their own flesh. As the word itself denotes, they are those who are hired to work for a reward. In today's Christian communities, the hirelings are those who do not spread the gospel Truth of the water and the Spirit, but instead preach false doctrines and pretend to be shepherds only to seek after their own interests.

Jesus said in John 10:14-15, *"I am the good shepherd; and I know My sheep, and am known by My own. As the Father knows Me, even so I know the Father; and I lay down My life for the sheep."* Jesus is our true Shepherd, and we are God's servants who believe in and preach the gospel of the water and the Spirit that Jesus Christ has given us. Because Jesus knew very well why we sin and what weaknesses we have, this true Shepherd accepted all our sins by being baptized by John the Baptist, and He bore the condemnation of our sins by giving up His own body on the Cross, all in order to save us. Jesus said in the above passage that the Good Shepherd lays down His life for the sheep. Just like this, Jesus obeyed the will of God the Father completely, to the point where He was baptized and even crucified to death.

The Lord told us, "You must spread the gospel of the water and the Spirit throughout the whole world, for there are many people who are yet to come into My sheepfold." Jesus accepts as God's children only those who believe in His baptism and blood. In other words, Jesus has given His grace of the remission of sins only to those who believe that He, who came by the water and the blood, has washed away all their sins, and it is only these people that He has turned into God's children. Just as the sacrificial offering of the Old Testament shed its blood and suffered death because of the laying on of hands, it was because Jesus was baptized by John the Baptist that He shed His blood and died on the Cross and rose from the dead again.

Seeing the faith of those who believe in this Truth, God has made them His own children. Jesus the Good Shepherd hears the prayers of the children of God, watches over them, leads them, protects them and blesses them. By believing in the gospel of the water and the Spirit with our hearts, therefore, we must receive the remission of sins, come into God's Church, walk with Jesus the Good Shepherd, and live blessed lives led by God. We must believe wholeheartedly that the Lord is our Savior and our Good Shepherd.

God Calls upon and Saves Sinners Who Are Like Goats

The truly pitiful people are the sinners who are mingled among the people of God. In the Bible, sheep generally refer to the people of God who believe in the gospel of the water and the Spirit, while goats refer to those who, despite professing to believe in Jesus, have not really received the remission of sins into their hearts. By and large, these goats come into God's Church by pretending to be sheep, and they deceive His servants and saints, as well as themselves. These goat-like people are so good at imitating sheep that they sound and act just like sheep, but they are the kind of people who do not repent even after revealing their true colors. But just as no goat can ever bear a lamb regardless of how well it imitates a sheep, such people are spiritually still sinners, no matter how virtuously they live in their lives in the flesh.

These goats, because they know that they are not the sheep, try to cover themselves with their own strength. So the goats look stronger than the sheep. But it is the sheep who have the Shepherd, and they are the ones who, having received the remission of sins by believing in the gospel of the water and the Spirit, are doing the Lord's work. There are billions of Christians throughout the whole world. Yet many of them are actually goats that still haven't received the remission of sins, and therefore we must all pray for them and preach the gospel of the water and the Spirit to them.

John 10:16 tells us, *"And other sheep I have which are not of this fold; them also I must bring, and they will hear My voice; and there will be one flock and one shepherd."* Our Lord said here that He has other sheep that are not of this fold of God's sheep, and that He has to bring them into the fold also. Bringing sinners, who still remain as goats, into the fold of God is what His servants do. The fold of God here refers to those who assist in this work. This is why Jesus said, "Sinners will receive the remission of sins and be under one Shepherd." In our hearts, you and I must truly believe in the gospel of the water and the Spirit, the Truth of salvation that Jesus Christ has given us, and by this faith live our lives in His Church with the Lord.

Jesus said in John 10:17, *"Therefore My Father loves Me, because I lay down My life that I may take it again."* Indeed, Jesus laid down His life to save our lives. He accepted our sins once and for all by being baptized by John the Baptist (Matthew 3:13), and He died in our place by giving up His life on the Cross (John 19:30). Jesus did all these things to save our lives, and that is why God the Father loves Jesus Christ and us.

That Jesus Christ came to this earth, was baptized, and shed His blood on the Cross was because God had commanded His Son to deliver us from our sins. To those who believe in the gospel of the water and the Spirit, God has given the right to remit away everyone's sins by spreading the gospel of the water and the Spirit. I give all my thanks to God the Father for remitting away all our sins with the water, the blood, and the Spirit, for making us His own children, for saving us from death, and for allowing us to live with Him forever in His Kingdom of Heaven. The power to turn us into God's own children belongs to Jesus. God the Father has given His Son the power and authority to save us from our sins. And to blot out our sins, Jesus fulfilled His work of salvation by bearing our sins through His baptism and dying for us on the Cross.

Fundamentally, Jesus is the Son of God and God Himself also. This means that God has become our own Savior. The birth of Jesus Christ the Messiah on this earth, the baptism He received from John the Baptist, His death on the Cross, His resurrection, and His ascension were all due to the fact that Jesus obeyed the Father's commands. Therefore, by being baptized, dying on the Cross, rising from the dead again for us, and now sitting at the right hand of the throne of God, Jesus has given the remission of sins, the Holy Spirit, and the eternal Kingdom of God to all who believe in the gospel of the water and the Spirit.

By believing in Jesus the Messiah, we have not only been saved from all our sins, but we have also received the blessing of glorifying God, for we have now become His own people. Now then, because only Jesus is the gate through which we can enter Heaven, we must be saved by knowing and believing in the gospel of the water and the Spirit that He has given us. We must infallibly know the Truth, that God Himself came to this earth, was baptized, died on the Cross, rose from the dead again, and has thereby saved us from all our sins and condemnation, and we must believe in this Truth without fail.

The gospel of the water and the Spirit was not made by man, but by God Himself. We were all made by God, and this Creator God Himself became a man to save His people from sin, was baptized by John the Baptist to take upon our sins, and was crucified and shed His precious blood to bear the condemnation of our sins. God has thereby brought the remission of sins and eternal life to those who believe in this Truth. It is when we know and believe in this Jesus as our Savior that we are able to glorify God. I give all thanks to the Lord for blessing us to believe in Jesus Christ and giving us the gospel of the water and the Spirit. We have received new life and become God's own children.

As we have become God's sinless children by believing in the Messiah's gospel of the water and the Spirit, we will enter the Millennial Kingdom and the eternal Kingdom of God, and we will enjoy all His blessings and authority forever. It is absolutely imperative for you to realize and believe here that you will all enjoy God's authority and live forever in Heaven in a sinless state. As the Messiah, Jesus received great authority from God the Father, and by exercising this authority, He has personally saved us from our sins with His baptism, blood, and resurrection. Every day, with our faith, we praise this Jesus Christ who is the door of the sheepfold, the door of salvation, and the gatekeeper of Heaven. ⊠

SERMON

8

We Must Believe That The Lord Is Our Good Shepherd

< John 10:1-18 >

"'Most assuredly, I say to you, he who does not enter the sheepfold by the door, but climbs up some other way, the same is a thief and a robber. But he who enters by the door is the shepherd of the sheep. To him the doorkeeper opens, and the sheep hear his voice; and he calls his own sheep by name and leads them out. And when he brings out his own sheep, he goes before them; and the sheep follow him, for they know his voice. Yet they will by no means follow a stranger, but will flee from him, for they do not know the voice of strangers.' Jesus used this illustration, but they did not understand the things which He spoke to them. Then Jesus said to them again, 'Most assuredly, I say to you, I am the door of the sheep. All who ever came before Me are thieves and robbers, but the sheep did not hear them. I am the door. If anyone enters by Me, he will be saved, and will go in and out and find pasture. The thief does not come except to steal, and to kill, and to destroy. I have come that they may have life, and that they may have it more abundantly. I am the good shepherd. The good shepherd gives His life for the sheep. But a hireling, he who is not the shepherd, one who does not own the sheep, sees the wolf coming and leaves the sheep and flees; and the

wolf catches the sheep and scatters them. The hireling flees because he is a hireling and does not care about the sheep. I am the good shepherd; and I know My sheep, and am known by My own. As the Father knows Me, even so I know the Father; and I lay down My life for the sheep. And other sheep I have which are not of this fold; them also I must bring, and they will hear My voice; and there will be one flock and one shepherd. Therefore My Father loves Me, because I lay down My life that I may take it again. No one takes it from Me, but I lay it down of Myself. I have power to lay it down, and I have power to take it again. This command I have received from My Father.'"

I don't know if the Lord has heard our prayer to have the gospel evangelized quickly, but our webmaster told me that the average number of hits on our homepage has increased to about 5,600 per a day. (Editor's note: the number recorded over 20,000 a day in 2006.) The response has been great since we have produced some more electronic books that contain the gospel of the water and the Spirit and uploaded them on the internet since we were not able to print many books in paper because of the financial difficulty. The request of the books increase by about 100 copies each time the number of visitors to our homepage increases by 1000 people. I am happy because the work of the Lord seems to be going well throughout the world.

There is much concern these days because there is a lot of arson being committed in Seoul these days. I think such crimes are increasing because life is becoming increasingly more difficult. Our weak hearts become even more damaged and anxious when such terrible things happen in our society. But it is so fortunate that God has taken care of us and blessed us so that we can serve the gospel of the water and the Spirit like this. I don't know how much longer we will be able to share this gospel, but I believe that God will give us strength and make us preach the gospel even more.

I will continue to share the gospel of the water and the Spirit to the entire world and write the books for the spiritual growth of the saints. And I believe the Lord will always work together with us so that the seeds of the gospel will blossom the flowers and bear fruit abundantly, and the flames of the gospel of the water and the Spirit will arise throughout the whole world.

But on the other hands, there are more saints who are leaving even after receiving the remission of sins than the new believers coming into our Church. Of course I think that could happen because we are weak human beings, but it is also true that I feel truly frustrated when I see the empty space left by the saints who have not set their mind firm with faith. But I truly want God to hold unto them until the end so that they would not become the adversaries of God. I have a desire in my heart that they would not become like the unfaithful servant who just returned the very one talent to the master and eventually faced condemnation as is recorded in the Scriptures.

I have a desire for you and me to complete all the work that has been entrusted to us until the day of the Lord's coming. I also think that this life of serving the gospel of the water and the Spirit and walking together with the Lord is truly happy. Though we are lacking, we are happy because we serve the gospel and we are comforted even when we are facing difficulties because we always abide in this gospel and the Lord. I sometimes wonder what I would have lived for if not for this gospel. Would we have true happiness if we lived only for our own flesh instead of serving the Lord came by the gospel of the water and the Spirit? Is it really a righteous life if you live only for yourself? No, it isn't. Living without knowing the Lord and the gospel of the water and the Spirit is really worthless, as it is written, *"A man who is in honor, yet does not understand, Is like the beasts that perish" (Psalm 49:20).*

The Scriptures Say the Sheep Must Enter through the Door of the Sheep

Today, we have read the Gospel of John chapter 10 together. When we look at the verses 1 to 5, we could see that our Lord is talking about the conventional practice in the world. He said, *"Most assuredly, I say to you, he who does not enter the sheepfold by the door, but climbs up some other way, the same is a thief and a robber. But he who enters by the door is the shepherd of the sheep. To him the doorkeeper opens, and the sheep hear his voice; and he calls his own sheep by name and leads them out. And when he brings out his own sheep, he goes before them; and the sheep follow him, for they know his voice. Yet they will by no means follow a stranger, but will flee from him, for they do not know the voice of strangers."*

As you know, the shepherd that takes care of the sheep opens the door for the sheep when the sheep come back after eating grass. Then the sheep come into the fold, and when the shepherd opens the door the next day and goes before them, the sheep follow him and eat grass. And the sheep recognize their shepherd perfectly and definitely. They only follow their own shepherd and do not follow anyone else even if that person wears the clothes of the shepherd. The sheep that remembers the shepherd's voice still follow their shepherd even if the fake one is disguised as the real shepherd. That is truly an bewildering and amazing thing, but it's true. The Lord spoke of the truly correct and real fact in the first part of the chapter 10.

In the Gospel of John chapter 10 verses 7 to 9, the Lord talks about the realistic and spiritual things here and our Lord portrayed Himself as the "door of the sheep": *"Then Jesus said to them again, 'Most assuredly, I say to you, I am the door of the sheep. All who ever came before Me are thieves and robbers, but the sheep did not hear them. I am the door. If anyone enters by Me, he will be saved, and will go in and out and find pasture.'"*

The Lord is our God. Jesus says He is the door of the sheep because He has become our Shepherd and led us, the flock of sheep, to the correct door and fed us the food of the salvation called the gospel of the water and the Spirit. And He continues on to say, *"All who ever came before Me are thieves and robber."* This is saying that anyone except the Lord who insists that he is the savior, the founder of a sect, or a religious leader are thieves and robbers. I am not trying to undermine other religions, but the teaching in Buddhism that all people can become Buddha and go to the nirvana is of a thief and a robber according to the Lord's Word here. The Lord said that only the Lord Himself is our true God and Savior and the Shepherd who leads us to the righteous path and gives us eternal life. He said, *"I am the door. If anyone enters by Me, he will be saved, and will go in and out and find pasture."*

If we believe in the Lord according to this Word of the Lord, if we believe that the Lord is our God, and if we believe that the Lord has blotted out all our sins through the gospel of the water and the Spirit, you and I can receive the remission of sins through that faith and become God's children and attain eternal life and go in and out through the door of the Lord and always eat the bread of life. That's because the Lord is the door of the sheep and the door of the Kingdom of Heaven as well as the door of salvation and the blessing at the same time. Probably, no one among the saints who believe in this fact does not know the Word, *"[The sheep] will go in and out and find pasture."* Who among the born-again does not know the fact that the Lord is the door that sends us to Heaven? But the important thing in our life of faith is 'faith' more than 'knowledge.' Through the Word in today's passage, I want you to reconfirm and believe in your heart this Truth that you have known well until now and have the heart of thanksgiving to the Lord.

The Lord Who Is the Good Shepherd Gives His Life for the Sheep

The Lord said in verse 11, *"I am the good shepherd. The good shepherd gives His life for the sheep."* The Lord says that He is the good Shepherd. The thieves come to kill and destroy, but the good Shepherd comes to this world to have the sheep attain heavenly life more abundantly. The Lord who gave us the true life and salvation is the good Shepherd: no one else but our Lord is the good shepherd. It means that there is none other than the Lord who can say, "I am the good shepherd." But what did the Lord say in following? The Lord said that the good shepherd dies for the sheep.

Giving up one's life is definitely not an easy thing. And there probably isn't anyone who would give up his life without hesitation to save others. But the Lord our God gave up His life and saved us because He loved you and me so much and had so much compassion for us. I am saying that the Lord came to this world and received the baptism to take all our sins upon Him and died in our place and saved us from the destruction. The Scriptures say that the good Shepherd gives up His life for the sheep. And the Lord gave up His life to save us. That's why we profess that the Lord is surely our good Shepherd.

Who is the good Shepherd who loved His sheep so much that He gave up His life for them and saved the sheep? Yes, He is none other than Jesus Christ. Can you and I give up our own life for the sheep? No, we can't. It is definitely not easy to give up our own life for others. Think of this story for a moment as an actual story for yourself and not just as the Word in the Scriptures. Our Lord did the work that no one else could do. The Lord who is the Almighty God came to this world as our Savior and paid the wages of all our sins by receiving the baptism on His body and giving up Himself to die on the Cross and resurrected again to perfectly save you and me. Therefore, the Lord said He is the good Shepherd. There really isn't anything more to say and explain any further about this clear Truth.

The Lord really is our God and the Savior who has saved you and me perfectly through the gospel of the water and the Spirit. He is the Shepherd that has never treated us like a doormat; rather He has treated us as His friends. We must confirm in our hearts of this faith that the Lord is the good Shepherd who has given us eternal life. Only those who understand this and believe in Him correctly are the people with the true faith.

But, what would happen if we do not believe that the Lord is our good Shepherd as we believe and follow the Lord? We just try to find a way out for ourselves and do not stand beside the Lord when we face a difficult situation. Then we stand against the Lord unwittingly. If we believe that the Lord really is our own Savior, we can uphold ourselves for the benefit of the gospel even when we are in a disadvantageous situation as we follow the Lord. We can do so because we believe clearly that the Lord would never harm you and me who are His sheep. You must remember that you can become the adversaries of the gospel some day if you do not acknowledge this fact and do not believe in this in your heart.

The Lord pointed to Himself and said, *"I am the good shepherd."* And He also said, *"The good shepherd gives up His life for the sheep."* We must understand that He is truly our good Shepherd and receive it with our hearts if the Lord definitely said this. We must become His sheep by believing that the Lord is the good Shepherd just like we have received the remission of sins by believing in the gospel of the water and the Spirit. We cannot really become His sheep and we are beings who can always depart from the Lord if we cannot accept this fact by faith.

I can also see such people around me that cannot live steadfastly as the Lord's sheep and depart from the Lord. Such people believe in the Lord, but suddenly turn from the Lord and stand against the Lord when their faith inflicts a loss on their lives. They should hold their hearts to unite with the work of preaching the gospel, but they instead are shaken like the chaff blown away by the wind. And they say, "When have I served the gospel?" regardless of whether it would harm the evangelization of the gospel or not. Such a person would become my adversary because he stands opposed to the Lord, but I think that is possible because he is a weak human being when I give it a second thought. Actually, you and I are beings that could become like that at any time if we do not truly believe in the Word that the Lord is our true Shepherd and the door to the Kingdom of Heaven.

Do you really believe that the Lord is the good Shepherd? I am sure you do. The deeper I think about it the clearer is the Truth that the Lord is the door of the sheep and the good Shepherd. We can understand definitely that the Lord is our door—the door to Heaven, the door of salvation, the door of the blessing, the door to eternal life—and the good Shepherd if we contemplate deeply, "What is really the relationship between the Lord and me?" or "Who is the Lord to me?" The Word the Lord spoke through today's Scripture passage is absolutely not exaggerated, forceful, or false. The Lord said, *"I am the good shepherd. The good shepherd gives up His life for the sheep."* The Lord who takes the responsibility of our present and future sins and gives us the eternal life is clearly our good Shepherd. Could we give up the Lord while living out our faith just because we face some difficulties and loses now that the Lord has paid the wages of all our sins by receiving the baptism and dying on the Cross and gave us the true salvation that we cannot receive by any other means? No, we can't. That is a wrong behavior that a born-again saint should not do.

Of course there appear some disappointing things among people and some wrong doings to one another when we follow the Lord and live out our faith. It's because our life of faith is also entangled with many humanistic relationships too, just as it is in our social life. But all problems are resolved naturally when we believe in the Lord and devote all our hearts to the preaching of the gospel. It means that I am able to overlook some one's shortcomings and understand him if he is a person who benefits the preaching of the gospel even though he has shortcomings and has done some wrong things to me. That's because a person who lives with his heart set for the benefit of the gospel is really a precious one.

People who serve the gospel of the water and the Spirit

and give their efforts for the preaching of the gospel are precious people regardless of their shortcomings and abilities. Anyone who has set his heart clearly for the gospel the Lord has given is a precious person. But what about a person who has not? He is in danger of his spiritual life. He is someone who could change at any time and become my enemy.

As you know all too well, there was a man named Judas Iscariot among the 12 disciples who followed Jesus. The Lord did not use him much although he was always at the side of the Lord because Jesus knew that he would later sell Him out. And this Judas who followed Jesus, listened to the Word from Jesus, and shared food to eat with Him actually sold Jesus out when Jesus didn't seem to do as he expected.

What can we realize from the account of Judas? It's that anyone who does not have unwavering faith can become an enemy to the gospel even if it's someone who has always lived a life of faith together with us. Therefore, we must set our hearts firmly and believe in Him so that we may not become like that. We must believe in the Truth that proclaims Jesus is the door of salvation, the door of Heaven, and the good Shepherd who would do good to us from the past, present, to our future eternally. The Lord will definitely not cast us out if we set this faith solid in our hearts and work for the benefit of the gospel of the water and the Spirit in the place that the Lord has permitted us.

The Apostle Paul said, *"For to be carnally minded is death, but to be spiritually minded is life and peace."* As this Word in the Scriptures says, if we take a closer look at people's thinking or emotion, it is really filthy. People do not even consider a good thing as a good thing when they start thinking about such things. The chain of thoughts that follow one after another inevitably reaches a negative conclusion. But how is the spiritual thinking? It brings a positive conclusion, true life, and peace.

Therefore, we, the people of faith, who have received the remission of sins by believing in the gospel of the water and the Spirit, do not need to bring in our own thinking into our faith. We just need to set our hearts firmly in the gospel and profess our faith, saying, "The Lord is my good Shepherd. The Lord is the door of the sheep and the door to all things. He saved us and gave us the eternal life and He does not harm us. He takes responsibility for all my past, present, and the future and also takes responsibility for our souls. He is a really good Shepherd to me. Therefore, I will serve the Lord in the situation that the Lord allows even though I am lacking." We must set our hearts firm in faith like this.

We Must Set Our Hearts for the Lord

I often say, "You must make up your mind to the Lord," to the believers and the servants of God. I mean that you must place your heart onto the upright work. Our hearts must take hold of the right place with the thinking, "This is my rightful place that God has given," and set our hearts down there as the plane in the air must land somewhere. If we set our hearts firmly in the faith, then the negative thinking that comes up as we live in this world cannot topple the faith. But what would happen if we were in a state that has not set the heart properly in faith. We might turn our backs to the Lord and stand in a position that stands against the gospel of the water and the Spirit because of the negative thinking that comes to us unavoidably for we are human beings. Therefore, today's Scripture passage is very important Word that is telling us we must set our hearts in the righteous thing and in the Lord who is the eternal Truth.

The Lord said that He is the good Shepherd. We must set this faith clearly in our hearts if we hear this Word and acknowledge that the Lord is really the good Shepherd. It means that we must actually accept this in our hearts and not just understand it as mere knowledge. We carry on our lives of faith through the heart not through the head. Your faith stays solid in its proper place no matter how the Devil shakes it and tries to pull it apart, if we understand the Word of God with the heart and set our faith solid on the Word with heart. But your faith will be shaken unintentionally when you just understand the Word without knowing it with the heart.

Some may think negatively saying, "The Lord is the good Shepherd. Why are you constantly repeating that when even I know that it is written in the Scriptures? Is it just to pass time?" This is a wrong faith. The Truth that "The Lord is my good Shepherd" would never be boring and make us feel grateful if we believed in the Lord's Word and got onboard on that Word.

Would it really be a proper faith if we who have received salvation through God and do the Lord's work did not believe in the Word God spoke in the Scriptures? I am asking whether you could really walk together with the Lord when you say, "That's Your Word. But my thinking is different. I think this is correct," in reply to the Lord's command that says, "Live your spiritual life this way. Everything will turn out well if you do it like this." Would you have the qualifications to receive the eternal blessing the Lord gives if you had such attitude? No, we wouldn't. It is right for you to reply, "I believe the Lord is our good Shepherd," when the Lord says, "I am the good Shepherd." This is really an easy and simple method.

The Lord cannot be disregarded as the good Shepherd or

become a less good Shepherd regardless of how much very intelligent people think and study about the matter. Just thinking simply, "I thought about it once again and I know the Lord is the good Shepherd as it is written in the Scriptures. It is clear that He is the good Shepherd that takes responsibility for my future and gives me the salvation and does not harm me," and believing it is the true faith. We may feel that such a person may seem to be foolish and dumb, but actually the person is truly wise. But the person who does much thinking on his own and is stubborn loses the true opportunity to attain proper faith because he is busy thinking deeply with his head. I am also one of the people who believe in the Lord simply like, "How could there be another god when the Lord really took all my sin by being baptized and died for me on the Cross, when the Lord has done all that for me? The Lord is my good Shepherd. That's it!"

All the religions in the world come to an end when we just say, "They are all garbage." There is only one mindset because the mind is set firmly in faith. Whether it's before being born again or after being born again, people have the desire to live according to the benefit of their own flesh because people are weak. But we will never be shaken no matter what temptation comes to us if we set our heart on the Word the Lord spoke and believe it as the Truth. No matter what situation we face, our hearts stand firm with the thinking, "The Lord is my Shepherd and the door to Heaven." This heart is not set upright automatically. Rather, we must set it upright by ourselves. It means that we must set the Truth and the heart that we think is right in ourselves. People who cannot set their hearts by themselves will not have the absolute Truth in their hearts even if tens of thousands of years passed. And they will eventually make reservations for the hottest seat in hell.

The Lord said, *"The hireling is not a shepherd and the sheep is not his own sheep. Therefore he flees when he sees the wolf and the wolf catches the sheep and harms them. The hireling flees because he is a hireling and does not care about the sheep. I am the good shepherd."* Here, the hireling means the people who just work for compensation just as the word implies and there are many religious hirelings around us that deceive the people and say they are the good shepherds. They minister in one church and then leave right away when another church says that they will pay him more. It is the characteristic of a hireling to quit the church that was entrusted to him without hesitation when yet another church says that it will give him more money.

But our Lord is different. The Lord said, *"I am the good shepherd; and I know My sheep, and am known by My own. As the Father knows Me, even so I know the Father; and I lay down My life for the sheep."* He said that He is the truly good Shepherd that gives up His life to save those souls. He said, *"Therefore My Father loves Me, because I lay down My life that I may take it again. No one takes it from Me, but I lay it down of Myself. I have power to lay it down, and I have power to take it again. This command I have received from My Father."* The Lord gave up His life out of His own volition to give new life to you and me exactly as this Word written in the Scriptures. The Lord took our sins upon Him through the baptism and gave up His life by giving up His body on the Cross, and the Lord says, *"No one takes it from Me, but I lay it down of Myself. I have power to lay it down, and I have power to take it again. This command I have received from My Father."* It is saying that He gave up His life on His own and no one takes it from Him, and for no other reason but to save you and me.

The Lord who loved us like this is our true God. The Lord truly is our Lord and our God. The great and almighty God who created the heavens and the earth gave up His life to save us that should die because of sin. That's why the Lord has to be our good Shepherd. There is none like the Lord in this planet and in the whole universe. The Lord is the good Shepherd who has saved us, and He leads us in the paths of righteousness. Do you also believe in this?

We must understand and believe this Word of the Lord with our hearts and engrave this firmly in each one of our hearts. We must confirm in our hearts this Truth that the Lord is the good Shepherd who gave up His life to save our souls and make us alive again. It is written that the Lord who has the authority to give up His life or receive it again laid His own life down for you and me. I really understand and believe so. All the people who have already received the remission of sins or those who have not must believe in this. We must set clearly in our hearts the fact that our Lord is our good Shepherd and follow the Lord by uniting together with God's Church and seeking the benefit of the gospel of the water and the Spirit.

Make up your mind now if you have yet to make up your heart as you live out your faith in these difficult times. The Lord said that He is our good Shepherd. There is no reason why you cannot place your mind on this certain Truth. Let's make up our mind once and for all by saying, "The Lord saved me through the gospel of the water and the Spirit. The Lord is my God and my Savior, and the One who gave me eternal life and the One who takes care of all things in the past, present, and the future. He is my good Shepherd that does good work through me." And we should live the rest of our life for the benefit of the gospel of the water and the Spirit. Let's live like that until we leave this world. The end of the world has drawn near. Regardless of whether you are young or old, whether you are a minister or a lay believer, I sincerely want all of you to make up your hearts before the presence of the Lord in same manner and believe it in your hearts and live this world that way until the last day.

The world right now is like the calm before the storm even though it looks peaceful to our eyes. It is precarious like the calm moment before the storm in every facet including political, economical, military, climactic, and natural realms. You and I are living in a dreadfully terrible time. This is the time to wake up from slumber and come back to the Church if anyone has departed from God's Church. But there are saints who still have not made up their minds and just continue to live for the benefit of their flesh. Jesus is the only One who gives peace and comfort to us during this time when all things are in a precarious state. Therefore, we must believe that the Lord is the good Shepherd and continue to store the Truth in our hearts as we read the Scriptural Word. We must make up our hearts firmly and draw out the faith once again and confirm it when the crisis rushes in or when the temptation arises from the heart as we live in this precarious world.

When your circumstance becomes disadvantageous and the greed from your flesh arises and hence comes a time when you do not seek the benefit of the gospel and just think about yourself, you then have to reconsider once again the Word, "The Lord is my Shepherd," by faith. And then turn your heart to thinking, "I should not be like this since the Lord is my good Shepherd. Shouldn't I be doing the good work as the Lord wishes since the Lord gave me the salvation and did not harm me?" This is the time you should stand before the Lord perfectly.

Actually, I live each day with the heart of one in the

battlefields these days. I do so because there could come a time when a more terrible war could erupt and I will not be able to do the Lord's work properly: I will regret it if I did not do this work today. I live each day with the heart to do the Lord's work as if we were involved in a war because we can at least work until now. There actually could be many crises for humanity due to various infectious diseases and natural catastrophes in the future as many people died in masses through the infectious disease called pest a long time ago.

We do not have much spare time. The Lord will come soon. We must be spiritually awakened right now at this moment. We must make up our hearts by knowing and believing absolutely that the Lord is the door of the sheep and our good Shepherd. We must give ourselves to the Lord serenely with our faith and commit ourselves to Him. And we must think of the work of God that has been entrusted to us as really precious work and faithfully carry out this work each and every day. I mean that we must live with the thinking, "I am a human being that could die any minute. I will take each moment preciously and work diligently because I might not have a chance to do it later." The foundation of such life is the faith in the truth that "The Lord is the good Shepherd."

The Lord really is the door of the sheep and the good Shepherd. Everything else is not much of a problem if we just believe in this. If we have received the remission of sins and become the righteous by believing in the gospel of the water and the Spirit, we must understand who the Person that has given us the remission of sins really is. We must believe in Him with the understanding that He is the Lord and our good Shepherd.

Living the life of faith is like that. It means that we must not just think of our salvation; we also must think of and believe in the Lord who has given us salvation. I will carry out the Lord's work diligently together with my coworkers and brothers and sisters today and tomorrow although I am lacking because it is the work that the Lord has entrusted to me.

I believe the Lord will guide us to the righteous path and protect us and make us serve the gospel. I give thanks to the Lord who is our good Shepherd. ⊠

SERMON

9

The Lord Is The Good Shepherd

< John 10:7-16 >

"Then Jesus said to them again, 'Most assuredly, I say to you, I am the door of the sheep. All who ever came before me are thieves and robbers, but the sheep did not hear them. I am the door. If anyone enters by me, he will be saved, and will go in and out and find pasture. The thief does not come except to steal, and to kill, and to destroy. I have come that they may have life, and that they may have it more abundantly. I am the good shepherd. The good shepherd gives His life for the sheep. But a hireling, he who is not the shepherd, one who does not own the sheep, sees the wolf coming and leaves the sheep and flees; and the wolf catches the sheep and scatters them. The hireling flees because he is a hireling and does not care about the sheep. I am the good shepherd; and I know my sheep, and am known by my own. As the Father knows me, even so I know the Father; and I lay down my life for the sheep. And other sheep I have which are not of this fold; them also I must bring, and they will hear my voice; and there will be one flock and one shepherd."

As a sequel to the sermon I preached this morning, I would like to share with you John chapter 10 again this evening. The Lord called Himself the door of the sheep. And He said, *"All who ever came before me are thieves and robbers, but the sheep did not hear them."* He also said, *"I am the door. If anyone enters by me, he will be saved, and will go in and out and find pasture."*

If we were to summarize John 10:7-10, the core message would be that the Lord is not only the door of the sheep, but also the Shepherd who grants salvation and blessings to people. The Lord also said in verse 10, *"The thief does not come except to steal, and to kill, and to destroy. I have come that they may have life, and that they may have it more abundantly."* As the Lord said, He is indeed the door of the sheep and our Savior. This Word is something that those who have not met our Lord can neither realize nor understand. The Lord told us that He is the door of the sheep and the good Shepherd, and that whereas the thief comes to kill, steal, and rob the sheep - He came to this earth so that the sheep may have life.

Although we professed to believe in Jesus as our Savior even before we really have met the Lord, when we were told that the Lord was our Shepherd and the door of the sheep, we couldn't quite understand it, and so we glossed over the matter, thinking to ourselves, "I guess that's true. Since it's what the Lord said, it must be true and real rather than a lie." But now that we have met and are abiding in the Lord who came by the gospel of the water and the Spirit, we can understand what it really means when the Lord said that He was the door of the sheep and the good Shepherd who was laying down His life for us. We can also grasp fully that as the Lord is the door of the sheep, the sheep go in and out, find pasture, and are saved. The Lord is indeed our good Shepherd. Even though some of us may not quite understand all the ins and outs of this passage, the Lord is clearly the good Shepherd and the door of the sheep.

The Lord Met with Me through the Gospel of the Water and the Spirit

I had been a Christian for about 10 years before I was really born again. And before I believed in Christianity, I had believed in Buddhism and even Confucianism. However, when I fell gravely ill and felt that life was meaningless, I believed in Jesus as my Savior. I believed in Jesus because as a gravely ill person facing his certain death, I wanted to tie up the loose ends of my life and solve the problem of sin in my heart. In reality, I didn't understand Jesus that well, but I hung onto the Lord since everyone told me that Jesus was the Savior of mankind, that He was crucified while shouldering all sins for the wicked and the sinful including me, that He rose from the dead again, and that anyone who believed in Him would be remitted from all sins. And I asked the Lord to forgive all the sins that I had ever committed until then. Although I believed in Jesus because I wanted to be washed from all my sins before dying, my sins were not actually washed away at that time. Yet I still continued to practice Christianity for a further 10 more years.

There is a Korean proverb that says ten years are enough for the mountains and the rivers to change. Nowadays, things change even more rapidly; a year is enough for the hills to disappear, tunnels to be opened, highways to be paved, apartment complexes to be built, and new streets to be laid. Yet even though I had been a Christian for a decade, my heart's sins did not disappear. Although my heart was elated when I first believed in Jesus, the problem of sin was not solved. So even as I believed in Jesus, I felt a lot of cynicism toward my faith. Despite the fact that I believed in Jesus sincerely and faithfully, whenever I looked into my heart, I saw all my sins still remaining intact, and even while I preached the Word of God to others, I myself struggled tremendously as I was too ashamed of my sinful self.

One day by God grace I eventually realized the gospel of the water and the Spirit written in the Bible, and I was remitted from all my heart's sins once and for all. I was so happy at that moment that laughter started bubbling up out from the depths of my heart. I realized why God the Father said when the Lord was baptized by John the Baptist and came out of the water, *"This is My beloved Son, in whom I am well pleased"(Matthew 3:17).* And I also realized why the Lord said just before He was baptized by John the Baptist, *"Permit it to be so now, for thus it is fitting for us to fulfill all righteousness."* When I reached this incredibly understanding, I could see the light of truth dawning on my heart. When I understood Matthew 3:13-17, it was like a brilliant and laser-sharp ray of light illuminating my heart from above. It is then that I realized, "The Lord bore all my sins by being baptized by John! Jesus Christ took upon not only my original sin but also my personal sins! He bore each and every sin I've ever committed throughout my entire lifetime from my childhood to the present!" I also realized that all the sins that I would come to commit in the future were also included in the sins of the world, and that these sins were all passed onto the Lord as well. Once I grasped this, peace came into my heart.

Before I met the Lord of salvation through the gospel of the water and the Spirit, my understanding was limited, and so I used to think, "The Lord is my Shepherd and my Savior. He alone is the Savior and the Son of God. There are four major religions in the world, but Christianity is not just the best amongst them. Only Jesus is the Truth, God Himself and my Savior." That was all that I understood, and the sins in my heart could not be removed by any means.

However, once I realized the gospel Truth of the water and the Spirit, the Truth of the remission of sins the Lord gave us, I grasped that the Lord took upon all my sins when I was truly destined to hell. So at that moment, a tiny little ripple broke out in my heart. Before my heart had been so very hard, frustrated and sinful, and I had been tormented inside even as I was laughing outside. But now that I finally obtained the washing of my sins, I let out a sigh of relief and was so happy, saying to myself, "My sins have now really disappeared like this! I have now received the remission of all my sins!"

But even after receiving the remission of sins, I was immediately worried about what to eat, what to drink and what to wear. That's because my flesh was still facing the problem of basic needs for clothing, food and housing, even though I knew very well that as I now had the Lord at my side, making money in this world was meaningless and the fame of the world and its riches didn't mean a thing. Moreover, now that I met the Lord I also felt a sense of duty, asking myself, "Shouldn't I serve the gospel of the Lord? Even though there are many Christians, they don't know the gospel Truth of the water and the Spirit. Isn't it then my duty to preach this gospel?" Yet to spread the gospel, I had to solve the problem of the basic needs for clothing, food and housing to support my family, and so I agonized over this issue and struggled a lot.

But one thing was very clear to me, and this was that the Lord had blotted out all my sins and the sins of the entire human race. So I tried to preach the gospel of the water and the Spirit, as I thought to myself, "It's not right for Christians to continue to agonize over the problem of sin. That's what the spiritually blind people do. People do not know this Truth. Is it not wrong for Christians to say that they have been remitted only from their original sin, and that they have to offer prayers of repentance to be remitted from their daily personal sins? How foolish they are! How pitiful they are to be imprisoned in their sins even though they believe in Jesus?" So I preached the gospel to everyone I met. Although many people were glad to hear the gospel, there also were some who stood against me. Yet despite this, the Lord has faithfully led me to where I am now.

Even after Meeting the Lord, I Still Faced Much Hardship

As the blind man written in John chapter 9 was driven out of the synagogue, I was also hated and despised by many of my old friends and acquaintances. But I didn't care. It didn't matter to me because the Lord was now the true Shepherd of my life. Just as the Lord said that He was the door of the sheep, He indeed became the door of salvation for me. He has become the door of salvation for you as well. As the Lord has become our Savior and our Shepherd, He takes delight in our hearts' desire to live for His gospel, and He continues to lead us and guide us, even though we are still weak and insufficient, sometimes wandering off and making many mistakes along the way. The Lord answered my prayers when I asked Him for things to use for the gospel of God rather than for my own flesh. God answered all my prayers asking, "Bless me, Lord! I need material means. I need a house to serve the gospel. Please give me a house. I need a job now, Lord; please give me a job."

I have encountered much hardship while serving the Lord and many difficult crises. When I experienced this I just prayed to God, and the Lord always came to my assistance. There were also many dangerous moments while serving the Lord, and crises that I had to overcome by faith. There were times when my health was not so good, when I faced a lot of urgent works to do for the Kingdom of God. At one time my health got so poor that it made me worry and think, “I am not going to last long like this. Maybe my time is coming soon.”

When the third English volume of my gospel book series came out, I had been so absorbed with the work to the detriment of my health that I came down with spondylitis, a type of arthritis that affects the spine. Apparently, I had this condition for a while, but I was not aware of it, and so I used to just ask my coworkers to massage my back, thinking that my back was getting stiff with old age. One of my coworkers then introduced me to Dr. Hong, a physician practicing traditional Korean medicine, and he gave me acupuncture with gold needles. I thought to myself, “I don’t care if the needles are made of gold or steel. I just hope I can be healed as soon as possible and continue to serve the Lord.” And true to my wish, it worked right away and I felt much better from that evening on. As not only I but also the whole Church prayed for me, I was healed. Although my health is not 100% yet, but it is a whole lot better.

I also had some problem with my throat, and so I went to see a doctor at a local hospital, but he told me that it was no big deal and just gave me a prescription. In reality though, there was a lump that was blocking my throat. Because this problem didn’t go away, I decided to go to a large hospital in Seoul for further diagnosis, and they found out the lump could turn cancerous if left alone. So I had it removed. Apart from this, I’ve had many other health problems as well, but every time God helped me to recover through medication and treatment, and through prayers of the fellow saints I have been able to maintain my health so far. God has also continued to lead His Church and help it.

I can now fully understand what the Lord meant when He said that He was the good Shepherd. I can appreciate it in my everyday life including my own experiences. In Psalm 23:1-2 David sang this incredible Hymn:

"The LORD is my shepherd;
I shall not want.
He makes me to lie down in green pastures;
He leads me beside the still waters."

David had lived by relying totally on the Lord, and just as God had bestowed His mercy and goodness on him throughout his entire life, I know that God is also bestowing the same blessings upon you and me alike. The Lord is indeed alive, and He is the door of the sheep, our Savior and our Shepherd. He is not only my Shepherd but also your Shepherd. The Lord helps us, protects us and bestows His many blessings on us.

When we read this passage, we can really grasp and appreciate just how much our Lord cares about us. But let's give some more in-depth consideration to see what it means when the Bible says that the Lord has become our Shepherd. The Lord said, *"I am the good shepherd. The good shepherd gives His life for the sheep."* The Lord gave His life to save us from sin. Born on this earth, the Lord took upon all the sins of mankind by being baptized by John the Baptist at the age of 30, and He loved us so much that He gave up His body on the Cross. Enduring all the appalling suffering, persecution and insults, the Lord bled to death on the Cross, shedding all His blood that was in His heart through His pierced hands and feet. He then rose from the dead, thereby becoming our Savior. He did all these things in order to save you and me from sin. Indeed, the Lord lacks nothing to be our Shepherd.

When you found yourself struggling after meeting the Lord, you also had to remove the dross of your heart that was still lingering in many places. You did this because you wanted to follow the Lord properly. The Lord has removed much of our carnal desires and thoughts. To do so He gave us many trials. But He still led us faithfully, for it was our sincere desire to follow Him in our lives by trusting in the righteousness of God. If we first think of the Lord's pleasure and live by faith seeking His Kingdom and His righteousness, then the Lord will bless us all the time. We now understand that God uses much persecution and hardship to cleanse our hearts, and then gives us blessings according to our faith. This is what the Lord has done to you and me. If there still is much dross in your heart and mine, then the Lord will permit these trials in our lives until it is removed, and through these trials, our faith will be refined and we will be shaped into God's useful instruments. And we know from our experience that it is from then on, when we thus become useful instruments of God, which the Lord works in our lives even more, helps us even more, and blesses us even more to spread the gospel of the water and the Spirit.

The Lord Is Our Good Shepherd

Just as the Lord knows us, we must also know Him. We cannot say that we do not know the Lord. It's so fortunate and gratifying that the Lord has become our Shepherd. He is our Chief Shepherd. He has met us through the gospel of the water and the Spirit and saved us from all our sins, and as our Shepherd, He is helping us and leading us to the way of righteousness for His name. As we keep the name of the Lord in our hearts, He helps us concretely and holds us steadfast with His guidance. It's so wonderful that we have a good Shepherd like this with us. Because Lord has become our Savior, it is considered a tremendous joy for us to carry out His work. That's because we had done so many useless things in this world. And it's also because we had been completely worthless beings.

There is a popular song in Korea that goes like this, "I drink, I sing and I dance, but all that remains in my heart is sadness." I haven't lived in this world as long as some of you, but I know that like words in this song, life is meaningless. It is completely futile. There is nothing but emptiness, as another line goes, "As I look around to find what to do, everything I see turns its back." Anything we try to do, there always are obstacles to overcome. There are times when we succeed and times when we fail—nothing is guaranteed. The winner may become the loser, and the loser may become the winner.

In the outskirts of a certain town is a motel called "Jackpot." Perhaps the owner named the motel "Jackpot" to reflect his wish to succeed with his business. This owner may have named his motel wishing for good luck, but we have the Lord who bestows great blessings on us. We have the Shepherd who came by the gospel of the water and the Spirit. Our Lord helps us and blesses all of us.

As I said before, I really enjoy doing God's work. That's because the work of the world and me are completely useless. If you were to work as a public servant for 30 years, you would probably retire with a few hundred thousand dollars in your savings account, but all this money means nothing before the Lord. You may work hard at your job, but this means nothing; you may run your business with all your passion, but this has no meaning; and you may make a lot of money, but this doesn't mean anything. After all, are all these things after all just to secure three meals a day? What a miserable life is this then?

Those who don't really appreciate all this may think that life is quite easy, but in reality, it is not so easy. In Korea military service is compulsory for all men, and so by the time Korean men start looking for a job after finishing school and serving in the military, most of them are already in their early 30s. And after getting married and having a couple of kids, they are already in their 40s. Life is like a journey of a vagabond. You come into this world empty-handed and you leave empty-handed. For our unmarried sisters as well, it won't take long before they get married, bear children and then hear others calling them grannies. There is no point in comparing our lives to someone else's life. All that results from this is a futile sense of superiority or inferiority.

Wealth doesn't mean much either. Although I have never been a wealthy man, I am so happy that I am now serving the gospel of the water and the Spirit. The haves and 'the have-nots' both eat only three meals a day. The rich depart from this world after spending their entire lifetime trying to manage their money to become even wealthier. There are times of success and times of failure. That's why life is like the sea. It never stays calm. There are good days and bad days, sunny days and cloudy days, and calm days and stormy days — and at the end of all this, life is over.

When I was young, my parents gave all their money to an indigenous Korean religion called *Daesonjinrihoe*. One of the doctrines of this religion is that when war breaks out, its followers would all ascend to the heavens in their shoes. It's so ridiculous and utter nonsense. Anyways, because my parents gave all their hard earned money to this religious group, I had a very rough childhood. Until I was 12 years old, my hope was that I would one day eat a full bowl of rice. You may think this rather funny, but I was born into a really poor family. And as I grew up in this poverty, I went through an exceptionally difficult childhood.

However, after I met the Lord through the gospel of the water and the Spirit, I saw that there were many opportunities to make money. If you open your eyes, look around, and make preparations little by little, then you will see many opportunities to make money, though not everyone can succeed all at once. I also saw how others were living. I myself worked as a salaried man for 14 months. I got paid $50 a day for working 8 hours. In 1980's, this was considered a good wage in Korea. But regardless of whether I get paid $500 or $5,000 a month, can this be even compared to preaching and serving the gospel of the water and the Spirit? Even if someone were to give me a truckload of money, can this be compared to doing God's work? No, it cannot! I will never exchange my ministry for anything! That's because no matter how much money I may be offered, not only do I think that my ministry is extremely valuable, but it really is worth every minute of my life. That's why I feel gratified. It's so gratifying to me that I am carrying out God's work.

Whenever our ministry workers get together I say to them, "You should be grateful to God. You should be thankful that you have met the Lord through the gospel of the water and the Spirit and are now serving Him. Do you think you met the Lord through your own effort, by trying to meet Him on your own? Certainly not! You could have never met the Lord on your own. And by yourself you could not have laid the foundation to serve the Lord either. With that kind of attitude and faith is that, you could not possibly serve the Lord even if you wanted to. Not just anyone can serve the gospel of the water and the Spirit. And the very fact that you are able to serve the gospel is something for which you should all be grateful." Admittedly there are some ministry workers who don't understand my point. They probably think quietly to themselves, "How can he tell us to be thankful when he gives us so much work? It's ridiculous!"

In reality, however it is in fact something for which we should all be grateful for. Having found the gospel of the water and the Spirit in our lives, you and I are now working hard to spread this true gospel. If we were not doing this work of spreading the gospel, what would we be doing? Would we not be just working to keep our bodies alive? We would all be working just to earn enough bread to feed ourselves. What a wretched life is this?

Let's say that you make $200 after working for the whole day. If you work every day without taking any days off, you would make $6,000 in a month. Is this a lot of money? Not really. In some ways, it may seem like a lot of money, but it really is not that much money, only enough to make a living. So let's say that you go out and work hard to make enough money to feed yourself, buy a house and the furniture to go with it, purchase a car to make your life a bit more comfortable, get some respect from the community, and people now call you 'the boss.' All this may seem like a big deal, but it's actually wretched to work just to keep your body alive. Your life would be on a treadmill, going through the same routine over and over, getting up in the morning to go to work, coming back home to get some sleep, and then starting the whole thing all over again the next morning. At the end of the day, when you look back to your day, you won't find any joy. There won't be anything worthwhile.

The Lord Has Enabled Those Who Hunger for Righteousness to Carry Out Many of His Works

The Lord said in Mathew chapter 5, *"Blessed are those who hunger and thirst for righteousness, For they shall be filled."* This means that those who truly yearn to do the righteous work of God will be filled. In other words, the Lord will give and entrust them with His work. It is to carry out this righteous work entrusted by the Lord that He fills us. My fellow believers, if you had to spend every hour, every day, every month, and every year only for yourself to ensure your own prosperity rather than doing something worthwhile now, then your life itself would be completely miserable. Some people are happy if only their basic needs for food, clothing and housing are met. Because of that, we call such people "pigs with a full stomach." They are like beasts. It's not because they live like beasts that they are no better than beasts, but it's because they only care about their own greed like pigs. Some philosopher said that he would rather be a hungry Socrates than a pig with a full stomach. There are many starving artists practicing their arts in poverty. Why do they do this? It's because they consider this more than worthwhile. They don't practice their arts just to feed themselves and make a living.

A Korean proverb says that when a tiger dies, it leaves its skin, but when a man dies, he leaves his name. What about you then? If you die after spending all your life just to feed yourself, then there will nothing meaningful to inscribe in your epitaph, other than the dates of your birth and death. There won't be anything to write on your epitaph. You must have something meaningful to write on your epitaph after you pass away, after you go to see God. You must have something good that you've done in your life. Try going to a cemetery and read some of the epitaphs there. Some epitaphs are inscribed with the names of all the descendants of the deceased. Those epitaphs just tell the visitors how many offspring the deceased had. Few epitaphs actually say something about the deceased themselves. Hardly any epitaph says that the man buried underneath was a righteous man.

The late Deacon Myoungchan Kim is buried in one of the public cemeteries in this city, and there you will find his tombstone. On that tombstone we inscribed, "Here sleeps the righteous Deacon Myoungchang Kim, waiting for the Lord's return." All the born-again Christians who believe in the gospel of the water and the Spirit wait for the Lord's return in their lives. But many people copy off this epitaph even as they have not been born again. In imitating us, they take out the word "righteous" and inscribe, "Here sleeps Elder so-and-so waiting for the Lord's return." To be honest, this is a violation of intellectual property rights. Yet these people don't really understand the real meaning of Deacon Kim's epitaph, but instead just think that it sounds good. That's probably why they can't use the word "righteous" and just inscribe, "Elder so-and-so, Deacon so-and-so, or Saint so-and-so sleeps here, waiting for the Lord's return."

There are two kinds of people in God's sight. Everyone is either a righteous person or a sinner. Those who have been saved from sin and received the remission of sins by meeting the Lord and believing in the gospel of the water and the Spirit are righteous people, but those who have still have sin even as they believe in Jesus - are sinners. Of course, those who don't know Jesus at all are also sinners.

There must be something worthwhile to inscribe in our epitaph. That's why we are so grateful that we've come to do God's work. We are doing what is right. There are many workers here in God's Church, and they should all thank God. And they should thank me as well, since I've given them a lot of work. Isn't this true? Why don't you answer? Perhaps you don't feel like saying anything. Perhaps some of you are thinking, "I am so sick and tired of work! All that he gives me is work and more work!" But my fellow believers think about what would happen if I did not give you any work at all. What would you do if I told you to take time off and do something else? You will probably do various things, but what would that be? They will all be perishable things. You will only do meaningless things. You will end up doing something that has no lasting meaning. Perhaps you will have a good time eating and drinking, and singing and dancing, but there will be nothing left when you wake up the next morning. That's why you should be thankful to God for entrusting His work to you.

The Lord said, *"I am the door. If anyone enters by me, he will be saved, and will go in and out and find pasture" (John 10:9)*. This means that as the Lord is the Shepherd of the sheep and the door of salvation, those who believe in Him will surely be saved. Salvation is not something that can be attained in any other way. It is attained only by believing in the gospel of the water and the Spirit given by the Lord. You must first be saved by believing in the Lord, and then you will be blessed in body and spirit, attending the Lord's Church and finding pasture there. Through the Church you will receive the blessings of Heaven and hear the Lord's Word, which is the bread for your soul, and you will carry out the blessed work of God. That's what you are supposed to do on this earth. As the Lord is the Shepherd, He will feed us in His sheepfold and His sovereignty. We must truly grasp that the Lord is the door of the sheep and that He is our Shepherd. We should not just end at receiving our salvation. The Lord said that He has given us eternal life.

He said that we would find pasture and He would feed us. None other than this is everlasting life.

That we can live forever with a perfect and immortal body means that we have received tremendous blessings. When our imperfect bodies are transformed into perfect and spiritual bodies to never fall ill again by become like God, we will never get old nor be imperfect again. It's a tremendous blessing for us to live forever in such a condition enjoying splendor and glory. That's how wonderful it is to believe in Jesus, and to receive the remission of sins and obtain everlasting life by believing in Jesus Christ, the door of salvation and in the gospel of the water and the Spirit. Our present lives are not all that there is to life.

The Lord has also granted us the Millennial Kingdom. He said that we will reign for a thousand years. We will find out the details of our reign when we get there. But the Lord also said clearly that after this Millennial Kingdom, He will give us the eternal Kingdom of God to enjoy 'everlasting life'. Do you believers believe in this? It's hard to imagine this because none of us has actually experienced everlasting life, but think about what it will be like when we are able to live forever as perfect beings. Imagine living forever as perfect beings, suffering no sickness and having no imperfection at all neither in our thoughts, nor in hearts, nor in our faith. And imagine enjoying splendor and glory. It's a wonderful blessing! The Lord says that because He is the door of the sheep and the Shepherd, those who come into Him will go in and out, receive salvation, and find pasture. In other words, they will receive eternal life. They will never thirst again nor die, but attain everlasting life.

The Lord will return to this earth soon, but we do not know exactly when. Nevertheless, He will come again for sure. At that time, those born-again Christians who had died and been buried in the ground will be transformed into perfect bodies and be lifted into the air, and then the righteous who are still alive will receive the Lord in the air, exactly as it is written in the Bible: *"For the Lord Himself will descend from heaven with a shout, with the voice of an archangel, and with the trumpet of God. And the dead in Christ will rise first. Then we who are alive and remain shall be caught up together with them in the clouds to meet the Lord in the air. And thus we shall always be with the Lord" (1 Thessalonians 4:16-17).* Then the Lord will make the new heavens and the new earth for us - to live there for a thousand years.

However, those whose hearts still remain sinful even as they profess to believe in Jesus—that is, those who claim to believe in Jesus even as they refuse to believe in the gospel of the water and the Spirit nor realize that Jesus is the door of the Sheep, the Savior, and the door of salvation—will not be able to receive Jesus on that day. After a thousand years, at the end of our splendid and glorious reign, God will resurrect them and bring them before the 'white throne' of judgment. Revelation chapter 21 says that those whose names are written in the Book of Life will receive everlasting life, but the rest will be cast into the everlasting fire of hell. The Bible says that this is the second death, meaning that every sinner will suffer forever.

Everyone must believe in Jesus Christ, who is the door of salvation and the door of the sheep, and thereby attain salvation and reach the pasture of everlasting life. Otherwise all will suffer forever. Once a sinner dies physically, both his soul and body will be cast into hell after the Millennial Kingdom, and that's why it's called the second death. That's why the blessings awaiting you and me as God's redeemed people are so wonderful. These blessings cannot be compared to any privileges enjoyed by even the most powerful rulers of the world. Such privileges last only as long as they hold onto their power. In contrast, we will enjoy our privileges for eternity. That's why we are so grateful to God.

Jesus also said in verse 16, "And other sheep I have which are not of this fold; them also I must bring, and they will hear my voice; and there will be one flock and one shepherd." This means that we must guide those who are still lost and wandering about. These people must indeed meet the righteous, hear the Truth about the gospel of the water and the Spirit in detail, come into the sheepfold of God, and receive the same blessings that we have received as the forerunners of faith.

What is the reason for our existence on this earth? What's the reason for us to be born on this earth? Man is born in order to meet the Lord, to be saved and to attain everlasting life. There is a single common purpose for which you are born, and it is for you to meet the Lord and be remitted from all your sins. If you fail do so then you were born all in vain. Like Judas Iscariot, it would have been better for you—not to be born at all.

Let us then lead all those who still have not come into the sheepfold, preach the gospel of the water and the Spirit to them, make them one flock with us in the sheepfold, and enable them to receive and enjoy the same blessings that we have received. ⌧

Sermon

10

The Lord Is Also Our Good Shepherd

< John 10:11-18 >

"I am the good shepherd. The good shepherd gives His life for the sheep. But a hireling, he who is not the shepherd, one who does not own the sheep, sees the wolf coming and leaves the sheep and flees; and the wolf catches the sheep and scatters them. The hireling flees because he is a hireling and does not care about the sheep. I am the good shepherd; and I know my sheep, and am known by my own. As the Father knows me, even so I know the Father; and I lay down my life for the sheep. And other sheep I have which are not of this fold; them also I must bring, and they will hear my voice; and there will be one flock and one shepherd. Therefore my Father loves me, because I lay down my life that I may take it again. No one takes it from me, but I lay it down of myself. I have power to lay it down, and I have power to take it again. This command I have received from My Father."

The Good Shepherd Even Gives up His Life for His Sheep

Our Lord illustrated here that He was the Good Shepherd and that the Good Shepherd even gives up his life for the sheep. It would be wonderful if there were only good shepherds like the Lord, but unfortunately there are many hirelings as mentioned in this verse amongst the ministers of this world who only work for pay. Just as good and evil coexist in this world, there are evil hirelings and good shepherds.

But our Lord referred to Himself as the Good Shepherd who gives up His life for the sheep. What was the basis of the Lord saying such a thing? We can understand this through the work of Jesus who received the baptism from John the Baptist and was crucified and died on the Cross in order to save mankind from sin, and thereby saved His sheep at once by being resurrected from the dead. The Lord saved us from sins by the gospel of the water and the Spirit and gave to us the true salvation as a gift, also to everyone who would believe in this genuine gospel.

Today's Scriptures passage tells us that a hireling leaves the sheep and flees when he sees a wolf approaching. But our Lord is not like that, He is the Good Shepherd who feeds and nurtures His sheep. Jesus came to this world for the sheep who were facing their certain deaths due to their sins, and saved them by receiving the baptism from John the Baptist, and giving up His life by being crucified on that cruel Cross, and being resurrected from the dead. Our Lord is the exceedingly Good Shepherd to those who truly believe in the gospel of the water and the Spirit. Even the sheep that have been wandering around and going astray due to not knowing where to go were also able to receive the true salvation by meeting the God given gospel of the water and the Spirit. The Lord saved us who were bound to die due to our original sins and our personal sins 'all at once' by the gospel of the water and the Spirit.

Before Jesus Christ came into this world, mankind was scurrying speedily towards the path of their destruction due to their many sins. You and I had been people like this who could not but commit sin throughout our entire lives, because we were originally born as offspring to sin. We were the people who could not but die spiritually and physically due to the many sins we commit.

But despite this our Lord gave up His life for our salvation. Jesus took all the sins of this world away by receiving His baptism from John the Baptist in the Jordan River, and He was also resurrected from dead after shedding His blood and dying on that Cross in agony. By doing all this Jesus saved all those who would believe in His gospel of the water and the Spirit 'all at once' and we were finally able to become Jesus Christ true sheep due to the baptism He received and the blood He shed.

Now you and I are able to receive the remission of our sins 'once and for all' and receive this true new life and possess eternal life by believing the Truth of salvation the Lord gave us, that is, the gospel of the water and the Spirit. Were we not the people who were destined to die due to our sins if it was not for our Lord who came by the gospel of the water and the Spirit? You and I were people who were destined for hell and be destroyed therein if the Lord had not come into this world. The unchangeable truth and fact is; we received our salvation because our Lord came to receive the baptism and die on that Cross.

In what situation were we ensnared before we were saved? Were we not such wicked people who could not but die and go to hell due to our many sins? But despite this we who know and believe in the gospel of the water and the Spirit, give praise, are thankful and give glory to God that the Lord is the Good Shepherd. We must never forget for even a moment the Truth of salvation that our Lord who is the Good Shepherd gave up His life on that Cross in order to save His sheep. I cannot but give thanks to God for this. Our Lord truly is the Good Shepherd for you and me who believe. I give glory to God.

Our Lord said these words to the Spiritual Thieves

In the Gospel of John chapter 10 verse 10, our Lord said, *"The thief does not come except to steal, and to kill, and to destroy. I have come that they may have life, and that they may have it more abundantly."* You should try and understand the deep meaning of these Word well. The Lord said, "The thief does not come except to steal, and to kill and to destroy." The Scriptures here refer directly to those ministers who swindle people spiritually as hirelings and thieves. A hireling literally is someone who works for a day's pay. Jesus illustrates here that spiritual swindlers and thieves are those who try to kill and destroy believers in their congregation as hirelings. A hireling is someone who comes to people and spreads the wrong faith so that they can steal their material possessions and their souls. Hirelings take everything away from believers and eventually destroy them.

You and I know this well, and are able understand the true nature of 'hirelings' by their spiritual fruit. I sometimes see famous pastors preaching on cable TV, and at times I feel aggrieved when I see those splendid church buildings; and I wonder if these ministers build these large and luxurious buildings just to compete against each other. I also get so frustrated when hearing their words; their sermons are all worldly that are so far-off from the gospel of the water and the Spirit. The basic content of their sermons are limited by telling their followers that one can become wealthy if they believe in Jesus as their Savior or if someone really desires to be a good Christian they should become a decent law abiding person and dedicate himself to Jesus. Putting it somewhat harshly, sermons like these are nothing more than an ulterior motive to fulfill their greed by overstressing the 'fear factor' those believers cannot receive blessing from God if they do not live like this.

The Lord harshly criticizes hireling's sermons, telling us that it is likened to taking away everything believers possess. How courteous do hirelings greet believers in their congregations! They greet believers in a gentle voice, "How are you?" They make themselves up so hypocritically and minister to believers as if they are gentle lambs or shepherds. They say, "You must live virtuously for the Lord," and use words carefully behaving in such a manner that their code of conduct will not be broken. They are the true spiritual hirelings.

They also preach like this. "Are you all really the people of God? If so then you should live a virtuous life. Because we are the people of God, we should live uprightly and not let Jesus be insulted because of us? Therefore we should turn away from sin and offer our prayers of repentance before the presence of God, and thereby become sanctified. By doing this you will become Godly. Only then will people start to discover Jesus in you and come to believe. So, how should we live? You should throw away your evil ways and become good Christians." They teach their followers like this by decorating their sermons up with all kinds of good words of this world. They are therefore classified as people who lead God's sheep in the wrong way, because they have not as yet received salvation by the God given gospel of the water and the Spirit.

Ministers, who believe correctly in the God given gospel of the water and the Spirit, preach the Word of nurturance to their sheep because they believe in the righteousness of God and follow the Lord. They do God's work by preaching the gospel of the water and the Spirit in many places. These true shepherds preach to the people the work of salvation our Lord had fulfilled, that is, the gospel of the water and the Spirit, and thereby give them the gift of new life to all who will accept this gospel. All those who follow the Lord's will like this and in turn preach to many souls the blessing of God through the gospel of the water and the Spirit are the true workers of God.

But we must know spiritual hirelings are not like this. These hirelings are people who approach others and minister to them with the sole purpose of stealing from them. They do not have weapons in their hands, but they are fundamentally the same as thieves. I can give you many examples of how they rob and steal from their congregations, spiritually and physically. For example, they acknowledge anyone who comes to their church as saints; they appoint them deacons if they come often enough; and soon these deacons become elders should they be rich and offer heaps of money. This is probably the reason why there are so many deacons and elders in these churches. But the truth is that these things are nothing more than methods of trying to rob and steal from you. This is because there is no one amongst them who can preach the gospel of the water and the Spirit.

So we see many ministers of the world confess Jesus as their Lord, but the Lord warns us that there are many hirelings amongst them who minister without knowing the gospel of the water and the Spirit. Jesus speaks clearly about these things through today's Scripture.

Just look around you. Although you and I who believe in the gospel of the water and the Spirit are the true sheep having received the true remission of sins before the presence of God, but these hirelings are even as bold to approach Gods sheep with the idea of stealing from them? God's sheep are those who have become the people of God by receiving salvation from all their sins by believing in the God given gospel of the water and the Spirit. They follow the Lord because they know His voice. The reason these true sheep follow the Lord is because they know how to distinguish the voice of the Shepherd from the voice of a hireling.

We, who believe in the righteousness of God, must know how to discern the words of a hireling from God's Word. It is written in the Book of Genesis 1: 6, *"Then God said, 'Let there be a firmament in the midst of the waters, and let it divide the waters from the waters.'"* This means that God had divided the water above the firmament from the muddy water on this earth. In other words, He divided the Word from the words of man. We therefore must discern all things based on the recorded Word of God. We should discern amongst the many ministers in Christianity today who the true servants of God are and who the hirelings are. We need to know that not anyone who says he has been born again just because he believes in Jesus as the Savior is a true Christian; not anyone can be regarded as a true Christian just because he has been appointed to deaconship or eldership in a church; and not anyone can be regarded as a true leader of God just because he has become a pastor in a Christian denomination. We therefore should know the gospel of the water and the Spirit and also believe it in order to discern who the spiritual thieves are and who the good shepherds are. We should check and see who really is following the Lord Jesus Christ by faith, and has become God's sheep and who truly believes in the gospel of the water and the Spirit.

Our Lord said that He knows His sheep and His sheep know Him well and follow the Good Shepherd only because they know the voice of this Shepherd. But amongst the many lost sheep in this world, there are those who have met the Lord by the gospel of the water and the Spirit, while there are others who have as yet not met Him. Tragically, these sheep who have not received the remission of their sins due to them not knowing the gospel of the water and the Spirit have as yet not become the Lord's sheep, the sheep of His fold. Everyone can meet the Lord if they would believe the gospel of the water and the Spirit, which says that Jesus Christ saved us from the sins of the world by His baptism He received from John the Baptist, His blood of the Cross and His resurrection. We should thus be able to discern what the gospel of the water and the Spirit is, and we must hold fast onto this genuine gospel.

Even amongst Christian leaders, there are those who believe in the gospel of the water and the Spirit, and there are those who refuse to believe in it and are actually evil hirelings. These hirelings use their sheep and try to become fat from all the many possessions they steal from their sheep. But the good shepherds have accepted the God given gospel of the water and the Spirit into their hearts and also serve the righteousness of God. These shepherds are the true leaders of God's Church.

There are many who have become spiritual hirelings. These are those who have graduated from theological seminaries, and do not have knowledge or believe in the gospel of the water and the Spirit, and earn a salary from their respective churches. They are ministering falsely with a value system based on material things. They are only interested in the things believers can fill their mouths with, and are not interested in God's sheep receiving salvation or even one soul receiving the true remission of sins. If these people are not the robbers and thieves mentioned by the Lord, then who are they really?

The true servants of God have keen interest in whether someone has received the remission of their sins by believing in the gospel of the water and the Spirit, and also how to increase the faith of these believing saints. Therefore the servants of God who believe in the gospel of the water and the Spirit are supplying sermons according to the Word for their spiritual growth. So when a servant of God preaches God's Word to those who have already become God's sheep, the Holy Spirit inside their hearts makes them accept it by saying "Amen" and then they consume it by faith. These true saints of God are obedient to God's recorded Word, and do not deviate from it. Because of this these saints and Jesus Christ become united in the will of God the Father. The Triune God is called the God of the Trinity because God has saved sinners from the sins of the world with one will and purpose.

We should be able to discern these hirelings and keep them at a distance including discerning the Truth from lies through 'the spiritual lens' called the gospel of the water and the Spirit. The Lord said, *"But a hireling, he who is not the shepherd, one who does not own the sheep, sees the wolf coming and leaves the sheep and flees; and the wolf catches the sheep and scatters them" (John 10:12).* How do sheep behave? Because they are the family members in God, they assist and fight for one another especially when one of them is in danger, and they care for one another and hope that they all would prosper because they are all one family. Because they have already become the righteous by believing in the Word of the gospel of the water and the Spirit and received the remission of sins, they care for one another to receive even more abundant faith and blessings from God. That is why we care for one another because we are one family who received this glorious salvation by the gospel of the water and the Spirit.

These ministers who truly have received the remission of sins desire deeply that the saints would prosper spiritually and physically. The Lord desires that everyone should truly believe in the gospel of the water and the Spirit, in order to receive many blessings from God in His Church, and to become a person of God. The Lord said, *"I have come that they may have life, and that they may have it more abundantly" (John 10:10).* He wants us to receive great blessing spiritually and physically. This is the very heart of God and the heart of a Good Shepherd.

We who believe in the gospel of the water and the Spirit are God's people. We are the sheep who have met Jesus Christ already and the Lord is our Shepherd. Because of this we must be able to discern the true shepherds from these hirelings, and live a life of a preacher who leads the lost sheep so that they can be herded towards the fold and help them to receive the abundant life also. The Lord told us to live like that. It is written, *"I am the good shepherd; and I know my sheep, and am known by my own. As the Father knows me, even so I know the Father; and I lay down my life for the sheep" (John 10:14-15).* Our Lord gave up His life for His sheep. Jesus received His baptism from John the Baptist and was crucified to death on the Cross in order to save us from the sins of the world and give us new life.

While doing God's work, there will be times when we become so tired and weary that we feel like dying. But when we give it much thought, we will once again realize, "The Lord is my Good Shepherd and He even gave up His life for me after receiving His baptism, but I am complaining that I have worked through one night even though I have eating delicious food to eat while working. I must therefore obey even if He requires my life. Why do I try to avoid even this much of sacrifice for Him?" We come to realize at a time like this just how lacking we are and what a Good Shepherd the Lord really is.

We Believe the Lord Is Truly the Good Shepherd

The Lord spoke of the reason why His Father loved Him

saying, *"Therefore My Father loves me, because I lay down my life that I may take it again" (John 10:17).* Although our Lord gave up His life He also intended to take it up again, so that He could give us new life. God the Father loved His Son, Jesus who is also our Savior. Many lost sheep received new life through Jesus as a result of Him receiving the baptism and giving up His life on that Cross. God loved Jesus Christ because He was His only begotten Son, and was also thankful and loved the work His Son had completed.

Even in human society, there can be no father who does not love his own beloved child. But a child seems even more lovable when he does something good and upright. Suppose a child saved another person's life, wouldn't the father be so proud that he had such a good son?

Think about it! Who has the power to threaten and kill the Lord when our Lord who saved you and me from our sins is the very God who created this universe? There will be no one who will be able to stand against Him.

That is why everyone should know that the Lord came to this world and volunteered to receive the baptism, and volunteered to receive the guilty verdict in Pilate's Court and died by having both His hands and feet nailed to that cruel Cross in order to make us, His sheep receive new life. Our Lord definitely did not surrender to the evil ones because He lacked power. All those who are lifted up as gods of this world are the servants of Satan. Our Lord is the true King of kings and the God of gods, the only Almighty God, the Good Shepherd and the God of salvation.

Brothers and sisters, we do not believe in one of the many religions of this world. We believe in the Lord who laid down His life voluntarily to save us from destruction. The Lord says in the Gospel of John chapter 10 verse 18, *"No one takes it from me, but I lay it down of myself. I have power to lay it down, and I have power to take it again. This command I have received from My Father."* This means that God the Father requested this from the Lord, and the Lord obeyed according to His Father's will. Our Lord truly is our Good Shepherd. Our Lord is the Good Shepherd who gave up His life to blot out all our sins and to make you and me receive new life. He is our true God and our Savior.

The God we believe in is different from all the idol gods of this world. And believing in the God given gospel of the water and the Spirit is the only way to receive this new life and the most secure way for us who believe to follow the Word of God. By believing in the gospel of the water and the Spirit, we come to meet the God of the Truth, and we follow Him who is our Good Shepherd. You and I have become the Lord's people and also the Lord's sheep by believing in the righteousness of our Lord.

People who have received the remission of their sins by believing in the gospel of the water and the Spirit today are the true sheep of God. The characteristics of these true believers are that they understand the voice of the Good Shepherd and follow this Shepherd. We also need to understand that they have an evil 'physical' aspect even though they have become the gentle sheep of God 'spiritually.' This is because the nature of sin is still in their flesh. But despite this we must not follow the evil desires of our flesh. We must believe in God's Word through the gospel of the water and the Spirit and follow God's voice with spiritual thoughts instead of fleshly thoughts by believing that the Lord has saved us from the sins of the world and that He is the Lord who gave us this new life. Therefore as the true sheep of God, we should listen carefully to the voice of the Shepherd and follow Him.

Although we might not give up our life like our Lord did who is the Good Shepherd who received the baptism from John the Baptist and shed His blood on that Cross for His sheep, but we must at least preach the gospel of the water and the Spirit to the souls around us who are still ensnared in their sins. This is because the Lord said that they too should come into His fold and belong to one Shepherd. We must now become the sheep who do good works so that all people will truly believe and receive salvation from their sins.

This evening I have preached about the Lord who is the Good Shepherd. I really desire that you all would believe in Jesus Christ who is the Good Shepherd by believing in the gospel of the water and the Spirit. We have by the Grace of God come to believe in the gospel of the water and the Spirit and lived until now because Jesus Christ who is the Good Shepherd who has saved you and me and led us into God's safe arms. Do you understand this? The Good Shepherd has saved us and He has always led us on the righteous path. Let us give thanks to God, to our Lord who is the Good Shepherd!

Since you have become God's sheep by believing in the gospel of the water and the Spirit, I really desire that you believe firmly and follow the voice of the shepherds God has appointed. If you hear and follow the voice of the Shepherd, you will receive even more abundant life and you and I will be able to live in this world sharing abundant life and all His blessings. The Lord has given this truly amazing blessing to His sheep through the gospel of the water and the Spirit.

Thank You, Lord. ⊠

Sermon

11

The Lord Is My Good Shepherd

< John 10:1-10 >

"'Most assuredly, I say to you, he who does not enter the sheepfold by the door, but climbs up some other way, the same is a thief and a robber. But he who enters by the door is the shepherd of the sheep. To him the doorkeeper opens, and the sheep hear his voice; and he calls his own sheep by name and leads them out. And when he brings out his own sheep, he goes before them; and the sheep follow him, for they know his voice. Yet they will by no means follow a stranger, but will flee from him, for they do not know the voice of strangers.' Jesus used this illustration, but they did not understand the things which He spoke to them. Then Jesus said to them again, 'Most assuredly, I say to you, I am the door of the sheep. All who ever came before Me are thieves and robbers, but the sheep did not hear them. I am the door. If anyone enters by Me, he will be saved, and will go in and out and find pasture. The thief does not come except to steal, and to kill, and to destroy. I have come that they may have life, and that they may have it more abundantly.'"

I felt as if I was returning to the world of children as I saw the snow piled up outside. I wanted to run around because the whole world became white. My heart also feels as if it became as white as snow. Like the dogs that run around in joy when the snow falls, I feel like hopping around because the sight of the snow falling is so beautiful. This is how I feel although people who have to shovel the piled up snow may feel annoyed. There is one thing that comes to mind when snow falls and the whole world is colored white in snow: it is the fact that our Lord blots out all our sin clean like the snow.

The Discipleship Training Camp will begin tomorrow, Monday, until Friday morning and the weather forecasts say there will be a lot of snow falling tomorrow as well. I hope none of our fellow saints get hurt on their way to the Camp, and I want you to be especially careful not to get into an accident. Let's pray to God for the safety during the Camp.

The world has changed much. The world has become a place where only the strong can survive. They say the law of the animal world is the 'survival of the fittest' and the strong prey upon the weak. The principle of the survival of the fittest that says only the strong survive and the weak become the prey of the strong has now gone beyond the animal world and the time has drawn near when this is realized in the human world as well. The time has come when the strong survive and rule over the weak and the weak become the prey of the strong and submit to the strong.

We live in such a world, but the fortunate thing is that we have met the Lord who is our Shepherd and received salvation at once by believing the gospel of the water and the Spirit that the Lord has given to us. Even if the whole world was destroyed now, we still have the heart of thanksgiving that we have met the Lord of the true salvation through the gospel of the water and the Spirit. We can have true rest in our hearts and have our hearts comforted like the fluffy cotton because we have met the Lord through the gospel of the water and the Spirit. Many worries and concerns that exist in this world always come before us, but we can receive salvation because we have in our hearts the Lord who is bigger than the universe, because the Lord rules over the universe, because our Lord will entrust the blessed and holy work upon us in the days to come, and because we believe in all this.

Do you live in this world with many worries? During those times, just look at the righteousness of the Lord who has become our Shepherd. Now you can become the true people of the Lord by receiving salvation from all sin by believing through the gospel of the water and the Spirit that the Lord has given to you and me. I want you to give thanks to God with this faith. I always have the thanksgiving for the fact that I have become one of God's people through the gospel of the water and the Spirit.

I know that you have many difficulties living in this world. There are many things that make us feel gloomy when we look at this world. It is true that my heart becomes depressed when I look at this dark world. I hear the sounds of pain from here and there as the period of unlimited competition has arrived in this world. Our hearts ache even more because you and I also live in this world together. Even so, all the depressing, visionless, hopeless, painful, and destructive things have already disappeared from us because our Lord lives. We have already died together with Christ and we have also been resurrected together with Christ.

I want you to know that the new Kingdom will again come upon the born-again by believing in the gospel of the water and the Spirit when the end of the world truly comes and the heavenly world will unfold from that moment. Therefore, I hope that you will live with the faith of believing the gospel of the water and the Spirit and God's promises. The righteous have nothing to be concerned about with the worldly matters.

We must just be concerned whether or not we are doing all the work of the evangelizing the gospel of the water and the Spirit to the whole world.

Who Are the People That Have Received Blessings from God?

The Lord said in today's Scripture passage, *"Most assuredly, I say to you, he who does not enter the sheepfold by the door, but climbs up some other way, the same is a thief and a robber. But he who enters by the door is the shepherd of the sheep. To him the doorkeeper opens, and the sheep hear his voice; and he calls his own sheep by name and leads them out. And when he brings out his own sheep, he goes before them; and the sheep follow him, for they know his voice. Yet they will by no means follow a stranger, but will flee from him, for they do not know the voice of strangers (John 10:1-5)."*

Our Lord is the doorkeeper of the Kingdom of Heaven and our Shepherd as well. It says therefore the Lord's sheep recognize the voice of the Lord and follow Him, but do not understand the voice of a stranger and do not follow him and run from him instead.

Do you have the faith that you have met the Lord by believing the gospel of the water and the Spirit and have become the Lord's sheep by receiving salvation from all the sins of the world? People with such faith have become the blessed people and have received immensely great blessing from God. We know that the people who have received the blessing before the presence of God are the servants of God that keep the Lord's sheep and preach the Word of the Lord.

All the sheep are the Shepherd's and the Shepherd is the

owner of the sheep. That's why we have the heart of thanksgiving toward God. Those who do not know how to be thankful for the fact that our Lord has become our Shepherd and that we have become the Lord's sheep are miserable people, but those who know how to be thankful to God are happy people. The people who know that they have become the Lord's sheep congratulate themselves for this blessing and always live each day with the joy in the hope of going to the Kingdom of God.

The people who believe with the clear understanding that they have become the people of God have received the very special love of God and the grace of salvation among all the people in this world. They are the people who have received immensely great blessing of becoming the Lord's people by believing the gospel of the water and the Spirit. Is it a small matter that we have become the people of the Lord by believing in the gospel of the water and the Spirit? Don't you understand what a great privilege and the blessing of salvation you have received?

What would have happened if we did not become the Lord's people? What would have happened if we did not become the Lord's own sheep? I wonder if the hirelings would have eaten us up, had we not truly become the Lord's sheep by believing in the gospel of the water and the Spirit. There are many livestock and wild animals in the earth; and, even among livestock, some are raised by humans and some are not. Therefore, the sheep inside the sheepfold sometimes are killed by the attack of the wild sheep outside the fence. Like this, we do not know when and who would come out and eat you up or harm you if we did not become the Lord's people. But the Lord's people have even greater safety because they are in the Lord and they are always protected in the Lord. That's why they are not harmed by the wolves and other wild animals. We are the secured and blessed people who live in the Lord's Kingdom.

Do You Know That There Is the Domain of the Evil Spirit in This World?

To put it in simple terms, it's asking whether you believe there are evil spirits or not. Devils of the evil spirits are the fallen angel and his followers that dwell in the earth that take control of people's soul to eventually kill them. We must understand this fact. There are more instances of people being harassed and killed by the evil spirits that we cannot see than the times when we are killed by a visible thing. The people who have not become the people of the Lord because they have not believed in the gospel of the water and the Spirit are headed to the darkness of hell after receiving much pain from the evil spirit that they cannot see. There are so many people in this world that become like that. The people who are used by the evil spirits are driven to do the evil things, see illusions, utter deliriously, and become depressed. And they sometimes commit suicide when the depression becomes severe. The hosts of evil spirits that exist in this world are like the wolves that wander in search of their prey. There are many evil spirits in this world and they look for the soul that could become their prey like the way the howling lion searches for the prey. Anyone who is ensnared by the evil spirits will face death.

No matter how intellectual and perfect one is and how much he possesses, the person will be caught by Satan the Devil and become a slave of Satan if he doesn't receive the remission of sins and become one of God's people by believing in the gospel of the water and the Spirit. Actually, many people born to this world live under the authority of the evil spirits until they are put to death. Do you know how great a number of people live under Satan's rule?

Satan the Devil gives much spiritual and physical pain to many people, make them suffer from the mental derangement, and also come into people's heart and become their master. Therefore, the Devil makes the people suffer and have difficult time in their lives.

That we have received the cleansing of our sins and become the Lord's people by believing in the gospel of the water and the Spirit from such dire situation is a great blessing. In other words, that we have become the Lord's sheep is truly a great blessing. The Lord said, *"I am the good shepherd. The good shepherd gives His life for the sheep."* The Lord is the doorkeeper of the sheep. That we have become the Lord's sheep is such a great blessing as we live in this troubled world because the Lord always protects His sheep. We have received a great blessing because the Lord protects us spiritually and physically. The reason why the evil one cannot do anything with us even if he tries to do something terrible to us who are the sheep is because the Lord protects us in body and spirit. We can live a normal life because the Lord protects us and, therefore, we would be harmed if the Lord did not protect us.

It says the Lord is the Shepherd. When I look at the darkening world and I see Satan the Devil running rampant in this world, and the greater difficulties I face, the more thankful I feel in my heart for the fact that I have become the Lord's people. I cannot help but be thankful to God as I see the pain and death that we would have exactly received if we did not become the Lord's people. In these end times, Satan the Devil is trying to kill the people and the cults that are Satan's servants are running wild trying to heal sickness and cast out demons and causing all kinds of commotion. How great is it that we have become the Lord's people in such a world where evil people are causing such commotion? What a great blessing we have received? We who have become the Lord's people among those born to this world are the people who have received immensely great blessing.

The single fact that we have become the Lord's people while we live in this perilous world is such a great blessing we have received as a gift from God. That we have become the Lord's people means that God protects us from the evil adversaries and I give thanks to the Lord for this. Just as you try to keep and take care of your things, God keeps and protects those who have become God's people even while the Satan the Devil is trying to harm all the people in the world including us who believe in the gospel of the water and the Spirit. We receive caring from the Lord as His people and we must believe with the understanding of what a great blessing this is. We must understand that the Lord has become your true Shepherd and the Savior. The people who truly believe in the gospel of the water and the Spirit that the Lord has given are the Lord's people and the Lord saved us from all our sins. And we have received the remission of all the sins of the heart by believing in the righteousness of the Lord and we have faith that we have become the Lord's own because of that. Therefore, the people who have become the Lord's people by believing in the gospel of the water and the Spirit are truly happy ones. They are the people who have received great blessing from God. In spite of everything, such people are the people who have received a great privilege in this world.

The Bible says that becoming His people is a great blessing. You must realize how great it is that the Lord has become our Shepherd! I give deepest thanks that words cannot express for the fact that our Lord has become our Shepherd and protects us. You and I might feel such amazing blessing in our hearts. Those who do not have the Lord as their Shepherd are outside the realm of the God's special privilege. Do you believe that the Lord has truly become our Shepherd when we believed in the gospel of the water and the Spirit? Do you believe that the Lord has become your Savior?

The Lord came to this world to save you and me. The Lord took over all your sins and mine upon Him by receiving the baptism from John the Baptist. Do you believe that the Lord died on the Cross for the price of all those sins and became the true Savior who still lives until now by being resurrected in three days? Those who truly believe in this Truth are blessed. Those who have been born again through the gospel of the water and the Spirit are the blessed people.

Many people buy lottery tickets called "Lotto" in Korea. It's not easy to win the first place in the lottery. They use the expression 'a wondrous reversion of life' when someone wins the first place in lotto, and many regard winning the lotto as a great fortune. The General Young Choi, the famous Korean general from long ago, said, "Look at a pot of gold as if it was a stone," and I agree with this saying and, therefore, I don't buy lotto tickets. But, anyway, the people who win the lotto are blessed people as they say in the world. But we must remember that we have received an even greater blessing than the lottery winners.

There is a lot of sand on the beach. Let's say that we have been chosen among many people that number as many as the sandstones to receive the special grace of salvation through the gospel of the water and the Spirit. Then, we who believe in this gospel of the water and the Spirit are very fortunate people who have been chosen to receive the blessing and had their 'wondrous reversion of life.' This is an amazing blessing that cannot be exchanged for any amount of money.

This gospel of salvation that manifested in our hearts by the gospel of the water and the Spirit becomes anew even with the passing of time. Those who reject the blessing that God gives will receive God's curse even more and suffer much more pain while living in this world, and they will continue living in that state. But as the time passes, we will come to know even more how great the blessing that we have received is. That's why God says, *"Those who are wise shall shine*

Like the brightness of the firmament,

And those who turn many to righteousness

Like the stars forever and ever" (Daniel 12:3). We live an even more righteous life that shines brightly in this world by believing in the gospel of the water and the Spirit. Such life is an astonishingly blessed life. Those who turn many to the righteousness will shine like the brightness of the firmament. You and I have received the amazing blessing of becoming the Lord's lambs and the Lord becoming our Shepherd by believing in the gospel of the water and the Spirit.

As the pearl hidden in the mud comes into the world and illuminate brightly in display, the blessing that we have received from God by believing in the gospel of the water and the Spirit manifest even greater value when the world is in greater trouble. As the pearl illuminates its brilliant color even more brightly in the mud, the righteous shine even more while they preach the gospel of the water and the Spirit among the sinners living in this darkening world. The righteous people have become the being that deliver the Truth of light as the light of salvation.

Meet the people who have not been born again. Does your

life truly shine in the gospel of the water and the Spirit, or not? That you are not same as those people will be revealed clearly. The righteous really experience that the light in them shines more brightly while they live in this gloomy world. You are happy because you always live in God's Church and share fellowship among the fellow born-again believers. And you should be even more thankful because you are doing God's work. Doesn't the light of the gospel of the water and the Spirit that you have seem to illuminate even more? The gospel of salvation that you have is much greater light than you can imagine. Soon, the people in the world will know how brightly we shine as you work in the world that does not know how to be born again.

It is truly a blessing that we have become the Lord's sheep by believing in the gospel of the water and the Spirit. The answer to the question "Whose sheep are we?" determines our fate, and all our conditions become guaranteed by the Lord because we are His sheep.

You would have been eaten up at once by the evil ones if you belonged to them. But you do not get eaten up and you instead grow well with proper care when you belong to the truly good One, Jesus Christ. The Good Shepherd knows His sheep and nurtures them properly and makes them receive even more bountiful life. Therefore the good Shepherd of this world will care for his sheep by doing his best and the Good Shepherd of the Kingdom of Heaven takes the born-again people as His own sheep and cares for them eternally and makes them live happily forever. We should know that the matter of 'whose sheep do we become' is really important.

You and I must believe that the Lord is our Shepherd and we must live with such faith in this world. Such faith results in great things. You will not be afraid of anything while living in this world if you have this faith. Whenever fear creeps into your heart, you must reconfirm the faith that the Lord is your Shepherd and make the faith firm that you are His sheep. You can overcome any problem if you have such faith. We can live in this world with His love, His blessings, and His grace.

Therefore, we must first have the faith that we are His sheep. Who do you belong to? You are now Jesus Christ's. Who is Jesus Christ? He is the one and the only Savior. He is the Lord and the eternally Good Shepherd who saved us from sin through the gospel of the water and the Spirit; He created the universe, rules and controls the eternal world. It means that we belong to such Lord. We can listen to the Lord's voice and follow the Lord from the moment that we understand the fact that we belong to the Lord and attain the faith in Him. We can follow the Lord with the faith of believing in the Lord.

We have lived with our own strength until now. Until now we have lived with our own fleshly means and methods and lived according to the direction we thought was right. But now we can listen to His voice and follow Him according to His directions after attaining the faith as His own. It is written that the sheep understand His voice. And the special characteristic of those who recognize the Shepherd is that they do not respond to the voice of others. But those who are not the Lord's sheep run away and do not follow after Him because they cannot recognize the Lord's voice.

We follow the Lord wherever He leads us as we realize that the Lord is our Shepherd and our Savior. Why? It's because we have the faith in us that we are His. A shepherd buys and sells sheep according to his need in this world, but the sheep in the Kingdom of God belong to the Shepherd eternally. The Shepherd is one with the sheep though He is also the owner of the sheep. We become one with Him when we believe in the fact that we are His. I don't want you to forget the fact that you are His own if you have received the remission of sins by believing in the gospel of the water and the Spirit. You belonged to the world and your family in the past, but you become His own after being born again through the water and the Spirit. You and I become His and live as His sheep and leave this world as His own.

All the Word you read today is talking about this. People who know that they are His sheep are very happy people and they are people who can follow His voice. And you will never be destroyed if you follow His voice. Instead, you will experience the new and wonderful world that you have never experienced before.

Do you believe in the Word of God that I have shared with you now? I also live with the belief that I am called to belong to Christ. I do not care much about what people say. What do the people of the world have to do with me? I am the Lord's own and therefore I don't have to be swayed by them. The Lord is my Shepherd. How can they match up against the Lord? I live with such faith and I know that you also must live with such faith.

We are one with the Lord. The Lord saved us by giving us His life and we have received salvation by believing in this Truth. We are one with the Lord just like the child born from a mother's womb is one with the mother because the baby is her other self. Everything will turn out great only if we have believed that we have become Christ's own by becoming born again through the water and the Spirit. It is all because we have indeed become His own. But it's impossible for a person who has not become His own to be one with Christ: they cannot be led by the Lord; and they instead run away when the Lord tries to lead them.

It is written that the Lord is the doorkeeper. The Lord is the doorkeeper of the Kingdom of Heaven. And the Lord is the gatekeeper of this Church. You and I can enter the Kingdom of God only through the Lord. We become the plundering wolves when we do not go into the Kingdom of God through the Lord. We are robbers, thieves, and evildoers deserving of death if we do not go into the Kingdom of God through the faith of believing the fact that the Lord has become our Savior by coming to this world and receiving the baptism, dying on the Cross and being resurrected from the death. And such people cannot enter the Kingdom of God and live there.

We must have the faith that the Lord is the doorkeeper of the Kingdom of Heaven. The Lord is not just any shepherd of the sheep, but He is the good and gracious Shepherd. He said those who do not enter through the door are the plundering wolves and the hirelings that kill the sheep, steal from the sheep, and destroy the sheep. If a thief comes into your home with a sword, what is he going to do? He is going to kill and plunder you of your possessions.

You cannot follow the Lord unless you are His sheep. It is difficult to follow Him if you don't understand the fact that you are His. Only those who have been born again by the Lord can recognize and follow the voice of the Lord who is the Shepherd; but those who have the separated mind from the Lord, that is, those who do not commit themselves to the Lord do not know the Lord's voice for they belong to another one. Those who are not God's people cannot follow God. And they cannot receive the blessing, either. Only those who have clearly been born again through the Lord can become His own and receive His caring and blessing.

I want you and me to live with such faith. Such faith is a great faith. This is a realistic point that decides whether or not you will be led by the Lord and be blessed by receiving salvation in this world. Do you have the faith that assures that you have become Christ's own? Have the faith that you have become Jesus Christ's own.

If you really have become the Lord's own, would the Lord care for you or would He not? The Lord loves you and cares for you. And would the Lord protect you, or would He not protect you? The Lord protects you. But the Lord cannot protect you even if the Devil tried to kill you if you are not the Lord's own. Satan the Devil will then steal all that you have through the people who have not been born again. And he will destroy you. The Devil definitely does not leave you alone if you have not become the Lord's own. But you can be protected if you have become the Lord's own, because the Lord protects you from then on.

That we have been born again through the gospel of the water and the Spirit is such a great blessing. The Lord said again in the Gospel of John chapter 10, *"To him the doorkeeper opens, and the sheep hear his voice; and he calls his own sheep by name and leads them out. And when he brings out his own sheep, he goes before them; and the sheep follow him, for they know his voice. Yet they will by no means follow a stranger, but will flee from him, for they do not know the voice of strangers" (John 10:3-5).* All these Words in the Scriptures speak about the great consequence that resulted from whether or not we have received salvation by believing the gospel of the water and the Spirit, now that the Lord has saved us perfectly.

I want you be confirmed in that faith if you have truly received salvation through the gospel of the water and the Spirit. If you have such faith, I don't want you to think, "Oh, well. I can't see much difference between receiving salvation and not receiving it," and consider it lightly. If you think so, you can be ensnared and taken away by Satan the Devil. You must learn about the faith and cultivate the foundation with clarity and certainty based on the definite Word in our spiritual walk.

I wanted to talk about this at this time. Those who believe in the Truth that the Lord came to this world and saved us through the water and the Spirit have become His own and they live in His caring and guidance. I want you to have faith that those who know this and have become His own people receive the blessing if they believe in Him and follow His voice and that the Lord cares for His people no matter how arduous this world becomes. And I want you to follow the Lord to the end.

I want to tell you that you need to follow the Lord with the faith that is built on the rock. For example, let's say there was a person who had a diamond but doubts everyday whether it is a genuine jewelry or not. Then someone can steal it in a split second while he is throwing it on the ground and picking it up again to check if it's real. I don't want you to become people who cannot keep the faith because you don't know how precious the gospel of the water and the Spirit is. The meaning of the life also disappears the moment you lose the Truth.

God's Word tells us that King Herod commanded his soldiers to kill all the children under the age of two in the vicinity of Bethlehem. What does that say? It says that Satan the Devil can slaughter the spiritually young believers while their faith is still wavering when it's been less than two years since they received the remission of sins. You are doing fine because you gather together in the Church and partake in every worship service and actually listen to the Word spoken from the Scriptures; but otherwise Satan the Devil would take you away. If this were not the God's Church, what would they say to you? They would tell you to bring money. If you say that you don't have money, they would tell you to bring the installment savings account. There are so many churches that have built 10 million dollar church buildings with such coercive donations. But the righteous shepherds never spend up 10 million dollars for a church building. He may spend 10 million dollars for the salvation of even one person's soul, but he would never put that much money up for a building.

It says that the thief comes to take away your belongings and to kill, and the good Shepherd comes to make the sheep attain life and make the sheep enjoy a more bountiful life. We must follow with correct understanding of what the true Church is like and what the truly good Shepherd is like. There is no other good Shepherd except Jesus Christ. Everyone except those who follow Him and believe in His Word is a thief and a swindler.

There are so many hirelings who only demand money from their congregation without shame in these difficult times. Wouldn't the hired workers groom themselves and come with a polished look when they try to swindle? They grease their hair, wear brand new shirts and suit, wear slick shoes that even a fly would slide down, and drive a luxurious car that costs nearly 100,000 dollars, but pretend to be so humble. When such swindlers meet a new believer, they say in a pious voice, "I wish the blessing of God for you." At first they are like that. But soon they say, "Bring your money. You don't have money? You have a job. Open the installment savings account and bring the account to me, and you make the installment every month." They are too much like robberies. Do you think this is a gross exaggeration? No, it is the reality of most churches in Korea. They seem like they are competing with each other in constructing mammoth church buildings. That's why all the believers are in debt. This is true. Some of you who still don't believe this, would you believe it after you have been exploited thoroughly? There really are so many outlandishly deceitful shepherds in this world. The blind sheep are prone to follow the false shepherd and be robbed because the sheep do not know the voice of their real Master.

Where in the world is another good shepherd like the Lord? Who else but the Lord would come to this world clothed in human flesh? Who else but the Lord would come and take all the sins you and I commit upon Himself by receiving the baptism from John the Baptist? Is there anyone else who would carry the sins of the world and die on the Cross for us? Is there anyone who could be resurrected after dying for us? Who else but the Lord would do this?

The Lord is the most righteous Shepherd because only the Lord did this work. It says that the sheep follow Him because they know His voice. Those who have been born again by believing in the gospel of the water and the Spirit have become the Lord's sheep, and the Lord who is the righteous Shepherd feeds the sheep and pours down the grace, blessing, and the glory. What a great blessing it is! You believe the Lord and God the Father when we believe the gospel of the water and the Spirit and follow the Lord. Believing the Lord is the proper door to the path of blessing. I want you and me to believe the Lord who is the true door to Heaven and the true way to salvation; I want you to believe in the righteous Shepherd and be born again through the water and the Spirit and become the blessed sheep that are led by the Lord.

Just as the snow comes down and covers the whole world in white, the Lord blotted out all our sins clean. The Lord came to the Jordan River, took all the sins of the world upon Himself by receiving the baptism, received the judgment on the Cross, shed His blood and died in our place, and was resurrected from death in three days, and thus became our Savior. I am so thankful when I think of the fact that the Lord made us His people who are without sin, perfect, and cleaner and whiter than the cleanest snow. I am so thankful when I think of the fact that we have become the Lord's people and I want us to follow His voice and preach His will all over the world. I have true thankfulness to Him in my heart.

Let us all follow the Lord with such faith in this life.

Halleluiah! ⌧

SERMON

12

Listen to the Voice Of the Shepherd

< John 10:1-18 >

"'Most assuredly, I say to you, he who does not enter the sheepfold by the door, but climbs up some other way, the same is a thief and a robber. But he who enters by the door is the shepherd of the sheep. To him the doorkeeper opens, and the sheep hear his voice; and he calls his own sheep by name and leads them out. And when he brings out his own sheep, he goes before them; and the sheep follow him, for they know his voice. Yet they will by no means follow a stranger, but will flee from him, for they do not know the voice of strangers.' Jesus used this illustration, but they did not understand the things which He spoke to them. Then Jesus said to them again, 'Most assuredly, I say to you, I am the door of the sheep. All who ever came before Me are thieves and robbers, but the sheep did not hear them. I am the door. If anyone enters by Me, he will be saved, and will go in and out and find pasture. The thief does not come except to steal, and to kill, and to destroy. I have come that they may have life, and that they may have it more abundantly. I am the good shepherd. The good shepherd gives His life for the sheep. But a hireling, he who is not the shepherd, one who does not own the sheep, sees the wolf coming and leaves the sheep and flees; and the wolf catches the sheep and scatters them. The hireling flees because he is a hireling and does not care about the sheep. I am the good shepherd; and I know My sheep, and am known by My own.

As the Father knows Me, even so I know the Father; and I lay down My life for the sheep. And other sheep I have which are not of this fold; them also I must bring, and they will hear My voice; and there will be one flock and one shepherd. Therefore My Father loves Me, because I lay down My life that I may take it again. No one takes it from Me, but I lay it down of Myself. I have power to lay it down, and I have power to take it again. This command I have received from My Father.'"

All human beings are made of the spirit, flesh, and the mind. People who have received the remission of sins in their hearts through the Lord can distinguish the spirit, flesh, and the mind; but the people who have not received the remission of sins cannot distinguish these and misunderstand the thought of the flesh as the spiritual thought.

The Gospel of John chapter 10 that we have read today shows very clearly how our Lord has saved our souls. Our Lord truly came to this world and saved our souls from all the sins by receiving the baptism and shedding blood on the Cross. Whenever I think of myself, I realize it is really a great blessing that my soul has received the remission of sins before the presence of God like this. I am sure that you also are very grateful to God. Therefore, understanding how God completely blotted out all the sins of our souls is the proper duty of us who have received such a great blessing. Today, we will have time to understand all these issues in detail through the Word from the Gospel of John chapter 10.

We Have Become the Sheep of the Lord, and the Lord Has Become the Door of the Sheep

Our Lord said in the Gospel of John chapter 10 verses 1-2, *"Most assuredly, I say to you, he who does not enter the sheepfold by the door, but climbs up some other way, the same is a thief and a robber. But he who enters by the door is the shepherd of the sheep."* And He said in John 10: 9, *"I am the door. If anyone enters by Me, he will be saved, and will go in and out and find pasture."* As we can see in this Word, the Lord said He is the door of the sheep and we are His sheep. And the Lord said that He prepared the Heaven and He is the door of the Heaven. The Lord says that He is the door of salvation itself because the Lord has already paid for all our sins completely.

God created the first humans, Adam and Eve. He made Adam with the dust of the ground and breathed life into his nostrils and the man became a living being. It means that human became a being that does not die eternally. But the human that was made in the image of the likeness of the majestic God fell to the temptation of Satan the Devil and committed sin. While the human was struggling in sin, God planned to blot out the sin that infiltrated our souls. The Lord already had the plan to be the door of salvation for us personally from that time. And the Lord's promise to blot out all our sins is recorded in many places in the Scriptures.

For example, Genesis chapter 3 verse15 says, *"And I will put enmity between you and the woman, And between your seed and her Seed; He shall bruise your head, And you shall bruise His heel."* It says here that the descendant of a woman shall bruise your head. Then, what does this mean? It means that Jesus would come to this world in flesh and destroy and eliminate Satan the Devil. And the Word *"You shall bruise His heel"* means that the Lord who received the baptism and shed blood on the Cross and fulfilled the just salvation would save our souls from sin. It is the promise of the Lord that He would save us and become the door of salvation, the door of the sheep, and the Shepherd of the sheep for us. Like this, the Truth that our Lord shall become the door of salvation for us is the plan of God that was set even before the foundation of the world, of course, before the fall of man by the temptation of Satan the Devil.

Like this, our God wanted to become our Shepherd and the Saviour from the time He created human being. God had the plan before the foundation of the world to become the good Shepherd for us and make us receive immortal life as we go in and out and receive the bread of eternal life and attain the blessing. Our God became the good Shepherd and led us to the upright path instead of leaving us alone. The Gospel of John chapter 10, verse 9 says, *"I am the door. If anyone enters by Me, he will be saved, and will go in and out and find pasture."* This tells us this plan and promise of the Lord. As this Word tells us, we receive new life and strength and spiritual and physical blessings through the Lord who is the door to our every blessing. Therefore, God is really our God and Saviour who became the friendly God whom the Devil cannot separate us from no matter how much he tries. Truly our Lord is our good Shepherd and the Lord of life and the Lord of judgment.

God blotted away the sins of our spirit clean at once through the gospel of the water and the Spirit and made us the believers His people. We have become perfect children of God without sin and the beloved sheep of God only through the righteousness of God, not through our effort. Our Lord personally received the baptism upon His body from John the Baptist and thereby took the sins of the world upon Him at once and become the perfect Saviour for those who believe in Him by giving up His body to be nailed on the Cross and being resurrected from the death. We were able to become the sheep of the Lord and be able to call Him our good Shepherd because of all such work of salvation that the Lord has fulfilled. Do not forget this fact.

Our souls would have still been tied to sin and couldn't have received the remission of sins forever if it had not been for our Lord. Our Lord saved our souls perfectly from the sins of the world. We were able to become the Lord's people and the Lord became our good Shepherd because of the Lord who has saved you and me from sin through the gospel of the water and the Spirit. We, humans, have spirit, mind, and body. And though the body has no choice but to live in this world committing sins, the soul has received salvation through the faith of believing the righteous work of the Lord: to atone for all the sins of the world, He has received the baptism and shed His blood on the Cross. And you and I, who believe in the gospel of the water and the Spirit that the Lord has given to us, have now become the people of God and the children of the Lord eternally. Nothing in the universe exists aimlessly, and rather, everything has instead been created to reveal the glory of God. I want you to know that the reason you and I have also been born to this world as creatures is in God's will, and it aims to make us become the children of God ultimately.

Let's Become the Thankful Believers

The Lord said that all those who believe with the gospel of the water and the Spirit become the children of God. And you and I have become God's children perfectly by believing in the gospel of the water and the Spirit that Jesus Christ has given to us. As I have said earlier, all of this work of salvation was within God's plan that was established even before the creation. We were born to this world within the plan of salvation in Jesus Christ and we have received the true remission of sins by believing in Jesus Christ who came by the gospel of the water and the Spirit. Now we will enter God's Kingdom that our Lord has prepared when the time comes for us to leave this world some day. We must always remember the fact that our souls have received the remission of sins through the gospel of the water and the Spirit before the presence of God and return glory to the Lord.

We humans have no choice but to follow the fleshly criteria rather than the spiritual criteria in all things we think about because we humans are beings with a body. But it is vastly wrong to follow these fleshly criteria even in the matter of the Lord's righteousness and faith. For example, it is wrong to think, "This is good for me. I have received the blessing from the Lord again" when our fleshly things go well, or think, "Why am I going through this suffering when I have believed in Jesus" when our flesh is sick and in troubles. The flesh is always unstable and goes through many changes. But we would be shaken every day like the chaff blown away by the wind if we placed our criteria in that flesh when we follow the Lord.

Like this, our flesh is imperfect and it must be totally changed in the future, but how are our souls? Our souls have received salvation from the sins of the world all at once through the gospel of the water and the Spirit the Lord has given us. That's why we can praise the righteousness of God and live happily in the Lord. Though our flesh commits sins while living in this world, we who have become the people of God must not judge others with the fleshly criteria and think it is right. We must go before the presence of God by believing in the righteousness of the Lord who has saved our souls from all the sins of the world. I know that we must become the sheep that always give thanks to the Lord by faith.

Do not forget the fact that you have become the lambs of God. And do not make any decision based on fleshly criteria, but think first before the presence of Jesus about the salvation of our souls the Lord has given and give thanks with the faith of believing this. Through Jesus Christ, we have truly received the remission of sins through the gospel of the water and the Spirit and received the special privilege of becoming the children of God as well. We must always keep in mind the Lord's purpose and blessing that gave us the birth in this world and become the saints who know how to come before the presence of God and offer up the worship service of thanksgiving.

Though We Are Weak

We have experienced many things while living in this world. There were many sufferings, sad things, good things, and also the things of God among those experiences. But we must think of all the fleshly things we have experienced for the survival in this world as just fleshly things when we come before the presence of God. I believe that we must first think of the grace of salvation that God has saved our souls from all the sins and praise God and give thanks and glory to God. God has really given you and me the blessing that cannot be expressed in words. Therefore, we must listen to God's Word and receive new strength in our souls by coming in and going out of His sheepfold. We must become the sheep of such faith whose souls praise God and sincerely give thanks to God.

We must not make a decision based on fleshly thinking no

matter what we do because we are all His children who have received the grace of salvation from God. We will look at the Word from Genesis chapter 1 to help your understanding.

God created the universe. God created the light in the world that was in chaos on the first day of His creation, and when God saw the light it was good. Then, He divided the waters that were above the firmament from the waters that the covered the earth on the second day. And He gathered the water that covered the earth together into one place on the third day and raised the earth gradually and divided the dry land from the water in the ocean. God called the dry land Earth, and the gathering together of the waters He called Seas. And God saw that it was good. And God said, *"And the earth brought forth grass, the herb that yields seed according to its kind, and the tree that yields fruit, whose seed is in itself according to its kind. And God saw that it was good."* It says clearly here that God saw everything He had created as good.

Then what about us who live in this world as the people of God? Does our appearance seem good to God when He sees us? No, it isn't. The fleshly thinking and the spiritual thinking run back and forth just like the way the ocean water rushes back and forth toward the shore. The fleshly thinking rises up endlessly like the ebb and flow of tides come and go away ceaselessly even though spiritual thinking arises in us and we praise God when we listen to God's Word. The fleshly sentiments, sadness, hurts and such things rise up unconsciously at times even while we are doing the spiritual work and thinking spiritual things.

At a time when we are consumed with the fleshly thinking that rises up like the flow tide, we must understand the fact that this is not our true self even though we are prone to think that way. This is just the seawater, that is, the fleshly thinking. I am saying that is not the true self but just a momentary thinking that comes up from the flesh, the emotion and greed.

When the ocean water reaches a full tide, if the tidal storm creates waves, the seashore is washed away by the tidal waves of over 10m high. And the trees on the seashore die from the salt that pours down on them when the ocean water rides the wind and invades the land. This is the same with the fleshly thinking of us the humans. The fleshly thoughts rise up often because we live in this world with flesh. And people whose essence is very friendly with the flesh at times misunderstand such fleshly thoughts that come up from time to time as those of their own self and their own essence. What would happen if they do not defeat this with faith? Whenever their weakness is revealed, they look at their weak selves and make wrong judgment that they are the blood of evil seed that cannot live out their faith. They fall into such despair and eventually depart from the Lord.

The Truth of salvation is always same for us humans. There is no other way. The flesh has limitations. Any variable thing cannot be the absolute Truth of salvation. We must realize that the flesh is not sanctified even though we have received the remission of sins, but it is our souls installed with good conscience that is headed toward God as it is written in 1 Peter 3:21, *"There is also an antitype which now saves us—baptism (not the removal of the filth of the flesh, but the answer of a good conscience toward God), through the resurrection of Jesus Christ."*

As there was never a time when the ocean water dried and there was never a time when the ebb and flow tides stopped flowing, the Lord always loves us. But our flesh always tries to lead us to death with selfish thoughts. However, you and I are not the people who shall live in defeat against the flesh. We are God's. The essence of you and I who have received salvation from sin eternally by believing in the gospel of the water and the

Spirit is that we are people of God and that we are His children and the Lord's sheep.

We who believe in the gospel of the water and the Spirit are actually very magnificent people before the presence of God, but the emotions and greed from our old selves rise up and down once in a while because we have the flesh. And the emotions of the flesh shake us up and even confuse our souls whenever the fleshly thinking rises up. Why is this so? It's because the fleshly thinking hurts ourselves like the way the ocean water hits the coastal land and the plants dry up and die because of the salt from the ocean water.

We must mend the hurt with the faith of believing the gospel of the water and the Spirit. And we must definitely remember that we are the people who have received salvation from sin eternally from God. That's the only way we can keep ourselves from getting immersed in the fleshly sentiments and getting hurt, and become even more formidable by faith. We must live with the faith of believing in the righteousness of God rather than our emotions. We must live with the faith in the recorded Word of God rather than relying on the fleshly thinking that rises up within us. Only then can we the saints praise the righteousness of God. We cannot help but become a loser eventually in the fight against the flesh and face death eternally if we do not live according to God's Word but live according to the fleshly thinking. Then we wouldn't be able to lead the spiritual life of faith properly and we wouldn't be able to give thanks to God, and we wouldn't be able to receive the spiritual food from Him. We can receive the spiritual food only when we have the faith of believing the righteousness of God. We receive the food for our hearts and receive new life, strength and the blessing through God's recorded Word of blessing and the bread of life as we meet God's servants in Jesus Christ.

How are you when the fleshly thoughts rise up within your heart? Do you think you cannot go forward any longer even though you have lived because of God's grace until now? Haven't you thought that you'd like to give up your spiritual life of faith because of that? Haven't you decided to go back to the former life like Peter went back to fishing again? We would go back if we could, but we have already become the born-again sheep of God by believing in the gospel of the water and the Spirit. Because there is a better homeland, that is, a heavenly one, to us the born-again, we need to look to that homeland and endure the present state as we go through this world. Those who have truly received the remission of sins by believing in the baptism of Jesus and His blood of the Cross can never go back to their old life.

Two Kinds of Warfare: The Spiritual Warfare and the Physical Warfare

A righteous person going back to the world means becoming the servant of this world that signifies the death of soul. Such a person wants to be one of the Israelites shackled to the chain of the Egyptian Emperor: they had worked desperately as slaves of Egypt just to get a piece of bread for their flesh everyday. Therefore, we who believe in the gospel of the water and the Spirit cannot go back to the former world and we do not want to as well. The only difference is that we who have received the remission of sins through the gospel of the water and the Spirit should live in two worlds simultaneously and that is a little difficult thing. That's what the physical life and the spiritual life are like.

Our souls are always comforted when we live with the faith

of believing in God's Word rather than with our fleshly thinking. The Holy Spirit within us gives us the confirmation, saying, "Yes, that's right!" and gives us new strength when we receive God's Word regardless of the fleshly thinking. Like this, our souls live in a peaceful and comfortable spiritual world without having anything to do with the flesh.

But how is our fleshly thinking that lives in the world of flesh? It stands against the spiritual thinking with the attitude, "What do you mean it is right? You can never live like that." That's why the spiritual warfare and the physical warfare erupt fiercely between the spirit and the flesh. How many people do you think can fight these two wars and win with their own strength? There are none other than the people of faith who believe in the righteousness of God who can win these wars.

We can never win the spiritual warfare and the physical warfare if we try to win these two kinds of warfare with the fleshly strength only. The victory in this war is possible only through the faith of believing in the righteousness of God. It may seem like our desires of flesh is limitless, but it is not actually like that. It may seem like we could swallow the whole universe when we are extremely hungry, but our flesh is satisfied when we are given just two bowls of boiled rice, two bowls of soup, and two glasses of water. It means that we can be liberated from the flesh and do not live as the slaves of flesh as long as we just do not follow the fleshly greed. But our souls cannot become upright just by our efforts. We can live spiritually only with the faith of believing in the righteousness of God. Even so, we put more emphasis on the desires of the flesh that we could overcome with our own effort.

Do not lose the spiritual fight just because of your desires for food, clothing, and shelter and the other the fleshly thoughts that rise up like the wave. Our Lord said that we should not worry about the things to eat and things to wear. And He said, *"Consider the lilies, how they grow: they neither toil nor spin; and yet I say to you, even Solomon in all his glory was not arrayed like one of these" (Luke 12:27).*

That's right. Take a look at the flowers. Each and every flower shows off its smiling face to the full. Like this, it is the duty of us creatures to always reveal the glory of God the Creator and to satisfy ourselves with our present circumstance. If God has given satisfaction to all the lowly flowers of the field like this, then how much more does God grant us who believe in the gospel of the water and the Spirit? The Lord clothes us and feeds us and quenches our thirst. The Lord has already filled us up in body and spirit, and He will continue to fill us up in the future as well.

People focus too much on their flesh and cannot think of the future of their souls because they do not have the faith of believing in the righteousness of God. They are wavering by fleshly thinking because they do not know well that their souls have received the remission of sins from God and how precious that remission of sins is. However, you and I should not be like that in our faith and in our spiritual life of faith. The truly important being is the inner person of the soul, not the outer person of the flesh that is satisfied if it is fed a little.

Our Lord planned and gave the true plan of salvation in the gospel of the water and the Spirit to save us from all the sins of the world. He actually saved us all at once through the gospel of the water and the Spirit. The Lord came to this world personally and saved us who believe in Him by taking our sins upon Him at once through the baptism received from John the Baptist and dying on the Cross to pay off the price for the sins of the world and resurrecting from death. Our Lord became the perfect Savior for you and me in this manner and became the door of the sheep and became the good Shepherd in our life.

The good Shepherd leads His sheep to the green pasture and feeds the grass and also gives them water by leading them beside the still waters. From human thinking, we may seem like we are living with our own strength. But with a closer look, we can see that we actually live with the things the Lord who is our Lord gives to us. We live like this now because the Lord gave us the fresh air, clean water, and all the circumstances and also the strength to work and the ability to earn money, and because the Lord protects us like that. That is true. We are the only ones who are not aware of the fact that we go on living because the Lord has become our Shepherd. Therefore, you and I must believe in the Lord and follow His voice, and we must think about the fact that we have received all the spiritual and physical blessings and live with the heart of thanksgiving before the presence of the Lord.

The Lord said that it is natural for our flesh to receive food from the Lord in all things if our souls have received the remission of sins by believing in the gospel of the water and the Spirit. We do not need to worry about the fleshly needs any more if we believe in this Word thoroughly. We must not be disappointed even if the things we have yearned for are not fulfilled shortly and we must not even look to the world with only the fleshly thoughts. The spiritual life of the people who have been born again through the gospel of the water and the Spirit is the life only for the gospel. Therefore, how could an imperfect nature of the flesh fit in with such a spiritual life? The war between the spirit and the flesh that exists in us is an eternal war. We just need to know that only the righteousness of God that saved us from the sins of the world is beautiful and that only the gospel of the water and the Spirit that gave us the eternal life to our souls is precious. Therefore, if we just do God's work quietly with such knowledge, it will be okay. And we who have been born again in that manner can receive the pasture from God in all things.

You and I must be treated preciously because we have become such precious souls since the moment we became born again by believing in the gospel of the water and the Spirit. We also must give priority to our soul more than our flesh, and we should consider it precious and treat it preciously. Then, the Lord who is the door of the sheep and the good Shepherd will protect our souls even more and lead us to the upright path. We have to give thanks by faith to the Lord who is our Shepherd and we have to continue to live in this world following the voice of the Shepherd. The Lord planned to become our Shepherd even before the creation. We shall receive the true food for the eternal life before the Lord in all things when we believe in the good Shepherd who saved our souls as God.

There Are Still Many Sheep That Are Not of This Fold

The Lord said in the Scripture passage that there are many sheep that are not of this fold yet. And He who is the good Shepherd said that He would give up His own life for the sheep and save them. You and I who have become the sheep of the Lord, the good Shepherd, by receiving His love must now join our hearts together with that Shepherd for the work of leading the sheep who have not yet come into our fold. To reiterate this, I am saying that we must live out our faith with the spiritual faith; we should not believe in the Lord just like people simply practice religions. I am sometimes afraid that you would not be able to live by faith and adhere too much on your physical weakness and shortcoming and eventually give up leading a spiritual life. But it is clear that a person who has become righteous once is righteous eternally before the presence of God and we have such faith. I believe this way.

Our Lord received the baptism to take over all our sins and became our true Savior by dying on the Cross. I give thanks again to the Lord who has given us such great faith. This work of salvation that God has given to you and me is such a precious and eternal thing. As that salvation is so precious, the soul that has been saved must also be treated very preciously. As we feed pets with food and take good care of them and nurture them carefully, it is the duty for us who are the sheep of the precious faith to feed the spiritual food to the souls that have not yet come into the Lord's fold and share the Lord's gospel with them so that they may receive the remission of sins.

We who have received the remission of sins in this world through the Lord are not people who draw back to perdition. We are not people who will be destroyed and die. Rather, we are people who have precious eternal life. Our souls are so precious and valuable when we think about them before the presence of God even if the outward man may seem lacking and have nothing to show off. Therefore, we don't need to be discouraged even if our flesh does not meet the expectations of the spiritual work. We are thankful just to give ourselves for the work of following the righteousness of the Lord. There are times when our hearts are hurt because we have to get rid of the desires of the flesh, but we can really become precious beings that bring much benefit to people if we endure this and do God's work with love and faith. I mean that there will arise within us the good conscience and faith to share the spiritual food as we follow the righteousness of the Lord. I give thanks again to God who has made us such righteous people.

Never look at your physical weakness and be discouraged. The Lord is your Shepherd and the door of salvation and your eternal Savior. We are now His children and His people since the Lord has blotted out all our sins and made us righteous. We will always be bright and full of life if we have this faith even though we live in this world that is like the desert. I want you to always rely on the Lord with faith and pray to the Lord and live in unity with the Church of God. I want you to be happy with faith and not become discouraged due to your flesh. The blessings of the soul will also transmit to the flesh, and there will come a time when the war between the spirit and the flesh will disappear when you live according to your faith.

Dear fellow believers, we are the truly blessed people. We are the people who will not be discouraged by such fleshly matters. I believe that we who are like that must live with the faith of believing in the righteousness of God even for the sake of our own soul and also share the Lord's gospel to the souls that have not come into this fold yet. That we have received the remission of sins before them have comes to us as thanksgiving rather than a burden. Let's not forget that we have the responsibility of sharing the merciful love of God with them.

The true faith grows gradually as time passes by: as one year, two years, three years, and four years pass by, your faith will grow accordingly. Always, the present is not the end of spiritual growth. We receive more spiritual food and our faith grows as much in all things that we do as the time passes. I want you to follow the Lord' s voice and have your mind set on the precious work and live the life of sharing the spiritual food with people based on such faith. ⊠

SERMON

13

Let Us Go Forth by Our Faith in the Word

< John 10:1-18 >

"'Most assuredly, I say to you, he who does not enter the sheepfold by the door, but climbs up some other way, the same is a thief and a robber. But he who enters by the door is the shepherd of the sheep. To him the doorkeeper opens, and the sheep hear his voice; and he calls his own sheep by name and leads them out. And when he brings out his own sheep, he goes before them; and the sheep follow him, for they know his voice. Yet they will by no means follow a stranger, but will flee from him, for they do not know the voice of strangers.' Jesus used this illustration, but they did not understand the things which He spoke to them. Then Jesus said to them again, 'Most assuredly, I say to you, I am the door of the sheep. All who ever came before Me are thieves and robbers, but the sheep did not hear them. I am the door. If anyone enters by Me, he will be saved, and will go in and out and find pasture. The thief does not come except to steal, and to kill, and to destroy. I have come that they may have life, and that they may have it more abundantly. I am the good shepherd. The good shepherd gives His life for the sheep. But a hireling, he who is not the shepherd, one who does not own the sheep, sees the wolf coming and leaves the sheep and flees; and the wolf catches the sheep and scatters them. The hireling flees because he is a hireling and does not care about the sheep. I am the good shepherd; and I know My sheep, and am

known by My own. As the Father knows Me, even so I know the Father; and I lay down My life for the sheep. And other sheep I have which are not of this fold; them also I must bring, and they will hear My voice; and there will be one flock and one shepherd. Therefore My Father loves Me, because I lay down My life that I may take it again. No one takes it from Me, but I lay it down of Myself. I have power to lay it down, and I have power to take it again. This command I have received from My Father.'"

Through today's Scripture passage, the Lord is speaking to us about the sheepfold. Let's read John 10:1-3 again here: *"'Most assuredly, I say to you, he who does not enter the sheepfold by the door, but climbs up some other way, the same is a thief and a robber. But he who enters by the door is the shepherd of the sheep. To him the doorkeeper opens, and the sheep hear his voice; and he calls his own sheep by name and leads them out" (John 10:1-3).*

Using the expression "most assuredly" to underscore His emphasis, the Lord said here that he who does not enter the sheepfold by the door and instead climbs up some other way is a thief and a robber. He then said that he who enters by the door is the real shepherd of the sheep. The Lord has made a door to the sheepfold for us. Having established the way of salvation to deliver us humans from sin, God sees anyone who tries to enter His Kingdom by any way other than this door as a thief and a robber. Only the Lord is the true Shepherd of the sheep and the door of the sheepfold. Jesus Christ alone can say such things to us. Of course, people can also make their own claims since they all have lips, but they cannot speak the truth like the Lord does. The Word of God is not some sort of dogma taught by many religions, nor is it something uttered by ordinary human beings. That's because it is the Word spoken by God Almighty, the supreme Creator who is omniscient and omnipotent, for whom nothing is impossible, and who is perfect.

The Lord has given us the gospel of the water and the Spirit, and He has told us that only He is our true Shepherd. Anyone who tries to enter the Kingdom of God without this gospel of the water and the Spirit given by Jesus is a thief and a robber. Who can claim to be the Shepherd of the entire human race? No one else but only Jesus Christ can say such a thing and actually has such authority.

Even the words of Confucius, Buddha, and Socrates, the so-called three great sages of this world, do not have this kind of authority. One of the more famous dictums spoken by Socrates is: "Know yourself." But this dictum is irrelevant to the problem of the soul; instead, it just means that one should realize his own ignorance. Buddha, on the other hand, did mule over mankind's problem of sin, but he failed to provide any real solution. All that he said is that death is the only way to be freed from one's sinful self. In the case of Confucius, he spoke of only ordinary ethical lessons, saying, "Keep good manners, be faithful to your country and your friends, and honor your parents."

Of course, what these people said is not a bad lesson. But none of their teachings can provide a fundamental solution to the issue of mankind's salvation from sin. Although anyone can talk about moral issues, what we really need is the door to Heaven and the Shepherd of the sheep to lead us there. Jesus has become such a door and Shepherd of the sheep. And He said that by believing in Him, the Shepherd of the sheep, through the gospel of the water and the Spirit, everyone can be saved and enter the Kingdom of Heaven.

Is the Lord Really Our Savior?

The Lord said that anyone who tries to attain salvation and enter Heaven without going through Jesus Christ is a thief and a robber. Jesus can say such things because He has the power and authority commensurate to His Word. Who is Jesus Christ? He is the One who created the universe and everything in it, and He not only made you and me, but He has also saved us perfectly from all sins through the gospel of the water and the Spirit. What's more, He did not just give us salvation, but He has also prepared your future and mine and made it possible for us to enter the everlasting and wonderful Kingdom of Heaven. That's why only Jesus Christ is the true God. This saying is not merely a matter of religious doctrine, but it is derived from true faith. There is no one else but only Jesus Christ who made the universe and all its hosts, and He alone guarantees your future and mine, assures our happiness, and takes care of our present as well.

We can see clearly just how exalted and powerful Jesus is. After all, who in this world could say with such confidence that anyone who doesn't believe in him is a thief and a robber? Although anyone can claim to be God, no one can show the evidence for this claim. In contrast, Jesus not only said that He was God Himself incarnated in the flesh of man, but He also showed all the evidence of His divinity through the gospel of the water and the Spirit. That's why He said confidently that anyone who does not go through Him is a thief and a robber. No one else can say that anyone who doesn't believe in him is a thief and a robber bound to hell. Only God Himself, who is omniscient and omnipotent, can say such things to all of us His creatures. God can say such things because He has the authority, and He says such things because He Himself is the Truth and our salvation. So we can believe that Jesus is almighty, that He is God Himself, and that He is our Savior.

The Lord Is Our Guide

Secondly, the Lord is speaking about the doorkeeper. He said that the doorkeeper opens the door for the shepherd, and the sheep hear his voice. When the shepherd, having come into the sheepfold, calls on his sheep, the sheep recognize his voice and follow him. In contrast, if someone else tries to mimic the voice of the shepherd to lead the flock, then far from following him, the sheep would actually run away as they won't recognize the pretender's voice. Here Jesus is not literally teaching us how to raise a flock of sheep, but He is speaking of the gospel of the water and the Spirit through a parable.

Do you understand what Jesus is saying here? He said, *"Most assuredly, I say to you, I am the door of the sheep. All who ever came before Me are thieves and robbers, but the sheep did not hear them" (John 10:7-8)*. This means that our Lord is the door, the doorkeeper, and the Shepherd of the sheep as well. That is so true! Since the Lord is our Savior, everyone who ever came before Him is a thief and a robber. That's why the Lord's sheep did not hear anyone else's voice and run away.

Even though you and I are weak and insufficient, we can still praise God aloud from the top of our lungs, and that's because we have been empowered by the Lord. It's because the Lord has saved us by His almighty power that we the saved are able to praise Him for His omnipotence. You and I praise the Lord not out of our own strength, but by the new spiritual power attained from the gospel of the water and the Spirit.

Jesus said that the sheep know their shepherd. People nowadays believe in many things. After all, just how many religions are there in this world? But can any of these religions really bring absolute salvation to mankind, preach only the exact Truth, lead people to the way of the perfect gospel, and protect their souls with any guarantee? No, none of them can do this. Only Jesus Christ can guide mankind perfectly to the true way of salvation. No one else can make such a claim, nor actually deliver on such a promise.

The Lord calls each sheep by name, and He walks in front of the flock to lead them. The sheep then follow Him, for they know His voice. The sheep do not follow anyone else. Only the Almighty God is your Savior and mine, and our Shepherd. Even though there are over 6 billion people living on this planet, the Lord knows everything about each and every one of them. He knows each of their names, understands each of their hearts, and also knows how they each have led their lives. He knows them all because He created them.

In particular, the Lord knows you and me, the believers in the gospel of the water and the Spirit, even better. That's because He has led us. He has saved a few in the east, a few in the west, a few from this tribe, and a few from that tribe. In fact, you and I have different family names, different households, different countries, and different skin colors. Yet despite this, God has saved us from every corner of the world and made us His children transcending race, gender, and age. And He also says that He will save even more people who still have not come into His sheepfold. We know very well that the Lord can achieve this because He is almighty. Because He is omnipotent,

He can take care of our every need and give us His guarantee.

No sheep can take care of itself. Without a shepherd, it cannot move even a step. Like such a sheep, we can be led to the right way of salvation only if we have Jesus Christ at our side, because He is our good Shepherd and God Himself. That's why the Lord said that He is the good Shepherd for His sheep. A good shepherd lays down even his own life to protect the flock. So did our Lord lay down His life to deliver us from sin, and He was also resurrected back to life. Only Jesus Christ has the power to rise from the dead again. Throughout His public life, Jesus had prophesied on several occasions that He would die and rise from the dead again, and He personally demonstrated the truthfulness of this prophecy. He called Himself a good Shepherd; He said that a good shepherd would forsake his life for the sake of the flock; and He actually demonstrated all this with His own body. The Lord could say such things to us precisely because only He is the true Messiah and the Son of God.

Our Lord is the same as God the Father. He is the Creator who made the entire universe and all its hosts; the Judge who will judge the believers and nonbelievers alike; and the only Savior who can grant all the happiness and blessings of the future. He is the Almighty God who can take care of all who believe in Him. Even though there are many religions in this world, nothing and no one can take care of not only our flesh but also our souls like Jesus does.

If Jesus, like a mere creature, had made all these promises only in words without actually having the power to deliver on them, then He would not be the Savior. That's because someone who is powerless can never be the Savior, nor guarantee happiness to his followers. Anyone can do anything with his words or in his plans, but if he doesn't have the real power, then it's all nothing but empty words. In contrast, the Lord is in fact omniscient and omnipotent, and He is also perfect. That's why He was able to become our Savior. This Jesus Christ we believe in cannot be compared to any creatures under the heavens. He is the omniscient and omnipotent God who cannot be compared to any idols on this earth.

This omniscient and omnipotent God has saved us through the water and the Spirit. I am so thankful to Him for thus saving us from sin. I am also thankful that the Lord is able to guarantee our future just as it's written in the Book of Revelation. He will render His terrifying judgment on all those who stood against Him. As slaves to sin, we had once also stood against the Lord with our sins. But despite this, the Lord loved us so much that He gave us the gospel of the water and the Spirit, and He delivered us from sin and destruction. That is why it is so worthwhile for us to always praise the Lord out loud.

The Lord has the power to guarantee our eternal future, and He is the only true God who has saved you and me. Therefore, it is only proper for us to take Him as our Shepherd and follow Him. We believe that He is our Shepherd. It's because Jesus is our Savior and our God that we are always thankful for His glory, His power, His love, and His mercy. Today also, we have gathered like this to thank the Lord. It's all because we have put on His grace that we are able to live happily and comfortably. It's all thanks to the gospel of the water and the Spirit, which we could never have obtained without Him. Do you then believe that our Lord is indeed God Almighty to all of us?

There is no reason for us to fear the future. That's because the Lord our Shepherd guarantees your future and mine. However, as far as those who don't believe in the Lord's righteousness are concerned, He will render His terrifying judgment on them. Such people should indeed fear God. You must realize here that although the Lord is the Shepherd for those who believe in the gospel of the water and the Spirit, for those who don't, He is the stern Judge.

The Lord says that He will cast out all those who don't believe in the gospel of the water and the Spirit into the fire of hell and make them suffer forever. It will be so hot that the Bible describes it as the place where everyone will be seasoned with fire (Mark 9:49). And it also says that once entered, no one can ever escape from it. Those who are cast into hell will tremble before the wrath of God, and they will gnash their teeth and wail over having rejected the gospel of the water and the Spirit while they were still alive.

While writing my commentaries on the Book of Revelation, I thanked God once again for the fact that I was saved from sin by believing in the gospel of the water and the Spirit. I was overwhelmed with gratitude just to think about how the Lord completely blotted out all the sins of my conscience and soul with the water and the blood. The fact that I was saved by believing in the gospel of the water and the Spirit was enough to make me thankful beyond all words, but even more gratefully, the Lord also gave the Holy Spirit into my heart, made me one of God's people and His servant, and gave me the Kingdom of Heaven as well. And even now I am still thankful. I am so grateful that I cannot help but praise His omnipotence. I want to thank Him again and again for His almighty power. Because it's the omniscient and omnipotent Lord who has enabled us to be born again and protected us, we can find all the more peace in our hearts.

If the Lord had been weak and powerless like us, then like Buddha, He would have just told us to reach Nirvana on our own and save ourselves by practicing asceticism. He would have said, "Just practice asceticism on your own. It would be good if you reach Nirvana and become divine in that way." If the Lord were such a powerless Being, then we would always have been gripped by anxiety over our sins. However, the Lord who has saved you and me is perfect, and there is nothing He cannot do. He has the power to do everything and anything. That's why our hearts are at peace, and why we are able to thank God always for enabling us to believe in Him.

Since receiving salvation by believing in the righteousness of God, we have been gathering together every day to worship Him. It's true that we are quite fatigued from working at our jobs and serving the gospel at the same time. But as tired as we are, the gospel work will prosper by that much. Just as a grain of wheat must sacrifice itself and die to bear many fruits, if we forsake and sacrifice ourselves, the work of the Lord will flourish even more. The Lord wants to fulfill His will through God's Church. Through the gospel that manifests His perfect love and His work of salvation, we will save all the lost sheep still wandering outside the sheepfold, all these pitiful sheep that still have not come across the gospel of the water and the Spirit.

Our hearts are grateful to the Lord for His omnipotence. There may be some worries in both your heart and mine, and when we look at our circumstances, we may sometimes be discouraged, but if we trust in the Lord's omnipotence and believe that He will perfect you and me and give us His perfect blessings, then we can still find peace of mind by trusting in His power. It's with this disposition that we should live the rest of our lives for the gospel work, and then meet our Lord face to face. Do you understand this? It's not so hard. We can do this step by step. I know very well just how busy you are. All of us are busy trying to carry out the gospel work, but I believe that we can renew our strength by faith daily.

The God who has saved you and me is an omniscient and omnipotent God. Christ is this omniscient and omnipotent God, and He is also our Savior. He is the only One who has the power to guarantee our eternal future and bring happiness to us. I ask you all to believe in this. Let us all live by faith in this truth.

Since you and I have been saved and become God's children, we should all trust in Jesus Christ and praise Him. Sometimes, we may feel that this is not such a big issue. When we judge based on our own fleshly thoughts, faith is hard to come by, but if we follow God by trusting in His Word, then even when we lose heart and lose strength as a result, we can still stand up again. That's why Isaiah 40:31 says,

"But those who wait on the LORD
Shall renew their strength;
They shall mount up with wings like eagles,
They shall run and not be weary,
They shall walk and not faint." If we really live waiting on God like this passage, then we will receive new strength and soar with wings like eagles.

Although there are many religions in the world, they are just quarreling with each other claiming to be better than the rest, and there is no true gospel of salvation. In such religions, there is no gospel of the water and the Spirit, and therefore no one can be born again nor can any heart find any comfort no matter how devotedly people may practice their religions. It is when our souls are truly born again through the gospel of the water and the Spirit that the Lord gives the Holy Spirit into our hearts, and thanks to this Holy Spirit and this gospel, we are able to comfort each other and encourage one another. Without the gospel of the water and the Spirit, it's also impossible to find any new strength to soar with wings like eagles.

Are you still unable to believe that Jesus Christ is God Almighty, your absolute Savior, and your Shepherd for both your body and soul? Are you still rejecting the gospel of the water and the Sprit from your heart, thinking that it is not the true gospel? If this is true, then you will have no choice but to live according to the prevailing current of the world. You will not find any comfort or strength. However, if you know the Truth and accept the gospel of the water and the Sprit trusting in God, then you can avoid falling into a useless religion and come to have true faith.

I am truly thankful to the Lord for giving us the gospel of the water and the Spirit and making us believe in this Word. I am also thankful that because of my faith in this gospel, I no longer worry about any uncertain future. If God were imperfect, then I would have been worried no matter how often I heard the Word, but because God is omniscient and omnipotent, I have absolutely no worry at all. If God were powerless despite having a good heart, then this would also have made me anxious, but because the Lord has not only saved me from sin but He is fundamentally the omniscient and omnipotent God, I am never anxious. He made the world. He is the Alpha and the Omega, the beginning and the end, and all things were made by Him. As I was writing my commentaries on the Book of Revelation, I became even more grateful to the Lord for the fact that everything was planned in Jesus Christ, and this plan is completed in Jesus Christ.

Let us all have faith in the gospel of the water and the Spirit and live by this faith. Although it's true that I've been very busy training our ministry workers, I feel indescribable joy whenever I stand here and preach. While training our ministry workers, I tested them to see whether or not they have received the true faith and the gospel-loving heart from God, and they all passed the test. It was such a joy for me to lead them by faith and see them standing firmly by faith.

There is a lot of work that we still need do. As our books are continually uploaded as e-books on our website, many more readers from all over the world will download and read them. Then the veritable wind of revival will stir up throughout Christian communities all over the world. People will be amazed to see us preaching the gospel of the water and the Spirit so boldly, and they will be even more amazed to see that everything we say is proven by the Bible.

The gospel of the water and the Spirit that we are spreading is the only breakthrough that can revive today's corrupted Christianity. Although everyone actually admits that Jesus Christ is the Truth and that there is something profoundly wrong with today's Christian doctrines, few have found any means to change this. However, as the gospel of the water and the Spirit is now providing the exact diagnosis of Christianity today and clearly pointing out the breakthrough that must be made, many people are amazed by this, saying to themselves, "I didn't know there was such an amazing thing!" In the days to come, countless more people will not only be amazed, but they will also come to have the same faith as ours.

For the entire Christian world that's trapped in despondent doctrines, its only breakthrough is the gospel of the water and the Spirit. Even though there are many misbelievers, because the gospel of the water and the Spirit is the Truth, if they believe in this Truth and follow it, then there will be even more people being born again all across the globe. This will come true without fail, for the Lord Jesus said, *"And other sheep I have which are not of this fold; them also I must bring, and they will hear My voice; and there will be one flock and one shepherd" (John 10:16)*. It is then our duty to work even more diligently to bring this work into reality.

Have you read the email sent by a man in the US who got a master's degree in theology? This man, who had finished graduate studies, was incarcerated for some crime, and while in the prison he read one of our books and received the remission of sins. And this man, now that he has become our brother, is the leader of a Bible study group in the prison. A man who had learned only about Christian doctrines irrelevant to the true gospel is now gathering convicted criminals and preaching about the true gospel and sin, about the work of John the Baptist and the baptism Jesus received. He is explaining in detail how all the sins of the world were passed onto Jesus, and how they were all remitted away.

The first English volume of our books is a very good guide for Bible study, as it explains the gospel of the water and the Spirit in concrete detail. American prisons are often visited by "feeding pastors." They are called "feeding pastors" because they bring a lot of good food to share and go home after just saying, "Let's live virtuously. When you are released from the prison, try to be a good person. Amen." These people are clearly different from our American brother in prison who is sharing the gospel of the water and the Spirit with his fellow inmates. Although he is a prison inmate, his heart has been freed from sin, and he is able to explain clearly to the other inmates why they and he alike couldn't help but commit crimes and find themselves in the prison.

Among the inmates, there must be some people with a long criminal record. Our brother is preaching the gospel of the water and the Spirit to such hardened criminals, saying to them, "Why do you commit crime again the moment you step out of the prison? The reason why you keep committing crime like this time after time is because sin is fundamentally in your nature. But, although you were born as someone who can't help but commit sin, the Lord has blotted out all your sins with the gospel of the water and the Spirit." Wouldn't all those who hear this gospel Word then be shocked? And many of them will believe in the gospel, receive the remission of sins, and live in joy. When they are thus released from the prison as born-again people, they will never commit any crime again or return to the prison.

My fellow believers, my heart is overwhelmed with joy that we now have a coworker in a US prison. I can easily imagine how amazed this brother must have been the moment he grasped the Word. When I read his letters, I can fully understand what's in his heart. As well, there are many coworkers throughout the whole world who are translating and revising our books, and whenever I read their letters, I can feel just how rejoiced the Holy Spirit in our hearts is. We have added another coworker ministering in the prison; among our translators, there are pastors as well; and many people all over the world are being born again by believing in the gospel of water and the blood that you and I believe in. It's such a joyful thing!

The gospel of the water and the Spirit, which is based on the Word of the Scriptures, has no flaw whatsoever to be presented to anyone and everyone throughout the whole world. You and I spread only the Word of God because we have already understood the gospel of the water and the Spirit, and we believe in Jesus Christ and preach what He has done for us. This Word that we are spreading is completely flawless and perfect no matter where it is told. That's because God has given it. And that's why people all over the world are receiving the remission of sins. We can hear voices from every corner of the world praising God. When our hymn book is translated into every language and shared by all, we will all be singing the same praises, and I am sure that this, too, will be very inspiring for all of us.

My fellow believers, I am someone who just loves to preach the Word. I can't imagine living without preaching the Word. As the Word of God fills me to fullness, there is abundant bread to share with the whole wide world. It pains me not to share the Word of God and feed it to people all over the world.

So let us train our ministry workers and live diligently by faith. I am not admonishing that we should just work diligently without trusting in God Almighty, but that we should live by trusting in the Almighty God who has saved us and be faithful to Him. Our hearts will then be rejoiced. Do you grasp this? Because of our shortcomings, our work cannot be carried out completely if we just rely on ourselves, and so in our hearts, let us put all our trust in God.

I am so happy that you and I have been saved. I am so thankful to the Lord that He has saved us perfectly despite our insufficiencies, and I also praise Him for his perfection. Does your heart have such a desire to praise the righteousness of God? Whenever I think of the Lord's salvation, my heart overflows with gratitude to the Lord, and I cannot help but praise His righteousness. I give all my thanks to the Lord. ✉

SERMON

14

Know Clearly That Jesus Is the Christ and Believe So Unwaveringly

< John 10:17-27 >

"'Therefore My Father loves me, because I lay down my life that I may take it again. No one takes it from me, but I lay it down of myself. I have power to lay it down, and I have power to take it again. This command I have received from My Father.' Therefore there was a division again among the Jews because of these sayings. And many of them said, 'He has a demon and is mad. Why do you listen to Him?' Others said, 'These are not the words of one who has a demon. Can a demon open the eyes of the blind?' Now it was the Feast of Dedication in Jerusalem, and it was winter. And Jesus walked in the temple, in Solomon's porch. Then the Jews surrounded Him and said to Him, 'How long do you keep us in doubt? If you are the Christ, tell us plainly.' Jesus answered them, 'I told you, and you do not believe. The works that I do in My Father's name, they bear witness of me. But you do not believe, because you are not of my sheep, as I said to you. My sheep hear my voice, and I know them, and they follow me.'"

In John chapter 10, the Lord continued to tell them that He was the Christ. It's written in verses 23-24, *"And Jesus walked in the temple, in Solomon's porch. Then the Jews surrounded Him and said to Him, 'How long do you keep us in doubt? If you are the Christ, tell us plainly.'"* When Jesus was on this earth, many Jews thought that they were being confused by Him. They thought that they were good Jews, but Jesus was now deceiving and misleading many of them to go astray. That's why they demanded Jesus to tell them plainly if He was really 'the Christ'.

The word Christ means to be anointed, which implies the approval of God the Father. Everyone who was approved, appointed and used by God in the Bible was an anointed man. The kings of Israel were appointed by God. The first king of Israel was Saul and the second king was David, both of whom were anointed by prophets. The 'anointed one' means that God has approved him. It means that his authority has been granted by God.

In addition to kings, prophets and priests were also all anointed. Sometimes olive oil was poured on the head of the peson being anointed. When kings, priests and prophets were appointed, they were all anointed on their heads. Spiritually speaking, this means that God the Father poured the Holy Spirit on them and made them His people to carry out His work.

The Jews said to Jesus, *"If you are the Christ, tell us plainly."* They had no clue that Jesus was actually the very Christ sent by the Father to carry out the work of saving all the people of this world from their sin. It was prophesied in the Old Testament, *"Behold, the virgin shall conceive and bear a Son, and shall call His name Immanuel,"* and the word Immanuel means God is with us. God the Father had promised repeatedly to send the Savior. This Savior is none other than Jesus Christ. The word 'Jesus' means 'the Savior' and the word 'Christ' means King. The Bible says that He is the King of kings, the Creator, and the Messiah who came to save us from sin, and He fulfilled the ministry of the Prophet by speaking this Truth to us.

The Jews said to Jesus, *"If you are the Christ, tell us plainly."* Jesus then said to them, *"I told you, and you do not believe. The works that I do in My Father's name, they bear witness of me. But you do not believe, because you are not of my sheep, as I said to you. My sheep hear my voice, and I know them, and they follow me."* Even though the Lord had told them plainly, they refused to believe. He had told them countless times that the Father had sent Him, that the Father was working through Him, and that the Father approved Him. It's written in John chapter one, *"In the beginning was the Word, and the Word was with God, and the Word was God. He was in the beginning with God. All things were made through Him, and without Him nothing was made that was made."*

The Bible speaks of this continuously from the very beginning. Jesus the Son of God, who came to save us from sin, made this world, came to shine the light of salvation to this world, and saved us by delivering us from darkness. God's prophets in the Old Testament had also spoken of Jesus as the Messiah and Savior to come, and when the time came, Jesus Christ came to this earth through the body of a virgin. Having thus come, Jesus carried out His work of salvation as promised and spoke plainly that He was the very Christ, but the Jews refused to believe. So Jesus told them that God was His Father and that He had existed even before Abraham, but they still did not believe. There is very little that you can say to stubborn incredulous people to convince them otherwise.

So the Lord said in verse 27, *"My sheep hear my voice, and I know them, and they follow me."* Jesus said that He is the Son of God, our Savior and our Creator and that He has saved us through the gospel Truth of the water and the Spirit. Those who believe in this believe that Jesus is the Son of God the Father, God Himself, the Creator, their Savior and the Messiah who has made them God's sons and daughters from utter darkness. That is what we believe. We believe that Jesus is not only the Son of God, but also the Creator who made the universe and the Savior who has saved us. Those who don't believe like this are not God's sheep.

Jesus said, *"My sheep hear my voice, and I know them, and they follow me."* Those who believe that God the Father loved the world so much that He sent His only begotten Son believe that God the Father indeed sent His only begotten Son to this world as their Savior, blotted out all their sins with the water and the blood, and thereby has saved them. There is no reason why anyone cannot believe in this, as it is written: "*For since the creation of the world His invisible attributes are clearly seen, being understood by the things that are made, even His eternal power and Godhead, so that they are without excuse" (Romans 1:20).* God has fully revealed to us what may be knowm of Him through the nature and His Word.

So if anyone recognizes God, then he will also recognize Jesus the Son of God. For us to be saved, Jesus had to come as the Savior, be baptized by John the Baptist in the Jordan River, die on the Cross, rise from the dead, and become the Savior of those of us who believe in the gospel of the water and the Spirit. There was no other way. The only way for you and me to be saved from sin was for Jesus to be born on this earth, be baptized by John the Baptist at the age of 30, die on that Cross, rise from the dead, and through this has save us; and it is by faith that we reach our salvation.

Would we be saved from sin by living virtuously and doing good deeds? Between all the countless millions of people, what is so superior about us 'the believers in the gospel of the water and the Spirit' that we would be saved from our sins, become God the Father's children, and be blessed in both body and spirit as the rising sun? There is no other way except our faith in Jeus. The Bible says, *"There is no other name under heaven given among men by which we must be saved" (Acts 4:12).* This means that it's impossible to attain salvation by believing in anyone else but Jesus.

It was said, *"My sheep hear my voice, and I know them, and they follow me."* The Lord said that He knows us 'the ones who believe in the gospel of the water and the Spirit'. Because of this fact we also know Him and follow Him. This is only natural. There are countless people living in this world, but some of them believe that Jesus is their Master, their Creator and their Savior, and that He has blotted out all their sins with the gospel of the water and the Spirit. On the other hand, there also are those who don't believe in the gospel of the water and the Spirit. In other words, some people in this world believe in the gospel of the water and the Spirit but others don't. Whether people believe in the gospel of the water and the Spirit depends on whether they are truly God's children or not. Put differently, this does not depend on one's will.

God is our Savior, the Truth, the Way and the Life. God is the Truth. Yet despite this, people cannot reach their salvation because their hearts are evil and full of doubts, and so they neither believe in nor recognize the righteousness of God, His love and the gospel of the God given water and the Spirit. But God is perfect. He said that He knows us. God knows all about us. There is no reason why we should not be able to follow Him. Does God lack anything that we would be unable to believe in Him and follow Him? Does Jesus Christ lack anything at all?

Those in this world who do not believe in the gospel of the water and the Spirit do not believe in 'this gospel' because they are not God's sheep. You may then wonder, "Did God choose some but not others?" The Bible says, *"For God so loved the world that He gave His only begotten Son, that whoever believes in Him should not perish but have everlasting life" (John 3:16).* God loved the world so much. It does not say here that He loved some but not others.

Of course, we may be able to find the notion in the Bible that God loves some people but not others where it is written, *"Yet Jacob I have loved; But Esau I have hated" (Malachi 1:2-3).* Those whom God loves are those who are like Jacob. Those whom God hates are those who are like Esau. Who are these people then? Those who are like Jacob are weak and deceitful, but they know themselves well and so rather than relying on themselves, they rely on the faith of their parents of the flesh—that is, they believe in the Lord God.

But people like Esau don't see any need for the God of their fathers and mothers. They believe in their own bows and their own arrows. People like these shoot and kill a wild boar and carry it home over their shoulders, to make a special meal and boast about how they shot an animal today and brag about their own strengths and abilities. But we must know that God hates those who are arrogant like this trusting in their own fleshly strength. Viewed spiritually, these kinds of people don't need to believe in the righteousness of God, since they think that they themselves are good, righteous, upright, strong and smart, while everyone else is unrighteous and just plain stupid. They are convinced that those who believe in Jesus are weak and fragile, and that only the feeble believe in and rely on God, while strong people like themselves have absolutely no need to rely on God. It's these kinds of people whom God hates. How smart could they be even if they were so smart? They would be dead in five minutes without breathing. What is there to be so arrogant about really? They are like midgets arguing over who is tall, when they cannot even survive being infected by one tiny little bacterium.

So God hates such people and loves those who know their insufficiencies and rely on God totally. Although God does love everyone in this world, He abhors those who boast of their own merits even doing this before His very presence saying, "I have no need for your help. I can live well on my own strength thank you very much; perhaps it's I who really should be helping you." God calls them arrogant and conceited, nothing more than the Devil's servants.

So we see that there are two kinds of people. There are those who know their insufficiencies and weaknesses, and who really desire to rely on God. Those who know that Jesus Christ sent by God the Father is not only the real God who created the Universe and their true Messiah who has saved them, but also the Lord of life who has given them everlasting life—it is to these very people whom God gives true salvation and everlasting life too through the gospel of the water and the Spirit. God loves such people who believe in the God-given Word exactly as it is, and who rely on God and follow Him because they are insufficient, for God knows all about their weaknesses.

So those who really know their shortcomings and listen to the Word of God say, "I believe in God no matter what others say. I rely on Him. The more I know Jesus Christ, the more majestic and precious He is." Such people are blessed before God. However, those who don't or refuse to believe in the righteousness of God think that they are too smart say the following, "Jesus cannot be the Son of God. Did He not call

Himself the Son of God? So doesn't this mean that He was made by God? If He was made by God the Father, how can He not be a creature, but divine?" Such people who believe in their own strengths, money, wisdom, and intelligence are all foolish people.

God spoke about fools in Psalms, saying that those who do not realize their honor are like the beasts that perish (Psalm 49:20). In order for God to make human beings His children, He created them in His very image. God allowed hardship in this world so that people would look for Him, rely on Him and thus receive the God-given blessings to be born again and enjoy everlasting blessings and eternal life. It is for this purpose that God made them, and yet some people still do not recognize this, don't realize their honor, don't realize and don't rely on the honor of God. Such people are doomed to perish. They are not God's children. The Lord said this many times while He was on this earth.

In John chapter 10's reading today Jesus said, *"Therefore My Father loves me, because I lay down my life that I may take it again. No one takes it from me, but I lay it down of myself. I have power to lay it down, and I have power to take it again. This command I have received from My Father."* In other words, the Savior said that He would lay down His life on this earth. God the Father loves Jesus like this because our Lord accepted all ours sins by being baptized and laid down His life on the Cross, because He carried out the work of saving us from sin in obedience to the will of God the Father. Jesus' life is not something that anyone else could take away, but it is something that He laid down of His own will. He said that He would forsake His life for the sake of His sheep and His people. He said that He had the power to lay it down and to take it up again. This means that Jesus received such powers from God the Father.

How simple is this passage then? Those who believe in the Word of God understand that Jesus did not die because He was 'powerless'. Although it's true that Jesus was crucified to death on this earth, it was not because He was powerless.

Let's turn to an example in the Bible. On the last night before being arrested, Jesus went to the Mount of Olives to pray, and while He prayed to God the Father to let His will be done, Judas came to Jesus accompanied by Roman soldiers and the chief priests. They came armed with swords, spears and torches. Judas then kissed Jesus. When the Jews greeted each other in those days, it was customary for them to wish peace to one another, saying 'Shalom,' and hug and kiss on both cheeks. This confirmed that they were not enemies.

Judas had told both the chief priests and the Roman soldiers that whomever he kissed would be Jesus whom they were looking for. The Bible describes this scene of Jesus' arrest in Gethsemane as follows: *"Then Judas, having received a detachment of troops, and officers from the chief priests and Pharisees, came there with lanterns, torches, and weapons. Jesus therefore, knowing all things that would come upon Him, went forward and said to them, 'Whom are you seeking?' They answered Him, 'Jesus of Nazareth.' Jesus said to them, 'I am He.' And Judas, who betrayed Him, also stood with them. Now when He said to them, 'I am He,' they drew back and fell to the ground" (John 18:3-6)*. Did Jesus try to attempt escape from them, or did He willingly give Himself up? He showed no resistence to His arrest, so that He could lay down His life for all of us.

The Lord is the Master who created the whole universe and all of mankind. The Roman soldiers could not prevail over Him with arms and weapons. Even if they had a million-strong army, Jesus could kill them all with a single utterance of His Word right on the spot. If He did this, they would all have died instantly. It's not because Jesus was powerless that He was arrested by the chief priests and the Roman soldiers and beaten by them. The Lord laid down His life willingly because He had taken upon all our sins once for all by being baptized, because He had to bear the condemnation of those sins, and because He could save us from sin, and to obey the will of God the Father He gave up His body on the Cross and died there in our place. The Life of Jesus was laid down and taken up again by Himself. That is how He has saved us 'the believers in the gospel of the water and the Spirit', by being baptized, dying on the Cross and rising from the dead for us. Those who believe in the gospel of the water and the Spirit can receive everlasting life and the remission of sins.

But those who don't or refuse to believe in the gospel of the water and the Spirit come up with all kinds of excuses for their disbelief. They say, "How can I believe in the gospel of the water and the Spirit? The Bible is the history of the Jews, and so how can I believe in it as the ultimate Truth of salvation?" They protest so vehemently even though their intelligence pales in comparison to the wisdom of God. They are foolish and ignorant, and what is worse they are so very stubborn. But they keep coming up with one excuse after another and stubbornly refuse to believe in God.

Through all the things that our Lord did on this earth 'in the name of Jesus', we can see that He is indeed the Son of God. Did He not go to the Mount of Olives to pray before He was crucified? Even though Jesus was God, He knew very well just how terrible it would be for Him to be crucified on a Roman Cross. That's why He prayed and earnestly asked the Father to take away His cup of suffering if possible. Since

Jesus had shouldered all the sins of the world, He had to to be crucified to bear the condemanation of these sins, but He still asked His Father if it were possible to make mankind sinless without Him being crucified.

But God the Father cannot lie and He cannot abolish the law of salvation and judgment that He established. Man speaks with a forked tongue of different things with his one mouth. While people may make promises and change them, God's promise can never be altered. So because God had said that the wages of sin is death and that He would infallibly judge and put to death all those with sin, He decided to send His Son to deliver us from sin and death. And by making Jesus receive baptism from John the Baptist; God had passed all our sins to Jesus once for all. Thus the Father had to render His judgment of sin on His Son Jesus Christ. In other words, He had to put Jesus to death in a physical way. This was none other than the terrible suffering of the Cross. That's why Jesus obeyed the will of God the Father.

When we look at what the Lord did when He came to this earth, we can see who God the Father really is. Although none of us have ever met God the Father with our naked eyes, we can still know who He is. In other words, through Jesus we see none other than God the Father. God has enabled us to realize, "Oh! That's who God the Father really is. He is the God of love. He is the Savior. He is the Messiah. He is the God of mercy. But He is also the God of justice. He saves those who deserve to be saved and judges those who deserve to be judged without fail." In short, through Jesus we can know who God the Father is. So those who believe in Jesus accept God the Father, and those who believe in God the Father can receive Jesus as their Savior.

Those who acknowledge the love of God can recognize

Jesus as their Savior who came by the gospel of the water and the Spirit. I acknowledge that Jesus is my Savior. I am not trying to coerc you to have faith. I believe that Jesus is the Son of God the Father, but at the same time He is also my God and my Savior; I believe that Jesus has saved me from sin through the gospel of the water and the Spirit; and I believe that Christ shouldered all my sins by being baptized, died on the Cross in my place, and rose from the dead again on my behalf to bring me back to life. Do you also believe in Jesus like this?

Those who do not believe that Jesus is really God, and who don't or refuse to believe in the gospel of the water and the Spirit, are neither God's sheep nor His people. There is no need to resent God's way of slavation. Why? Because God loves everyone equally, He has indiscriminately blotted out everyone's sins with the gospel of the water and the Spirit. For His part, God the Father has blotted out all sins with the gospel of the water and the Spirit through Jesus Christ. What kind of people would then believe in the love of God and the gospel of the water and the Spirit, and what kind of people would not believe? Those who are like Jacob believe in God's love and the gospel of the water and the Spirit, while those who are like Esau do not believe. Can you understand this?

Are you spiritually a Jacob or an Esau? Are you cunning in your flesh? Are you not in fact quite cunning? Don't you have many evils and weaknesses? Are any of you like Esau? Those who are like Esau say, "I'm muscular like this, I've taken various supplements, and I think I can do anything if I make up my mind to do it. So I don't need to rely on the love of God and the God given gospel of the water and the Spirit. I don't believe in anything else but my own strength. So I can do anything and anybody. I despise religious people. I especially look down on anyone who claims to have been saved from sin by believing in the righteousness of God and the gospel of the water and the Spirit. They are all idiots!" In reality, it's actually these very people who are the foolish ones. For communism, materials are its gods. Communism is a materialist ideology. So its adherents only seek after materials. Even though there is a God who made these materials, they don't rely on this God but these materials.

Who then are the blessed by God? They are those who are like Jacob. When I consider myself, I am like Jacob. One of our ministers once lifted a barbell weighing 80 kilos with one arm and asked for a heavier weight, saying that it was too light. I imagine with both arms He could have easily lifted 160 kilos. If this minister only relied on his strength, he would have become a man like Esau. However, he relied on God and continues to do so even though he is such a powerful man, and he has led the saints by faith instead of relying on himself.

How about our bodies and spirits? Are we overflowing with strength? Are we such people who are full of own abilities, wizards at making money, don't lack anything including fame, have no need to rely on anyone else, and call those who rely on God complete idiots? We know that this is not who we are. We are all insufficient.

Human beings may seem like great achievers, but they are actually nothing. It's often said that people's dreams change as they grow old. A kid may dream of becoming the President, but his dream turns less ambitious as he grows older, wanting to become a doctor later on, then a public servant and then just wishing to have any job at all. We must know how weak our flesh really is, how powerless we are, and how insignificant we are before God; we must realize His love and the gospel of the water and the Spirit He has given us. It's these kinds of people who rely on God.

If anyone has any strength at all, it's God who has given him this strength. People like Jacob live by relying totally on God. And being saved by believing in the love of God and the gospel of the water and the Spirit is also achieved by relying on God. It is simply impossible for anyone to attain salvation on his own strength. Relying on God and His work is what faith is all about. Relying on God to help us even in our everday affairs is also faith. Why? It is because we know the omnipotent power of God. This is what our living Lord is saying to us today. The Lord has fulfilled all righteousness with His baptism and blood, and now sits at the right hand of the throne of God the Father as the living Savior of all who believe in the gospel of the water and the Spirit.

When Jesus was on this earth, most people at that time could not believe that He was their Savior or Mesiah. Did everyone not believe then? No, many people did believe. But there were more people who refused to believe. In this age also, the question is whether one believes that Jesus is the Savior who was born on this earth, took upon the sins of this world by being baptized by John the Baptist at the age of 30, was crucified to shed His blood to death, rose from the dead again, and now sits at the right hand of the throne of God and is still alive. Now as before, many people do not believe in Jesus as their Savior, and even those professing to believe in Jesus preach 'only' His death on the Cross rather than the gospel of the water and the Spirit. However, there also are many who believe in this Truth. We the true believers believe and profess that Jesus took upon our sins by being baptized, died on the Cross, rose from the dead, and has thereby become our Savior. His baptism means that He bore our sins. His death is our death to sin and destruction, and His resurrection is our resurrection. As we rely on Jesus Christ, we are sinless for He has saved us.

I am sure that you also believe like this.

Why am I saying these things? It's to ask you if you really believe that Jesus is indeed the Son of God and our Savior who has saved us through the gospel of the water and the Spirit. In other words, do you really believe that Jesus is our Savior? I'm asking you to truly believe in the gospel of the water and the Spirit. I'm admonishing you to believe that Jesus is the real God, the Creator and our Savior.

The word 'Christ' means the 'anointed One' who fulfills the will of God the Father—that is, the One who saves us from sin. As God the Father sent His Son Jesus Christ to this earth, He took upon all our sins by being baptized, died on the Cross, rose from the dead, and thereby saved us from sin once for all. You must believe clearly that Jesus Christ is 'the Christ.' A few people have started to believe in this, but why do so many Christians still refuse to believe in this Jesus? The reason is because they open the Bible and receive only teaching of morals and ethics, and their leaders tell them to practice virtue. "Give a lot of offerings. If you serve a lot and do a lot, you will be honored in the church and become a deacon or an elder." This in a nutshell is what they teach. Since Christians are encouraged only to compete against each other, they are not interested in who Jesus really is and how He has blotted out their sins with the gospel of the water and the Spirit, but instead they just want to keep doing things on their own all to be commended and approved.

That's why they are perishing away spiritually. Simply put, spiritual fraud is rampant where the teaching of the gospel of the water and the Spirit is missing. It's the same as the multi-level marketing schemes. What is multi-level marketing scheme or simply put a pyramid scheme? Someone forms a sales organization, subscribes more and more people into it as salesmen or saleswomen, and makes a lot of money for himself very rapidly. Churches are the same. "If you evangelize and bring in a lot of people, your rank in that church will go up." This is what pastors are really saying to their congregations. If a church attendee evangelizes a lot, makes a lot of offerings, and works hard for the church, then he is approved regardless of whether he has received the remission of sins or not. That's why today's Christianity has turned itself into a mere wordly business. It is a gathering place of charlatans defrauding each other using religion.

I believe that Jesus came to this earth 2,000 years ago to save us, took upon all our sins by being baptized at the age of 30, was crucified to death while shouldering the sins of the world, rose from the dead, and then ascended to the right hand of God the Father. Jesus Christ has therefore become our perfect Savior by coming to this earth by the gospel of the water and the Spirit. You must all believe in this. You must know it clearly and believe in it. If you believe in the gospel of the water and the Spirit, you will most certainly be saved. The gospel of the water and the Spirit is worthy of believing together with Jesus. Because we are weak, it is worth relying on.

If we believe in Jesus and the gospel of the water and the Spirit, we will be saved and become God's children. When a baby turns one year old, he should be able stand by himself and take his first step, and this brings a great deal of joy to his parents. Likewise, after becoming God's child, if you walk step by step according to the will of the Father and His pleasure by believing in the gospel of the water and the Spirit, your faith will start growing as you listen to the Word, then this in its self makes you the object of God's love. This is not achieved by offering something of your own.

Just how different is the gospel of the water and the Spirit from the gospel of the Cross is when compared with each other? People do not know the difference between the two gospels, but they are in fact fundamentally different from each other. How wonderful would it be if pastors in this world were to preach and teach the gospel of the water and the Spirit to the congregation and thus blot out people's sins first, and then tell them to serve the Lord? But that is not what they do, but instead they just teach catechism and baptize anyone who attends church unconditionally. When a church member serves well, pastors make him a deacon, and if he is even more slavish and hypocritical, they make him an elder. If someone in the congregation fails at business, they tell him to go to a seminary saying that God is calling him through these hardships. Something is wrong here. Does a Christian go to a theological seminary and become a servant of God only if he turns out to be a failure?

We must know and believe clearly that Jesus is our God and our Savior. We must believe like this clearly. As the Bible says, *"You shall know the truth, and the truth shall make you free,"* we must unmistakably know 'this Truth', that is, the gospel of the water and the Spirit. Otherwise we will go straight to hell from our warm church pews. A famous pastor once said that while those outside church were going to hell because they did not know Jesus, the Devil takes countless Christians to hell from church pews. Even though this pastor had no clue as to how to be born again, his words were right literally because he knew that there were lots of Christians who were not born again. What do I mean when I say that countless people are going to hell from church pews? It means that even though people attend church regularly, those who don't or refuse to believe in the gospel of the water and the Spirit will most certainly go to hell.

So what is the most urgent thing that you must know and believe in? It is none other than the gospel of the water and the Spirit. One must first be born again before he can grow in his faith, and then he can do what is right and serve the Lord. Only if you believe in the gospel of the water and the Spirit, receive the remission of sins, and are born again spiritually, can you then really grow up. How then is it possible to grow spiritually when you are not even born again yet? Does a baby grow in the womb even when the mother is not pregnant?

This is called imaginary pregnancy, a condition in which a woman shows all the signs of pregrancy even though she is not actually pregnant. This happens to animals as well. My dog once had this condition. Her abdomen kept enlarging as though she were pregrant, but when I took her to the veterinary surgeon; they told me that she had imaginary pregnancy. Even animals go through this. When it comes to salvation, there are many Christians who display this salvation imaginary. It's ridiculous. They imagine themselves to have been saved even though they still have sin saying, "Jesus, You are my Savior. Even though I am sinful, because I believe in You, You approve me as being sinless." This is preposterous.

The Bible says, 'Believe in the Lord Jesus. You and your household will then be saved. Whoever receives Him, those who believe in His name, He gave them the right to become God's own children. Does this then mean that anyone is saved if he just receives Jesus in whatever way they decide?" No certainly not. Exactly how do we receive Him then? We receive Jesus only if we accept that He has saved us by coming to this earth by the gospel of the water and the Spirit. We must have a clear understanding of when, where, how and why Jesus became our Savior. Salvation is reached only if we believe in

Jesus with this clear and sound understanding. Is it okay to just say that we believe even if we don't really understand?

You can receive Jesus Christ properly only when you know in detail what He has done for you. If some complete stranger passed by your house, would you just recklessly open the door and welcome him in warmly? No, of course you won't. You would instead say, "What are you here for? What brought you here? If you don't have any business, please go away." Just as you would not welcome such a stranger to your home, likewise Jesus will not welcome anyone who does not really know Him. Unfortunately today's Christians do not really know Jesus even though they all claim to believe in Him and carry on like they do. They are, in essence, claiming to trust a total stranger. But such blind faith without understanding is useless; before you can really believe in Jesus, you must first understand what He has done to save you.

You must clearly realize that Jesus is your Savior who came to this earth by the gospel of the water and the Spirit. You must believe in this Truth. You shouldn't just wildly claim to believe in Jesus and preach about Him and do not actually know the gospel of the water and the Spirit. This gospel of the water and the Spirit is dynamite. It brings the joyful news that the Lord has blotted out all the sins of the world. Yet too many Christians are ignorant of this true gospel and say that anyone can be saved if he just believes in Jesus blindly.

When these kinds of Christians are asked, "Since you believe in Jesus, you must be sinless, right?" they say, "No, that's not necessarily the case. Although I believe in Jesus, I still have sin, because no one is without sin."

"Then what do you do about the daily sins you commit?" They reply:

"I've already obtained the remission of my original sin by

repenting, but I have to continue to offer prayers of repentance every day to receive the remission of my personal sins."

"So then you are telling me that you have sin?"

"Yes, I still have sin in my heart."

How can there be any sin left if the gospel of dynamite has already exploded and destroyed everything? This means that 'Christian sinners' still do not know the gospel of the water and the Spirit. These people really have no idea that Jesus is the Son of God and our Savior. The Lord came to this earth as the Son of God and spoke the gospel Truth of the water and the Spirit as the Prophet. And as the High Priest of the Kingdom of Heaven, He bore all the sins of mankind on His body 'once for all' by being baptized, shed all His blood on the Cross while shouldering the sins of this world, rose from the dead, and has through this saved us completely. We must have a clear understanding of this Truth and believe in it plainly. We must admit this gospel Truth with our hearts.

Do you acknowledge the gospel Truth of the water and the Spirit? While you should believe in God with your heart, this does not mean that you can just arbitarilarly throw away your head and allow yourself to be overwhelmed by your own emotions. If tears well up, don't let your own emotion overpower you. Why do you need to cry? You may be true to your feeling when you shed tears, but once the tears dry up, you will have a different feeling. When you cry, you feel overwhelmed by grief, but what happens when you stop crying? Does this feeling not disappear in little while? Don't you find yourself laughing at some funny TV show? Emotions change, but what about knowledge? Does it also change? No, it doesn't. What about the gospel Truth? Does the Truth change? No, it does not. That's why faith is not just about our emotions, but it is founded on our knowledge of the gospel Truth and our will to embrace this Truth. In other words, we must first know the Truth before we can believe in it and accept it willingly.

We must know the righteousness of God. We must know about righteousness, about sin and about judgment. What is the righteousness of God? It is the work of salvation that Jesus Christ has fulfilled for us. What is sin then? Not to or refusing to believe in this righteousness of God is the greatest sin. Not to believe in the gospel of the water and the Spirit is the most grievous of sins. The greatest sin is not to believe that Jesus is the Son of God, the Creator and the Savior, and not to believe that He came to this earth to save us through the gospel of the water and the Spirit. What about judgment then? It is the final judgment awaiting everyone: Whoever does not believe in the gospel Truth of the water and the Spirit will be cast into the everlasting fire of hell, but whoever believes in this Truth will enter into - everlasting life.

The Truth of salvation is plain and clear for everyone to understand and to believe in it. If you think it's too late, think again; there is still time for you to turn around even now and believe in the gospel of the water and the Spirit. All that you have to do is just listen to the Word now and believe in it. That is what faith is all about. Faith is always ongoing. It doesn't matter whether you have been a Christian for a long time or not, but what matters is whether or not you believe in the gospel Word of the water and the Spirit right now at this very moment.

I trust and pray that you would all believe in this true gospel and receive the remission of all your sins once and for all. ⌧

SERMON

15

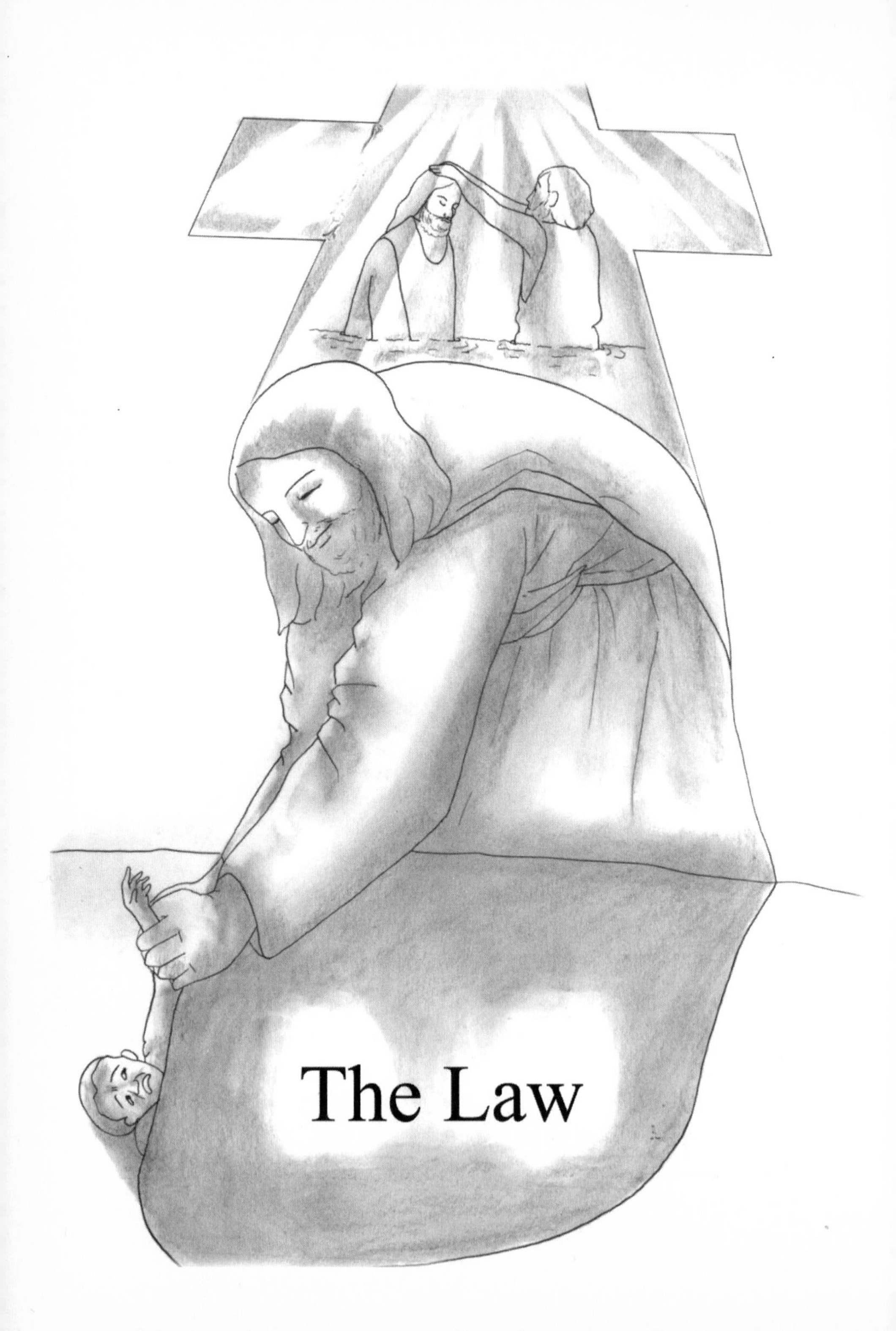
The Law

The Lord Resurrected Lazarus

< John 11:1-44 >

"Now a certain man was sick, Lazarus of Bethany, the town of Mary and her sister Martha. It was that Mary who anointed the Lord with fragrant oil and wiped His feet with her hair, whose brother Lazarus was sick. Therefore the sisters sent to Him, saying, 'Lord, behold, he whom you love is sick.' When Jesus heard that, He said, 'This sickness is not unto death, but for the glory of God, that the Son of God may be glorified through it.' Now Jesus loved Martha and her sister and Lazarus. So, when He heard that he was sick, He stayed two more days in the place where He was. Then after this He said to the disciples, 'Let us go to Judea again.' The disciples said to Him, 'Rabbi, lately the Jews sought to stone you, and are you going there again?' Jesus answered, 'Are there not twelve hours in the day? If anyone walks in the day, he does not stumble, because he sees the light of this world. But if one walks in the night, he stumbles, because the light is not in him.' These things He said, and after that He said to them, 'Our friend Lazarus sleeps, but I go that I may wake him up.' Then His disciples said, 'Lord, if he sleeps he will get well.' However, Jesus spoke of his death, but they thought that He was speaking about taking rest in sleep. Then Jesus said to them plainly, 'Lazarus is dead. And I am glad for your sakes that I was not there, that you may believe. Nevertheless let us go to him.' Then Thomas, who is called the Twin, said to his

fellow disciples, 'Let us also go, that we may die with Him.' So when Jesus came, He found that he had already been in the tomb four days. Now Bethany was near Jerusalem, about two miles away. And many of the Jews had joined the women around Martha and Mary, to comfort them concerning their brother. Now Martha, as soon as she heard that Jesus was coming, went and met Him, but Mary was sitting in the house. Now Martha said to Jesus, 'Lord, if you had been here, my brother would not have died. But even now I know that whatever you ask of God, God will give you.' Jesus said to her, 'Your brother will rise again.' Martha said to Him, 'I know that he will rise again in the resurrection at the last day.' Jesus said to her, 'I am the resurrection and the life. He who believes in me, though he may die, he shall live. And whoever lives and believes in me shall never die. Do you believe this?' She said to Him, 'Yes, Lord, I believe that you are the Christ, the Son of God, who is to come into the world.' And when she had said these things, she went her way and secretly called Mary her sister, saying, "The Teacher has come and is calling for you.' As soon as she heard that, she arose quickly and came to Him. Now Jesus had not yet come into the town, but was in the place where Martha met Him. Then the Jews who were with her in the house, and comforting her, when they saw that Mary rose up quickly and went out, followed her, saying, 'She is going to the tomb to weep there.' Then, when Mary came where Jesus was, and saw Him, she fell down at His feet, saying to Him, 'Lord, if you had been here, my brother would not have died.' Therefore, when Jesus saw her weeping, and the Jews who came with her weeping, He groaned in the spirit and was troubled. And He said, 'Where have you laid him?' They said to Him, 'Lord, come

and see.' Jesus wept. Then the Jews said, 'See how He loved him!' And some of them said, 'Could not this Man, who opened the eyes of the blind, also have kept this man from dying?' Then Jesus, again groaning in Himself, came to the tomb. It was a cave, and a stone lay against it. Jesus said, 'Take away the stone.' Martha, the sister of him who was dead, said to Him, 'Lord, by this time there is a stench, for he has been dead four days.' Jesus said to her, 'Did I not say to you that if you would believe you would see the glory of God?' Then they took away the stone from the place where the dead man was lying. And Jesus lifted up His eyes and said, 'Father, I thank you that you have heard Me. And I know that You always hear Me, but because of the people who are standing by I said this, that they may believe that You sent Me.' Now when He had said these things, He cried with a loud voice, 'Lazarus, come forth!' And he who had died came out bound hand and foot with graveclothes, and his face was wrapped with a cloth. Jesus said to them, 'Loose him, and let him go.'"

Through Lazarus' death that is so vividly described in today's Scripture passage, the Lord is saying the following to us: Every human being, no matter how meritorious he may be is limited in his faculty; therefore no one can be saved on his own without knowing and believing in the Word of God.

What Is the Lord Trying to Teach Us?

When Jesus was still on this earth, He displayed a special fondness to three siblings mentioned in today's Scripture reading namely, Mary, Martha, and Lazarus—therefore He used to visit their hometown Bethany quite often during his travels. One day while Jesus and His disciples were far away from Bethany, an urgent message was delivered to Jesus. It was a request from one of these siblings asking the Lord to urgently return to Bethany because Lazarus whom Jesus loved was very sick. However even after hearing this urgent message, Jesus tarried there for a further two days and did not return to Bethany right away.

Only on the third day He said to His disciples, *"Our friend Lazarus sleeps, but I go that I may wake him up."* The disciples misunderstood the Lord's words and thought that Lazarus had literally fallen asleep and they were going there to wake him up. It is quite clear to witness the disciples' ignorance of Jesus. Contrary to the disciples' interpretation of the words of our Lord when He said, "Lazarus is asleep," what He really meant was that Lazarus was dead, and that He was going to Bethany to resurrect him. When the Lord finally told them that Lazarus was dead, Thomas one of Jesus' disciples said, "Let's also go and die with the Lord." Since Jesus said to the disciples that He was going to Bethany to wake up Lazarus even though he was already dead, Thomas thought that Jesus was going there to face His own death, and so he thought that the disciples should also go there and face death together with their teacher. Here we see that Thomas was a loyal disciple. When viewed from the human point of view, Thomas was truly loyal, brave, innocent and worthy of emulation. But when we look at the faith of the disciples of Jesus from a spiritual viewpoint, we can see that they had as yet not matured spiritually.

Although the disciples followed Jesus to Bethany thinking that they were going to face their deaths, but Jesus went there to raise Lazarus from the dead. When someone is fast asleep; it would imply from a human prospective that he will wake up eventually. It's because the Lord was going to resurrect Lazarus from the dead that He drew an analogy to sleeping when He spoke about Lazarus' death. My fellow believers, you should all realize that this applies not only to Lazarus but to us as well. Like Lazarus, you and I and everyone else will not simply cease to exist when we die, but we will be raised from the dead by the Lord. That's because one day the Lord will come back to resurrect us perfectly from the dead. This passage where Jesus expressed death as 'sleeping' holds a profound implication concerning the resurrection.

When Jesus arrived at Bethany with the disciples, Martha, Lazarus' sister ran out to Jesus and fell down at His feet. And she said to Him, *"Lord, if you had been here, my brother would not have died. But even now I know that whatever you ask of God, God will give you."* Jesus then said to her, *"Your brother will rise again,"* to which Martha answered, *"I know that he will rise again in the resurrection at the last day."* Through the death of Lazarus Jesus wanted to make it known that He was the Lord of the Resurrection.

After this Jesus remained where He was and called for one of Lazarus sisters, that being Mary. Hearing that the Lord was looking for her, Mary rushed to the Lord hurriedly and said to Him, *"Lord, if you had been here, my brother would not have died."* We can see Mary's heart while wailing at the feet of the Lord, probably with mixed emotions that included some resentment towards the Lord for showing up so late. She was able to say this because she clearly had the faith that the Lord could have saved Lazarus. Everyone around that village wept, not just Mary and Martha but also all the Jews who had come to pay their respects. The Bible says that Jesus was moved to tears when He saw them crying.

The Bible records no less than three instances when our Lord wept while living on this earth. He wept once over the death of Lazarus. And He wept while praying to God His Father on the Mount of Gethsemane. It is written in Hebrews 5:7-8, *"Who, in the days of His flesh, when He had offered up prayers and supplications, with vehement cries and tears to Him who was able to save Him from death, and was heard because of His godly fear, though He was a Son, yet He learned obedience by the things which He suffered."*

The Lord also wept when He entered Jerusalem this was to lay down His life knowing that Israel would be destroyed. He wept over the fate of Israel, foreseeing how it would be completely conquered and destroyed, and how its people would all be taken into captivity and slavery. It's written in Luke 19:41-44: *"Now as He drew near, He saw the city and wept over it, saying, 'If you had known, even you, especially in this your day, the things that make for your peace! But now they are hidden from your eyes. For days will come upon you when your enemies will build an embankment around you, surround you and close you in on every side, and level you, and your children within you, to the ground; and they will not leave in you one stone upon another, because you did not know the time of your visitation.'"*

As we can see from this passage, our Lord was deeply saddened that people refused listen to His Word even though He had personally had come to this earth. It hurt His heart tremendously to think about the coming woes that these people would soon face. That's why He wept when looking at the city of Jerusalem and its people who were destined for destruction. We need to remember although the Lord is God Himself; we can see here that He has warm human feelings just like us.

Returning to today's Scripture passage, we read how the Lord groaned in the spirit and was greatly troubled over Lazarus' death. Distressed to see how His loved ones were weeping in despair, He also wept in his heart. Of course when Jesus said earlier that He was going to Bethany to wake up Lazarus, He meant that He was going to resurrect him, but Jesus experienced grief in His heart over the sadness of the people He loved. It's written, *"And He said, 'Where have you laid him?' They said to Him, 'Lord, come and see.' Jesus wept. Then the Jews said, 'See how He loved him!' And some of them said, 'Could not this Man, who opened the eyes of the blind, also have kept this man from dying?' Then Jesus, again groaning in Himself, came to the tomb. It was a cave, and a stone lay against it. Jesus said, 'Take away the stone'" (John 11:34-39).*

We can clearly see from this passage had Jesus been with Lazarus, he would not have died. That's because Jesus is the Almighty God with the power to raise the dead to life and heal the blind and the sick. However Jesus had not been in Bethany at this time, and even when He heard that Lazarus was critically ill, He deliberately stayed for another two more days before finally coming. My fellow believers, what do you think was the reason for this? It was for the glory of God.

Does the Word of the Lord Have Power?

Having shared with the people's grief, Jesus now sought to raise Lazarus back to life, and so He asked, *"Where have you laid him?"* He then was led to Lazarus' stone tomb and said, *"Take away the stone."* Then Martha, Lazarus' sister said to Him, *"Lord, by this time there is a stench, for he has been dead four days."* The people there were thinking, "There is already a foul smell as it's been four days since Lazarus' dead. It's an impossible task, no matter how powerful the Lord really is." Herein lies the reason why our Lord had put off coming to Bethany for these two days after He heard that Lazarus was so very ill. It's here that we can solve the puzzling question as to why Jesus had not come before Lazarus' had died. It was the Lord's clear intention to manifest the glory of God to us through this incredible incident. He said to Martha, *"Did I not say to you that if you would believe you would see the glory of God?"* Jesus then prayed to God the Father and then afterwards said in a loud voice, *"Lazarus, come forth!"* Then Lazarus, who had been dead, walked out of the grave with his hands and feet still wrapped in linen.

My fellow believers, we need to examine carefully here what the Lord is trying to say to us. Our Lord is telling us that human beings are fundamentally incapable of solving the problem of their sins on their own. In other words, no one can save himself from sin no matter how virtuous and decent his character may be. That's because unlike God, human beings are insufficient and their faculty is limited. The Bible therefore says, *"There is no other name under heaven given among men by which we must be saved" (Acts 4:12)*. There is no name other than Jesus Christ that can grant true salvation to mankind. This is what the Bible is telling us.

For you and me gathered here today; it is only by faith and our belief in the God given gospel of the water and the Spirit that we have been saved from all our sins? Yet despite this fact are there not countless people still trying to solve the problem of their sins through their own efforts? Don't many Christians expect that once enough time has gone by since they had believed in Jesus, their characters would somehow change and they would not commit so much sin? But we need to remember there is nothing good that man can expect from within himself. Our only hope is found in Jesus Christ, the Almighty who came by the gospel of the water and the Spirit. No matter how well we know the righteousness of the Lord and no matter how we have received the complete remission of sins, our flesh is still flesh and the Spirit is still the Spirit. Just because we have believed in Jesus for years, are our characters changed so much that when someone strikes our left cheek we can somehow turn the right cheek and ask him to strike that side as well? That is certainly not the case. Our insufficient flesh still remains insufficient. We must therefore always trust in the righteousness of the Lord and rely in it until the day the life of our flesh expires. Only then can we live by faith until the end of this world.

Here lies the very reason why it is so absolutely imperative for us to continue to rely on the righteousness of the Lord. Through our own human righteousness we can never be saved from our sins nor be perfected. No matter how long we may have led our lives of faith in Christ, we must continue to trust and rely on the righteousness of God, and we must keep our hearts sinless by believing in the gospel of the water and the Spirit. If we fail to hold onto the power of this gospel even for a moment, then we can never say that we are righteous people.

We must realize that through today's Scripture passage, our Lord is telling us that salvation from the sins of the world is neither attained by trying to keep the Law nor reached through human virtues or willpower. Therefore we should not rely on our own righteousness. If you rely on your own righteousness, then no matter how hard you try to be morally upright, you will falter and will only stress you out even more.

In other words, trying to be saved from your sins through your own effort is all in vain. It is nothing more than a misconceived notion for us to think, "I've been saved from sin by believing in the righteousness of the Lord, but even so, would not my life somehow be better off if I just tried to be more virtuous with my acts?"

Although you do rely on the righteousness of Lord, I can sometimes see that some of you still cannot rely on it 100%. This is because there still is some righteousness of your own flesh remaining in you. It is because you rely on the righteousness of God only to the extent that your own righteousness is not undermined, and you still want to live on your own. But make no mistake: This is a completely flawed thought of the flesh. When we rely 100% on the righteousness of the Lord, it's not enough to rely just to a certain extent. We must rely on it entirely for 100 percent. This means that we should continue to abide by our faith in the righteousness of the Lord. If you live even just for an hour without being mindful of the righteousness of the Lord, then you will fall into your own carnal thoughts and end up living your life with a great deal of regrets.

A life like this cannot be said to be a proper life of a righteous person. Unless we rely on the Lord's righteousness every minute of the day, we cannot call ourselves as those who follow the light illuminated by the Lord. Yet there are times when our carnal thoughts arise unconsciously in us which makes us think, "I am now sick and tired of this life of faith. I've been a good Christian all this time, and so I think I can now stop living out my faith. From now on I will lead my life the way I see fit!" So there will be times when some of us will end up leading this kind of life, but this is foolishness. Why is it foolishness? It's foolish because it is an attempt to serve God with one's own carnal efforts. When this happens we end up living a life that hides the glory of God rather than glorifying Him. We have received the remission of sins by believing in the righteousness of the Lord, but in our flesh we are still imperfect and not strong enough, therefore we feel the limits of our insufficient selves. Isn't this true? But this is only natural. Although we have received the remission of sins by believing in the gospel of the water and the Spirit, it does not mean that our flesh has been changed, that is why there is all the more reason for us to rein in our own thoughts by trusting in the righteousness of God. In our flesh we are always insufficient, always weak and always wicked. It's because that is the fundamental nature of the flesh of man.

Fellow believers I am now going to speak to spiritual people. It's a known fact that those who are physically healthy are also mentally healthy. Amongst our organs it's the liver that helps us to diffuse stress, and healthy people have a healthy liver, and so they can cope with stress better and their minds are more relaxed. Since they can manage themselves quite well, they have enough room to be more understanding of others. But what about those whose health is not so good, and whose livers are failing them? When they get stressed out, their bodily organs become dysfunctional and even their mental health deteriorates. They want to be more understanding of others, but their tolerance levels are very limited, and so when they face even the slightest outside pressure or annoyance, they crumble. After all how could anyone be sympathetic to others when he is struggling with his own physical ailments?

Whilst on this subject, the so-called sages or the so called virtuous of this world must have had quite healthy livers. They were after all so patient and understanding that they were called "sages." However fellow believers, these people neither knew nor believed in the gospel of the water and the Spirit, and therefore they cannot be called 'truly righteous people'. Even these so-called sages must have had human limitations; it's just that we are not aware of them. There must have been some stress that they could not resolve even with their healthy livers, and their minds probably were not that relaxed. Everyone is the same; the sages of the world are no different from you and me.

In our flesh we all are imperfect. We are nothing unless we rely on the righteousness of the Lord. If we don't trust in His righteousness even for a moment, then we cannot call ourselves righteous people before God, nor can we stand unashamed before Him, that is why we must always believe in the gospel of the water and the Spirit and rely on it all the time. If we know ourselves well and recognize the righteousness of God before His presence, then we will always remain righteous.

Let's return to today's Scripture passage. Lazarus was laid to rest in a cave carved out of the rock and the entrance was blocked and sealed with a large boulder. It was customary for Israelites to carve out a cave out of a rocky mountain to bury their dead, and seal the entrance with a boulder. The dead body was then protected from scavenging animals and went through the natural decomposition process inside the hot cave. It's because of this Jewish custom that the entrance to Lazarus' grave was blocked and sealed off. When the people removed this boulder as instructed by the Lord, He said in a loud voice, *"Lazarus, come forth!"*

What happened then? Lazarus who was dead got up and walked out of the grave, all wrapped in linen cloth. The Lord had told the people clearly that they would see the glory of God if they believed in Him, and at that moment they indeed saw God's glory. Lazarus' resurrection from the dead was to the glory of God. On the last day God will also resurrect our dead bodies just like this. And we know that if anyone believes in the Word of Jesus Christ right now, God the Father will resurrect both his soul and body and clothe him in His glory. I give all my thanks to God for this.

Legalistic Faith That Is Not Placed in the Righteousness of God Cannot Be the Real Faith

Today the Lord is telling us that no life can be saved through the Law or anything else. He said that salvation is possible only by His power, and the Lord did in fact save a life. When the Lord said, *"Lazarus, come forth,"* Lazarus came out of the cave grave wrapped in linen cloth. Our Lord has such power.

My fellow believers and me included, it is only by the righteousness of the Lord that we have received salvation from sin, not by anything else. It is because the Lord has raised us back to life by His power of salvation that we have obtained our salvation from sin. In other words, the Lord has brought back to life our souls that had been dead because of our sins, and He has given us this new life. It is the Lord who has brought us back to life, which neither the Law nor any good deeds of our own could ever achieve. Our existence is such that without the righteousness of God, we can never be saved from sin, and even if we were saved, we could not be made perfect unless we believed in the Lord. Our righteousness is imperfect, but the righteousness of the Lord is perfect and everlasting.

What would happen if we did not believe in this righteousness of God to the end? We would then always remain imperfect; and will be nothing more than piles of sin. That is why we believe that the righteousness of the Lord is far greater than our own righteousness. We trust in the Lord's righteousness every single day, every hour, every minute and every second. We are now living before God having been made perfect and have attained new life by believing in the righteousness of the Lord. You and I are such people, those who believe in the gospel of the water and the Spirit.

As human beings we often find ourselves bound by our own weaknesses. Even though we have received the remission of sins through the gospel of the water and the Spirit, we still tend to tie ourselves down with our own thoughts. This is likened as to how Lazarus' dead body was tightly wrapped with linen cloth. When Lazarus died he was wrapped in bandages from his head to his toes. That's why when Lazarus walked out of the tomb when the Lord called him out; he walked out alive still wrapped and bound in linen cloth.

What do you think the Lord is trying to teach us about this incident? The implication here is that even if you are brought back to life, unless you remove that which binds you, you will not be able to lead your life properly. That is why the Lord told the disciples to unbind Lazarus and let him go free, so that he would live a new life.

Spiritually speaking fellow believers, we were exactly like Lazarus. Just as the Lord raised Lazarus back to life with His Word, so He has also raised us back to life with the gospel of the water and the Spirit. He has saved us perfectly not by the Law but by the forever-unchanging righteousness of God. However not everything ends with this. We have been saved from sin, but the next important step is to be freed from what binds us, just as Lazarus could live normally only when the bound linen around his body was unbound. Only then can we lead our lives properly as righteous people. We need to know this, it does not matter just how we are saved from sin and have become righteous people if you still have many ties around you that bind you then you cannot possibly fulfill your role as a righteous person. By our faith in the Lord, we must set ourselves free from whatever binds us i.e. from our weaknesses, our wickedness and our shortcomings etc.

We must continue to meditate on the righteousness of the Lord and believe in it with our whole hearts. Although the power of our faith will last forever once we believe, but as human beings we are still at times prone to be bound by ourselves, and therefore as often as we are bound, we have to untie ourselves by trusting in the gospel of the water and the Spirit. I therefore ask you to examine yourself carefully to see what it is that binds you down now. If you are bound by legalistic beliefs or fleshly thoughts, then you must set yourself free from them as soon as possible. That's because only then can you live an upright life abiding in God.

My fellow believers, to be freed from our bondages we must look toward the righteousness of our Lord. The Lord saved you and me because we believed in the gospel of the water and the Spirit. This righteousness of God is the forever-unchanging Truth of salvation. The Lord said, *"I am the Alpha and the Omega, the Beginning and the End" (Revelation 22:13)*. As this passage makes it clear that the Lord is the only God of salvation who never changes from the beginning to the end. This Lord has saved us from sin. Believing that the Lord has saved us from sin through the gospel of the water and the Spirit, we must surrender ourselves into God's possession forever. The only way for us to escape from sin, our weaknesses, and our insufficiencies is to live righteously and to believe in the righteousness of the Lord and trust in the Lord.

The Lord's Word is indeed right when it says that no one can be saved from sin through the Law. We can never attain our salvation from sin by keeping the Law. That's because it's impossible for anyone in this world to keep the Law to perfection. Yet even as we realize this we still allow ourselves to be bound by the Law. We think to ourselves, "How can I lead a life of faith when I cannot even keep this one little commandment? When I am so insufficient, my circumstances become so very challenging, and I feel an abject failure, therefore it too preposterous for me to even try to lead a life of faith?"

My fellow believers, whenever you have thoughts like this, I admonish you to remember what our Lord said in today's Scripture reading: *"Take away the stone."* The stone implies our old faith. We are now new creatures in Christ because our old faith was removed. The Law is definitely not the way to reach salvation from sin. Just as the stone was removed, so must you also remove your legalistic faith and believe in the righteousness of God. It is only by the righteousness of God that we have been saved, not by anything else. The gospel Truth of the water and the Spirit teaches us that it is the righteousness of God that has brought us back to life, and that the salvation of God is what has delivered us. I admonish you all too once again believe in this gospel Truth at this hour and to thank God for it. And I ask you to look toward the Lord's righteousness. You will then begin to experience a renewal of your heart, new strength springing forth, and the God of Truth being with you, as though your liver was restored to health and all your stress was removed.

It is by the grace of the God-given salvation that we gain new strength and live once again. That we are actually serving the Lord and even alive now is all thanks to the grace of God. Were it not for the grace of God, how could we who were all sinners, have ever become the Lord's sheep? Unless we believe in the gospel of the water and the Spirit, we could never ever practice the righteousness of the Lord, and could not ever follow Him? If we can barely cope with our own lives, how is it that we could ever save other souls? The very fact that we believe in God's righteousness and we now abide in God is itself all due to God's grace. That is why today as always, we admit in our hearts that it is by the grace of God that we are alive, and we live forward by trusting in this. Were it not for the grace of God, we would have all perished in both body and spirit by now. We were all sinners destined forever to wander lost in sin.

We often come across people who are strong-willed or those who have accomplished a huge amount of virtuous deeds, all rejecting the righteousness of God. These people are the foolish ones. I am absolutely convinced without a doubt in my mind that it is fundamentally impossible for any human being to perfect himself no matter how hard he tries in his flesh. One could try all his life, but it's simply impossible and a waste of time. Many people think, "If I reach a certain point in my efforts to escape from evil, I should be ok." But this is completely misguided. Man's flesh is unchangeable. That's why it is important to remember to always live in the grace of God. Never forgetting the Lord, we must always abide in His redemption and look toward the Lord who has saved us from our sins; made us His children and His people, and has become our own Shepherd. You and I must live a life like this without fail.

My fellow believers, we can have true faith only if we look toward the righteousness of the Lord in our lives. From the account where Lazarus was raised from the dead, what spiritual lessons have been able to learn there from? Our lessons are the following: "Salvation can never be reached through the righteousness of man. There is no one in this world who can keep the Law to perfection, nor anyone who can live by the Law. Salvation can never be attained through this Law."

It is this truth of salvation that the Lord is teaching us at this hour. Our Lord said, *"Lazarus, come forth,"* and Lazarus was indeed raised back to life. It is no one else but the Lord who saved Lazarus and it is also the Lord who has saved you and me from sin through His Word. It's because the Lord loved you and me that He saved us from all the sins of the world through the gospel of the water and the Spirit. Let us then always remember that we must rely on this righteousness of Lord, and let us all live by faith.

May God bless you all! Halleluiah! ✉

SERMON

16

Let Us Live with Hope of Everlasting Life And Resurrection Given by the Lord

< John 11:15-46 >

"'And I am glad for your sakes that I was not there, that you may believe. Nevertheless let us go to him.' Then Thomas, who is called the Twin, said to his fellow disciples, 'Let us also go, that we may die with Him.' So when Jesus came, He found that he had already been in the tomb four days. Now Bethany was near Jerusalem, about two miles away. And many of the Jews had joined the women around Martha and Mary, to comfort them concerning their brother. Now Martha, as soon as she heard that Jesus was coming, went and met Him, but Mary was sitting in the house. Now Martha said to Jesus, 'Lord, if you had been here, my brother would not have died. But even now I know that whatever you ask of God, God will give you.' Jesus said to her, 'Your brother will rise again.' Martha said to Him, 'I know that he will rise again in the resurrection at the last day.' Jesus said to her, 'I am the resurrection and the life. He who believes in me, though he may die, he shall live. And whoever lives and believes in me shall never die. Do you believe this?' She said to Him, 'Yes, Lord, I believe that you are the Christ, the Son of God, who

is to come into the world.' And when she had said these things, she went her way and secretly called Mary her sister, saying, "The Teacher has come and is calling for you.' As soon as she heard that, she arose quickly and came to Him. Now Jesus had not yet come into the town, but was in the place where Martha met Him. Then the Jews who were with her in the house, and comforting her, when they saw that Mary rose up quickly and went out, followed her, saying, 'She is going to the tomb to weep there.' Then, when Mary came where Jesus was, and saw Him, she fell down at His feet, saying to Him, 'Lord, if you had been here, my brother would not have died.' Therefore, when Jesus saw her weeping, and the Jews who came with her weeping, He groaned in the spirit and was troubled. And He said, 'Where have you laid him?' They said to Him, 'Lord, come and see.' Jesus wept. Then the Jews said, 'See how He loved him!' And some of them said, 'Could not this Man, who opened the eyes of the blind, also have kept this man from dying?' Then Jesus, again groaning in Himself, came to the tomb. It was a cave, and a stone lay against it. Jesus said, 'Take away the stone.' Martha, the sister of him who was dead, said to Him, 'Lord, by this time there is a stench, for he has been dead four days.' Jesus said to her, 'Did I not say to you that if you would believe you would see the glory of God?' Then they took away the stone from the place where the dead man was lying. And Jesus lifted up His eyes and said, 'Father, I thank you that you have heard Me. And I know that You always hear Me, but because of the people who are standing by I said this, that they may believe that You sent Me.' Now when He had said these things, He cried with a loud voice, 'Lazarus, come forth!' And he who had died came out bound hand and foot

with grave clothes, and his face was wrapped with a cloth. Jesus said to them, 'Loose him, and let him go.' Then many of the Jews who had come to Mary, and had seen the things Jesus did, believed in Him. But some of them went away to the Pharisees and told them the things Jesus did."

Jesus Raised Lazarus from the Dead

John chapter 11 gives the account of the death of Lazarus as an example to explain the resurrection of the dead. The story developed here starts with three siblings who lived together, a brother named Lazarus and two sisters named Martha and Mary, and it begins with Lazarus falling gravely ill and dying from it. The key protagonist in John chapter 11 is Mary. Through this account, the Lord is speaking about the resurrection to come.

As described in today's Scripture reading, even after the Lord heard of Lazarus' serious condition, He stayed for a further two more days and did not go to see Lazarus right away. When He was finally on His way to Bethany He said, *"Our friend Lazarus sleeps, but I go that I may wake him up."* Amongst the disciples at that time was a man named Thomas, also called the Twin, and this disciple thought that Jesus was asking them to go to Lazarus to all there die together. But the Lord said clearly, "Lazarus is dead, but I go to wake him up." Thomas clearly misunderstood what the Lord was talking about, but on the other hand in some ways he seems to have been the most loyal disciple of them all. The other disciples understood what Jesus meant when He asked them to go with Him to wake Lazarus up, but Thomas misunderstood this to mean that Jesus was asking them to go to face there deaths. In fact Thomas was a man of little faith until he actually met the resurrected Jesus physically. He is the disciple who believed in Jesus' resurrection only after he had touched Him by putting his fingers into His side.

Although Jesus said, "Lazarus is not dead but asleep," He was informed that Lazarus had already died. Martha then spoke to Jesus in a resentful way, *"If only you had been here, my brother would not have died."* As we can see from today's Scripture passage, there was some resentment when Martha said to Jesus, "Why did you not hurry? You lingered for two long days and did not come until now, only after Lazarus had died."

However despite this Martha also said, *"Even now I know that whatever you ask of God, God will give you."* She too believed that Jesus was the Son of God and the Savior. When the Lord said to her, *"Your brother will rise again,"* Martha replied, *"I know that he will rise again in the resurrection at the last day."* This belief is also held by all the saints attending God's Church today.

Jesus then asked Martha, *"I am the resurrection and the life. He who believes in me, though he may die, he shall live. And whoever lives and believes in me shall never die. Do you believe this?"* Then Martha confessed to Him, *"Yes, Lord. I believe that you are the Christ, the Son of God, who is to come into the world."* When the Lord said, *"Your brother will rise again,"* He meant it literally. But Martha still had not realized that He was about to raise him from the dead that very day. That's why she confessed, "I believe that you will raise him on the last day and give him eternal life." In other words, although Martha believed that the Lord would resurrect her brother and give him everlasting life, she could not ever imagine that Jesus would raise him right away. Having taken Jesus' Word from her own perspective and digested it in her mind, Martha then told her sister that the Teacher was calling for her.

As soon as Mary heard this, she got up and dashed over to Jesus. It is written, *"Now Jesus had not yet come into the town, but was in the place where Martha met Him. Then the Jews who were with her in the house, and comforting her, when they saw that Mary rose up quickly and went out, followed her, saying, 'She is going to the tomb to weep there.' Then, when Mary came where Jesus was, and saw Him, she fell down at His feet, saying to Him, 'Lord, if you had been here, my brother would not have died.'"*

Do you also have the faith to believe that whenever you encounter any problems, the Lord will solve it for you? It's a great faith to believe that the Lord will take care of your problems without fail. Mary had such faith; she believed that if the Lord had been there before her brother's death, he would not have died. I wonder if you also have faith like this today.

Let us continue with today's Scripture reading. It's written here that Mary, Martha, and everyone in the town were crying in grief, and when Jesus witnessed this He too was troubled to see this. Jesus knew how heart-broken they all were. He shared the grief of not only Mary and Martha, but also of the friends and neighbors of these three siblings and all the Jews in that village. People there wept while remembering Lazarus's living days while they comforted Mary and Martha. It must have been unavoidable for Jesus to be troubled to see this. It must have hurt His heart to see how all these people were crying because they were powerless to do anything even though they wanted to help, and that must be why Jesus wept.

Then the Lord asked them where they had laid Lazarus. There were a handful of occasions when Jesus wept while on this earth, and here we can see just how much Jesus loved this family and Lazarus in particular. The people there were wondering, "Jesus opened the eyes of the blind, and so could He not have also kept Lazarus from dying?" And Jesus when hearing this groaned within Himself seeing that His people were completely helpless before their deaths.

When Jesus reached Lazarus' tomb He told the people to remove the stone blocking the tomb. In Jewish culture at that time, it was customary to lay the dead in a stone tomb. From the ancient forefathers to the descendants to come, all kinfolks' bodies were laid in a cave or tomb and the grave was blocked off with a large stone, and in time the corpses would rot away leaving only bones.

When the Lord ordered the stone to be removed, Martha said that there would be a stench as three days had already gone by since Lazarus' was laid to rest. But Jesus repeated, "Did I not say that if you believed in My Word, you would see the glory of God? Take away that stone." So Martha obliged and organized the stone to be removed, and Jesus then looked up to the heavens and prayed: *"Father, I thank you that you have heard Me. And I know that you always hear me, but because of the people who are standing by I said this, that they may believe that you sent me."* After praying like this, Jesus shouted out in a loud voice, *"Lazarus, come forth!"* At this command, Lazarus arose from the dead and walked out of the grave still wrapped in linen like a bound up mummy. The Lord then ordered the people to loosen him so that he could walk freely, and the many people who witnessed this event came to believe in the Lord.

Those Who Believe in the Righteousness of God Will Live Again

That there is 'the resurrection' means that those who have been born again by believing in the gospel of the water and the Spirit will for sure live again. We must realize that all those who were born again through the gospel of the water and the Spirit will be resurrected for sure when the Lord comes again. God will raise them back to life and make them live again enjoying the glory and splendor of Heaven. The Lord has shown the righteous that they will live again. We must latch on to this that there is resurrection for us, and that we will live again. Do you believe that we will live forever? Do you believe that the Lord has given us everlasting life?

Resurrection is found amongst the righteous. If we are to attain new life after death and reign for a thousand years with the Lord, we ought to think about what we should do for our remaining lives on this earth. The Lord said that He would give us eternal life. Just as He enabled us to be born again, He will also give us everlasting life. We will be raised back to life after death, and we will live forever with the Lord. When we think about living forever above all else, we are compelled to think about what it is that we should live for now, what should be the purpose of our live now, and what we should do whilst we are still alive on this earth.

There are several passages in the Bible addressing this issue. In particular when we turn to 1 Corinthians 15:48-58, we can verify what the Word says about our resurrection: *"As was the man of dust, so also are those who are made of dust; and as is the heavenly Man, so also are those who are heavenly. And as we have borne the image of the man of dust, we shall also bear the image of the heavenly Man. Now this I say, brethren, that flesh and blood cannot inherit the kingdom of God; nor does corruption inherit incorruption. Behold, I tell you a mystery: We shall not all sleep, but we shall all be changed—in a moment, in the twinkling of an eye, at the last trumpet. For the trumpet will sound, and the dead will be raised incorruptible, and we shall be changed. For this corruptible must put on incorruption, and this mortal must put on immortality. So when this corruptible has put on incorruption, and this mortal has put on immortality, then shall be brought to pass the saying that is written: 'Death is swallowed up in victory.' 'O Death, where is your sting? O Hades, where is your victory?' The sting of death is sin, and the strength of sin is the law. But thanks are to God, who gives us the victory through our Lord Jesus Christ. Therefore, my beloved brethren, be steadfast, immovable, always abounding in the work of the Lord, knowing that your labor is not in vain in the Lord."* Like this the Apostle Paul wrote in His letters that when the last trumpet sounds, the dead will be raised incorruptible, and we will also be transformed.

Those Who Will Partake in the First Resurrection

Everyone who is 'truly born again' will partake in the first resurrection. As a sign of the end of the Great Tribulation, the last trumpet symbolizes the final day of planet earth. The Bible says that when the corruptible puts on incorruption, death will be swallowed up in victory. This means that the born-again will live again. In other words, it refers to the resurrection of the born-again. That's why the dead are expressed as 'sleeping' rather than dead. Those who are asleep can wake up again, but those who are dead cannot wake up, and so in the Lord's sight, our death is like sleeping; He will therefore raise us back to life. Such amazing blessings await all of us who believe. That is why the Apostle Paul told us, "Be steadfast, immovable, always abounding in the work of the Lord, and knowing that your labor is not in vain in the Lord." Put differently, Paul is telling us that that since our death will be only temporary and we will be resurrected to receive eternal life, we should think about how we ought to live now until that time.

There also are passages in the Bible that speak about the salvation and everlasting life God has given us. It's written in Ephesians 1:4-6: *"Just as He chose us in Him before the foundation of the world, that we should be holy and without blame before Him in love, having predestined us to adoption as sons by Jesus Christ to Himself, according to the good pleasure of His will, to the praise of the glory of His grace, by which He made us accepted in the Beloved."* As you can see, this passage uses the expression "glory" here. It refers to a magnificently shining life. That the Lord has given us the grace of resurrection means that He will raise us from the dead to live with Him forever, so that we may praise the glory His grace. In other words, it literally means that we will live a glorious life praising God for all His blessings, having received the God-given gifts of everlasting life, salvation and the resurrection.

I often think about what exactly a glorious life entails, and what exactly is meant by the resurrection. What is everlasting life? It is immortality. When God raises us back to life, He will not resurrect us into imperfection. Instead, we will put on the same spiritual body as that of Christ, as our imperfections will be perfected, the corruptible will put on incorruption and our bodies will never fall ill again.

The Bible also tells us that the lives of the born-again will be to the praise of the glory of God's grace. This means God will make us praise Him not only for saving us from sin but also blessing us to live a glorious life with Him. What is a glorious life? When we grow old, our bodies will fail us like a worn out tent and will eventually perish. However, because we believe in the gospel of the water and the Spirit we have not only been saved from our sins, but our dead bodies will also live again. None other than this is 'the resurrection'.

What will we do after the resurrection then? What will we do when we eventually go to the Kingdom of the Lord? We will live a heavenly life, the perfect and glorious life of God. Glory means brilliance, and therefore it implies that we will live unimaginably splendid lives. Such a life is beyond our comprehension, just as we cannot quite grasp just how life is in Buckingham Palace, because none of us has ever lived there.

Can You Imagine the Privileges of Living in the Kingdom of God?

I once had very expensive Chinese noodle dish costing over $70, when they normally cost only about $3 in most places in Korea. This happened when I visited a hospital in Seoul. I was accompanied by several coworkers, and as it was getting near lunch time, we looked for a restaurant, but we couldn't find any parking lot. So we decided to go to a nearby hotel where parking was readily available, as most hotels in Korea usually have a buffet restaurant. But when we got on the elevator, we saw from the hotel guide that there was a Chinese restaurant on the second floor, and so we went to this restaurant. When we sat down and opened the menu, we saw that a bowl of Chinese noodle cost $7 at that restaurant. It was a bit more expensive than the usual price, but we decided to try it anyways and ordered the dish. But before the Chinese noodle dish was served, we were served with other smaller dishes. So we ate each dish whenever it was served, and the main dish was served in the end. After finishing the main dish, we asked if this was all, and the server told us that it was the last dish. So we asked for the bill and to our utter surprise, we found out that the meal actually cost $70 each rather than $7. We had thought $7 was expensive enough, but the meal cost no less than $70. I asked the waiter to bring the menu once again, and I found that I had misread its price. But haggling over the price would only have embarrassed us, and so we ended up paying the full amount. This happened because we were totally clueless; we simply did not know just how expensive some restaurant could be, since we had never been to such a posh restaurant before.

Let me tell you another story, but this time it's about a former president of South Korea. This episode happened when President Park Chung Hee, who had come to power by a military coup in 1961, visited a power plant in Busan almost 40 years ago. At that time the road to that power plant was untared, nor was there any trees planted along the road. Korea in those days was such a poor country that many people were still relying on firewood for heating, and so understandably there were hardly any tree left standing.

But when it was announced that the President was visiting that power plant, huge pine trees were planted along the route. Actually they were not really planted, as the trees were cut at the stump and just planted into the ground alongside this road. As though this was not enough, the whole town went through a major cleanup to prepare for the President's visit, and people lined up along the road to wave the flag. In those days South Korea was under such an authoritarian regime that people didn't even dare to mention the President by his name. In less than a month since the President's visit, the road was all paved. But the pine trees were all taken out to be used as firewood. Rumor had it that on his way to the power plant, the President complained to his staff about the bumpy ride, and based on this comment alone his underlings had the road paved without delay. This episode illustrates the privileges enjoyed by the powerful. Yet we cannot quite grasp it because we have never led such a privileged life.

Recently I saw a documentary on the life cycle of a dragonfly on TV. From this documentary I learned that dragonflies lay their eggs underwater, and once hatched the larvae continue to live in the water for a while feeding on tiny insects. But eventually they climb up a tree and morph or change into fully-grown dragonflies, opening their wings to fly. Dragonflies have four wings, but amazingly each wing moves independently. They can maneuver in the air freely, sometimes by flapping just one wing, and they can make sharp, 90-degree turns and swoop in all of a sudden. How mysterious and glorious is it that the larvae living underwater can fly when fully matured? The same thing happens with maggots. If you go to an unplumbed outhouse, you can see maggots swimming in the refuse below and crawling up in time to become flies. After repeatedly falling down and crawling back up again, they finally make it out and turn into flies. Isn't this what's really glorious?

Can you now appreciate even if by a small degree what the Bible means when it says, *"To the praise of the glory of His grace"*? Do you feel that while you can understand everything about grace, salvation and everlasting life, you still cannot really grasp what is meant by a glorious life, as you've never lived a life like this before?

Didn't Jesus pass through a stone wall after His

resurrection? When Thomas was told about Jesus' resurrection, he was reluctant to believe the fact saying that he will not believe until he actually puts his hand into Jesus' side. Jesus then walked through the wall and appeared before Thomas, rebuking him, "Why are you so faithless? Put your hand into my side and your finger into the wounds of my hands. Believe that I have risen from the dead." Only after Thomas touched Him by putting his hand into the side of Jesus did he finally believe in His resurrection.

Although you may say that you just cannot grasp what is meant by a glorious life as you've never lived such a life, let me assure you that when you put on your spiritual body, you will be able to transcend time and space. Our Lord rose from the dead, and He fulfilled everything exactly as He had said. Moreover He rules over all creation, both spiritual and physical, and everything in the universe submits to Him. Just how glorious is this then? We too will live such a glorious life because we have been saved by believing in the Lord.

I give all my praise to Jesus who solved the problem of sin and death and rose from the dead. I praise Him for saving us from the sins of the world. Just as it is written in the Book of Revelation that the people of God will look down on the earth from the sea of glass and praise God, countless people in His Kingdom will praise God for saving them. They will praise God for giving them heavenly bodies that will never fall ill again, for granting them unsurpassed privileges as the children of God, and for allowing them to live glorious and splendid lives as kings. This are not all; as there is so much more grace of glory that the Lord has given us, we will all live glorious lives praising the righteousness of God. This is the honor reserved for the righteous. For the believers in the gospel of the water and the Spirit, their honor is found in the very glory of

God.

I myself, though a righteous man sometimes feel frustrated because I am still insufficient and many things do not go my way, but in the end I will live a glorious life. I will never die but enjoy splendor and glory forever.

When you turn to the Book of Revelation, you will see a beautiful place described there a place that has houses built with 12 precious stones surrounded by a sea of glass. In the middle of its street, and on either side of the river, is the tree of life that bears twelve fruits every month. The leaves of the tree are for the healing of the nations (Revelation 22:2). It's akin to the ancient Garden of Eden, often called simply Paradise on earth. This is the place where there is neither evil nor death, but only splendor and glory. The Lord has given the resurrection of glory to all of us the righteous; in this resurrection there is everlasting life; and a life of glory is found in this everlasting life. None of this can be understood unless we meditate deeply on it.

For God Has Given to Us Not Only Salvation but Also Everlasting Life, We Will Enjoy Glory and Splendor in Heaven

It's wonderful enough that we have been saved from sin by believing in the gospel of the water and the Spirit while living on this earth. Yet as though this were not enough, we have also received everlasting life. That the Lord raised Lazarus back to life is the concrete proof of our resurrection to come.

Then what kind of life will we live in the future? Remember what the Bible said here, that we have been saved "to the praise of the glory of His grace." To praise God means to extol and adore Him. Soccer fans adore players like Ronaldo of the Brazilian team and Zidane of the French team. We Koreans are very proud of the fact that our team made it to the semifinals in the 2002 World Cup. Less than 10 countries have ever advanced to the semifinals since the first World Cup games began in 1930. In 2002 Japan made it only to the knockout stage and China didn't even survive through the regional qualifying games. If the subject of soccer ever comes up and people from other countries look down on Korea, we can now say to them, "Our team made it to the semifinals in the 2002 World Cup. Did your team make it to even the quarterfinals? Of some 200 countries around the world, less then ten countries have ever advanced to the semifinals." Like this, just as we are proud of our soccer team and adore our players, we praise God for His blessings. With such praise and thanksgiving, we will also enjoy the splendor and glory of Heaven.

The life that awaits us in Heaven is not a humble, ordinary life. Instead it is an amazing, marvelous life of glory. Though it is hard to imagine, I would like to fly on the back of an angel and rule the dominion of creation as a son of the King. We don't actually grasp what it means to live a splendid and glorious life. We have only a vague idea how the millionaires are living in so much opulence, but waiting for us is an incomparably more glorious life. So I am very happy.

The Lord will surely resurrect us the believers in the gospel of the water and the Spirit. Deacon Myungchan Kim is asleep in his grave. He is asleep waiting for the return of the Lord. And the Lord will come to wake him up. If he had died forever, he would have no hope, but as those who are asleep will be waken anew, a new and glorious life awaits Deacon

Kim.

I don't know exactly what you will be doing in the Millennial Kingdom. But let's think about it here based on the Word of God. You will live a glorious life, it will be impossible for you to have any heartache or face any hardships, and there will be nothing lacking in your heart, your mind or your body. If we were to just barely live there, then our lives would be no different from that of a dog or a pig, but we will live a glorious life. Our hearts will be filled only with joy, and our bodies and our minds will be able to live in perfection without any conflicts that trouble life. That's why the resurrection is so beautiful.

Although we may get weary from serving the Lord every day, and our lives of faith may suffer as a result, we must renew our strength, remembering that the Lord has given us new life and the resurrection, and that He has enabled us to enjoy glory and splendor. We must believe that because the Lord has given us everlasting life, we have the resurrection waiting for us, and that just as the Lord raised Lazarus back to life, He will also raise us. If there were no resurrection of the Lord, Jesus would have had to end His ministry with His baptism and His death on the Cross. But the Lord not only blotted out all our sins, but He also rose from the dead again in order to give us a new and glorious life. Through His resurrection, He has affirmed us of our resurrection and given us hope. Although it is hard for us to imagine life after resurrection, we are convinced that such a glorious life awaits us, for the Bible says that only those who are Holy can walk in the Kingdom of Heaven, a place with royal roads and palaces where there is no one evil, nor any harm, nor any tears. So we thank God for this.

Do you also believe that there is the resurrection? Those

who believe in the gospel of the water and the Spirit can believe in their resurrection as a matter of course because they have the Holy Spirit in their hearts. If you don't have such hope, then you should look and examine yourself carefully. Some of you may have a hard time even thinking about the life that awaits you since you haven't even lived it yet, but you should examine yourself to see if this is not because you are too busy, weary and exhausted from the reality of your everyday life.

Let Us Live with Hope

The Bible says that faith, hope and love will abide always, but the foremost of these is love. Because the Lord loves us, He has saved us from all our sins once and for all through the gospel of the water and the Spirit, made us God's children and enabled us to live a glorious life. We must therefore have hope. This present age in particular needs hope. Hope is absolutely indispensable to you and me especially as those who have received the remission of sins. Our Lord has given us everlasting life, and there is resurrection waiting all of us. Unless we have this hope, we cannot endure when the Antichrist appears. Although we are renewed, the world gets worse and will turn increasingly destructive.

Have you heard of RFID? The acronym stands for Radio Frequency Identification. These are small electronic chips that are inserted in products and scanned to identify them. It's said that these chips, once they are miniaturized, will eventually be implanted in human bodies as well. Not only can scanners identify someone implanted with the chip over a hundred meters away, but even satellites can keep track of the bearer.

Europeans began developing this technology about 4 or 5 years ago and they've done some rudimentary research, but recently South Korea made a breakthrough and developed far more advanced chips. Buyers from around the world are competing with each other to get their hands on this technology.

It's said that in about 4 or 5 years down the road, the whole world will be using such electronic chips. The only issue remaining is how to make them inexpensively and as small as possible. Once this issue is resolved, it will be possible to insert electronic chips into everything. To illustrate, when consumers purchase products at a supermarket nowadays, each product has to be scanned at the cashier, but when RFID chips are inserted, there won't be any need to scan the products individually no matter how full the shopping cart is. You can just pass by the scanner and everything in the cart will be calculated automatically.

Microchips are already being used to keep track of pets and cattle. Tiny chips are inserted underneath the skin of a dog or a cat, and simple scanning makes it possible to identify the owner and all the vaccination information. Similar systems are often used by governments. Transit passes, for instance have a chip in them. As each pass has a unique serial number, it can be traced back to the purchaser. Such memory chips are called RFID devices, and this technology is gaining widespread use around the world. There is now a growing demand for such technology, as more people go missing and more things get lost.

Time is coming when everyone will be required to receive the mark of 666, and once a world dictator emerges and uses this technology, he will rule over everyone. The rise of this dictator will mean the fulfillment of the Book of Revelation. I've studied this closely and what I've seen is completely astounding. Of course, it's true that bar codes are already used commonly now. This particular technology was already commercialized, but for now it's used on products, not on people. In the future, however, even ordinary people will be tracked. As people get increasingly nervous about their safety and want to protect their families and possessions, they will look for a way to keep track of everything and eventually, such a system whereby everything is assigned a unique serial number will spread around the world rapidly.

We must therefore have hope. The Bible says that God has given us everlasting life, and that no one can take us away from Him. The Lord has given us eternal life, and because He has this power, He will not lose us to anyone.

And the Lord spoke of the resurrection. Through His 33 years of life, He taught us that we would die once and be resurrected. He showed us the resurrection. Like this, we have the resurrection awaiting us. We should therefore stand firm in the Lord, and we should devote ourselves even more to the work of the Lord. We must realize that our labor in the Lord will not be in vain. Rather than looking at all the things of this world, we must remember what the Lord said to us. In other words, we should think about not only our salvation but also the many blessings that God has given us, and we should live in anticipation of enjoying these blessings in the future.

Although I am yet to live in the Millennial Kingdom, I am overjoyed to think about how I would live there. First of all, I would like to play some soccer. How much fun would I have, since I would not get hurt even if I fell? What about our sisters? What would you like to do then? Sister Yunok what would you like to do? Would you like to travel all over? What are you going to do in your travels? Would you like to fly around on an angel's back when you get bored and try every delicious food there? The Bible says that there is abundant food there. It's written, *"In the middle of its street, and on either side of the river, was the tree of life, which bore twelve fruits, each tree yielding its fruit every month" (Revelation 22:2)*. It's a wonderful place.

What about Brother Myungsun Jang? What would you do when you live there? You would probably want to go fishing, wouldn't you? You will be able to catch all kinds of fish you want. Brother Jongman, what would you like to do? Play soccer? What about you, brother Pilsu? Would you like to eat a lot of tasty snacks? Brother Jungyong, what do you want to do? Do you want to travel around the world? You will travel not just around the world but the whole universe. What about brother Dongwook? What do you want to do? Do you also want to try every delicious dish you can ever imagine? Sister Yu, what would you like to do? Would you like to travel? You can travel with sister Yunok then. Like this, I am sure that when that day comes, all of us will enjoy tens of millions of times more wealth and glory than what we can ever imagine. I give all thanks to our God for giving us such wonderful blessings! ✉

SERMON

17

Jesus Christ Who Has Solved The Problem of Death

< John 12:20-33 >

"Now there were certain Greeks among those who came up to worship at the feast. Then they came to Philip, who was from Bethsaida of Galilee, and asked him, saying, 'Sir, we wish to see Jesus.' Philip came and told Andrew, and in turn Andrew and Philip told Jesus. But Jesus answered them, saying, 'The hour has come that the Son of Man should be glorified. Most assuredly, I say to you, unless a grain of wheat falls into the ground and dies, it remains alone; but if it dies, it produces much grain. He who loves his life will lose it, and he who hates his life in this world will keep it for eternal life. If anyone serves Me, let him follow Me; and where I am, there My servant will be also. If anyone serves Me, him My Father will honor. Now My soul is troubled, and what shall I say? 'Father, save Me from this hour? But for this purpose I came to this hour. Father, glorify Your name.' Then a voice came from heaven, saying, 'I have both glorified it and will glorify it again.' Therefore the people who stood by and heard it said that it had thundered. Others said, 'An angel has spoken to Him.' Jesus answered and said, 'This voice did not come because of Me, but for your sake. Now is the judgment of this world; now the ruler of this world will be cast out. And

I, if I am lifted up from the earth, will draw all peoples to Myself.' This He said, signifying by what death He would die."

It is a fact that from the ancient times to now, humanity has been trying to solve the problem of death. From kings to the ordinary people, all human beings have tried everything to solve the problem of their death. There was, however, no one on this earth who could solve this problem, but only Jesus Christ could give the correct solution to this intractable problem.

In ancient burial custom, mummies were quite common. What we can find out from these mummies is that mankind has had a fundamental hope for eternal life. People used to offer sacrificial offerings to such gods of their own making as the sun god, begging for blessings. For some gods, such sacrificial offerings were at times human beings themselves. Why did they do so? Because they believed that there would be glorious life waiting for them in the world beyond their death. They believed, in other words, that there would be their resurrection. People who gave offerings to a god thought that the wrath of this god would end as they gave offerings to him. We can see from this fact just how many people had dreamt of the next world and lived their lives for the purpose of attaining eternal life.

We can see this from the ancient kings of history also. The first emperor of China, Qin Shi Huang, was one of those who sought to live forever in this world. He ordered his servants to find the elixir of eternal youth, and many of his servants sent out in search of the elixir were lost in far away places and never made it back. He had made them search for a magic herb that would put a stop to the death of the flesh in this world and enable him to live forever. However, he died at the age of 50 in spite of his desperate endeavors. Like this, it has been everyone's common hope to solve the problem of death.

Most people believe in their afterlife. We can verify this fact from the discovery of the archeological artifacts of the Emperor Qin, who upon his death had hundreds of thousands of terracotta armies buried along with his own dead body. The Emperor Qin, wanting to be protected by his armies even after his death, certainly dreamt of living and enjoying his power and authority forever. When we see this, we can realize that everyone has this desire to be freed from death and live forever.

The Problem of Everyone's Death Has Been Resolved by the Death of Jesus

When the Passover approached, Jews went up to Jerusalem where the Temple was located. There were certain Greeks at the time who requested Philip, a disciple of Jesus, "We would like to see Jesus; could you for us ask Him to see us?" When Jesus heard of this request from Andrew and Philip, He said, *"The hour has come that the Son of Man should be glorified."* This means that now the time had come for the Lord to rise from the dead again and reign forever to solve the problem of death, something that all the people of the world eagerly sought after. Jesus had come to this earth to solve all the problems of the death of mankind and the condemnation of sin, and He said here that the time had now come for Him to fulfill this.

Jesus said this to let it be known that the day for Him to be crucified and die was nearing, as He had already been baptized by John and had thereby shouldered the sins of the world once and for all. Our Lord said in John 12:24, *"Most assuredly, I say to you, unless a grain of wheat falls into the ground and dies, it remains alone; but if it dies, it produces much grain."* Jesus said this in reference to His own sacrifice. The reason why Jesus was sacrificed was because He had shouldered the sins of the world by being baptized by John.

The reason why Jesus said here that He would become a grain of wheat was because now, once He is crucified and rises from the dead again, He could enable many people to receive eternal life by believing in Him as the Savior, for He had already received the baptism that passed the sins of the world onto Him. He said this because if He does not fall on the ground and die, He would remain as a grain, but once He is crucified, shed His blood and die, and rise from the dead again, He would solve the problem of death for many people and enable them to receive eternal life. Had Jesus who was baptized by John not shouldered the sins of the world, not died on the Cross, and not borne the condemnation of death, everyone's problem of the remission of sin and death would forever have remained unresolved.

Because Jesus was to reach His death to pay the wages of the sins of all people, He shouldered the sins of the world and was vicariously crucified to death in their place. Therefore, if we do not have the faith that believes in the baptism and death of Jesus, then there would be no eternal life for believers. This is why Jesus said about His own death, *"unless a grain of wheat falls into the ground and dies, it remains alone; but if it dies, it produces much grain."* All of us must realize that Jesus Christ came to this earth to accomplish the task of washing away the sins of the world and resolve the problem of death.

Our Lord said, "But for this purpose I came to this hour." Jesus came to this earth to wash away the sins of mankind and solve the problem of death for them.

Having come to this earth in the flesh of a man and been baptized by John the Baptist at the age of 30, Jesus had already accepted all the sins of the world. He therefore knew that if He would only die on the Cross and then rise from the dead again, His mission to wash away the sin of the world and solve the problem of death would all be accomplished. Because Jesus was crucified and bled to death, all those who believe are now able to overcome death and receive eternal life. Because Jesus had taken upon our sins through His baptism, with His death on the Cross He now had to pay all the wages of sin in our place. This is why Jesus gave Himself up to be crucified. The Lord Himself was baptized for us the entire mankind, shed His blood on the Cross, and died vicariously in our place all in accordance to the Law that declares the wages of sin to be death. Jesus has thereby fulfilled His purpose to bring everyone alive.

All people were born into this world as sinners, for Adam and Eve, the ancestors of mankind, had fallen into the temptation of Satan and sinned against God (Romans 5:12). All human beings therefore could not but be conceived in sin from the very moment they were made in the wombs of their mothers and be born in iniquity (Psalm 51:5). From the very birth, mankind could not but die for the sin that they inherited from their ancestors. Once people are born into this world and time goes by, they grow old, fall ill and are visited by death inevitably, and this was a fate from which they could forever not escape. As such, for Jesus Christ the Lord of all humanity, there was no other solution but for Himself to come to this earth in the flesh of a man, be baptized, be hung on the Cross and shed His blood, rise form the dead again, and thereby give us mankind His true salvation, so that He would solve not only the problem of aging and illness, but also to wash away all the sins of mankind, solve the problem of their death, and give them eternal life (Psalms 103:3-4).

So by shedding His blood and dying on the Cross, Jesus has enabled all those who believe in Him to get all the problems of their sins and death solved once for all. By being baptized and shedding His blood on the Cross, the Lord has enabled all those who believe in Him as their own Lord to be washed of their sins, to be delivered from their death, and to receive eternal life, and He has enabled anyone to have the problem of eternal death resolved by faith. As such, our Lord is the very One who has forever solved away the problem of death for us.

The reason why Jesus Christ was baptized by John and bled to death on the Cross was for us to receive eternal life. Our Lord is the Savior who has completely solved away the problem of our sin and death all at once. Because Jesus took upon the sins of the world by being baptized, He died as a result and rose from the dead again. This was the Lord's righteous judgment, death and resurrection that were fulfilled for us who believe in the gospel of the water and the Spirit. As Jesus was hung on the Cross and died on it, it is by believing in this fact that we have been delivered from all the condemnation of sin and death.

Jesus said in John 12:31, *"Now is the judgment of this world; now the ruler of this world will be cast out."* The Lord said here that this world is now to be judged. This means that because the Lord took upon the sins of the world by being baptized by John, when He dies on the Cross He would be vicariously suffering even the death of all those who would be born in this world in the future for their sins also, and so the power of Satan, who can reign in only where there is sin, would now disappear. As such, because the Lord accepted all the sins of the world through the baptism that He received from John, by being crucified and vicariously suffering the death of everyone, He has enabled all to escape from the condemnation of their sins. It is by believing in this truth that we can solve our problem of sin and death.

Had Jesus not died on the Cross even as He had been baptized, the problem of our death would not have been solved. But because He took upon our sins with His baptism, He shed His blood on the Cross, rose from the dead again, and has thereby given true salvation to those who believe. Had Jesus not been crucified to death, the condemnation of our sins would not have been resolved, and this would then mean that we would have to die for our sins. But instead of us having to die for our sins, the Lord was baptized and died for our sins, being crucified and shedding His blood, and He has thereby resolved everyone's problem of sin.

Have You Truly Agonized over the Problem of Death?

What mankind must actually be most agonized about is the problem of death. Isn't there a way for humans to live forever? How wonderful would it be if there were no death for everyone living on this earth? There are countless people who die without solving the problem of death, but the Lord has solved all these things for us. Given this, how could we not thank Him and believe? We can only thank the Lord, for He became a grain of wheat and fell on the ground, solving all the problems of sin by being baptized and dying on the Cross. Jesus our Lord solved our problem of sin and death once for all by being crucified. Now, those who believe in this will take part in the resurrection of the Lord (1 Corinthians 15:22-23). Those who believe in the gospel of the water and the Spirit are, by believing in this gospel, now washed of all sins, their problem of death is resolved, and they have thereby received eternal life.

Our Lord said, "I, if I am lifted up from the earth, will draw all peoples to Myself." Being "lifted up from the earth" here mean none other than the death of Jesus on the Cross. When Jesus was crucified to death while shouldering the sins of the world, His feet did not touch the ground, as His body was lifted up from the earth. This clearly tells us that the death of Jesus has solved our problem of death. People who think about their death and sins come to thank God, for they come to realize that Jesus Christ has solved all their problems of death by taking upon their sins through His baptism and dying on the Cross in their instead. This is the faith that believes in the truth.

Unless the problem of their death is resolved, people cannot avoid but be constantly worried. But to solve the problem of death in our lives, Jesus Christ came to this earth, was baptized, died on the Cross, and has thereby saved us mankind from sin and solved our problem of death. We must realize that the Lord has given new life to those of us who believe in His life-giving ministries. We can attain this new life only when we believe in this truth. Yet most of today's Christians believe in Jesus without knowing this truth, a situation that is deeply saddening and disturbing.

This morning, I visited the tomb of Deacon Kim, who passed away a few years ago. I went there with a few colleagues of mine to know whether the tomb was well maintained; I wanted to check if the grass was growing well, whether or not there was any risk of landslide with the coming Monsoon season, and various other such safety issues. We didn't pour drinks and bowed down before the tomb like the people of the world do. Instead, we just meditated once again on how the Lord has solved the problem of death for us, and we gave thanks to God. We prayed for a while before his tomb, and we ruminated on our faith again, that the Lord would raise him and us to live and see one another once again.

Because the Lord has solved our problem of death once for all with the baptism that He received from John and the blood of the Cross, it is by believing in this that the problem of sin and death is resolved for us (Romans 8:1-2). When our Lord makes His angels sound the last trumpet, we will once again come face to face to those with the true faith who had fallen asleep in their tombs (1 Thessalonians 4:14-18).

Through the baptism that Jesus Christ received and His bloodshed, our problem of death has now been all solved. That Jesus died on the Cross was because He had shouldered our sins through His baptism. Therefore, His death is our own death. And His resurrection is the resurrection of us who believe (Romans 6:3-6). This is not just a doctrine, but it is the actual truth of salvation.

Everyone must think about death, though at different depths. Why? Because the Bible tells us that it is appointed for men to die once, and the more serious problem is that this would be followed by the judgment of their sins (Hebrews 9:27-28). That people, once born in this world, must die once for sin is utterly true. It is only a matter of course for us to die once, but we must think about how we are to solve the problem of the second death that follows the first death. This second death is none other than the eternal punishment of hell for our sins. The problem of this second death had been like a great task assigned to the entire mankind, but now with the coming of the faith that believes in the gospel of the water and the Spirit, this problem has been all resolved. All of us know very well that because Jesus was baptized, shed His blood on the Cross, and rose from the dead again, all these problems of death and sin have now been resolved for us, and that there will be resurrection for us. I give my thanks to the Lord, for by believing that Jesus has solved our problem of eternal death by dying in our place, we are now able to follow God by faith, no longer burdened by our worries about our own death.

Do You Know That Jesus Christ Has Solved the Problem of Death for Everyone?

Jesus has truly solved our problem of sin and death. He has permitted new life to us who believe to live forever. If we believe in Jesus and in His ministries of the water and the Spirit that He fulfilled for us, we can receive all these blessings by faith. In John 14:6, Jesus said, *"I am the way, the truth, and the life. No one comes to the Father except through Me."* In John 11:25-26, He also said, *"I am the resurrection and the life. He who believes in Me, though he may die, he shall live. And whoever lives and believes in Me shall never die. Do you believe this?"*

Those who believe in Jesus Christ will live even as their bodies die, and those who live and believe in Jesus will forever not die. If we are still alive when the Lord returns, we will really come before God without ever tasting death. If we believe in Jesus and have been resolved of this problem by faith, then we will live again even as our bodies die. And if we live through the coming Great Tribulation without being martyred by the Antichrist, then our bodies too will receive eternal life without tasting death. We must thank the Lord for thus giving us eternal life also.

When we believe in Jesus, we must get the problem of death resolved along with the washing of sin. All these things are resolved by believing in the true gospel of the water and the Spirit. Think about it yourselves. How has your problem of sin and death been resolved? As Jesus was baptized, was crucified to death, and rose from the dead again, it is by believing in this truth that our problem of death has been resolved. The Cross where Jesus died is not just symbolic, but it is the place where Jesus actually solved the problem of our death. The baptism of Jesus solved our problem of sin; His blood on the Cross solved the problem of death; and His resurrection from the dead, by giving us new and eternal life, solved our human desire to live forever. For us, Jesus Christ is truly the Savior, our resurrection and life, the Lord who has enabled us to be resolved of the problem of sin, the problem of death, and the problem of eternal life once for all. We must therefore believe that the Lord is the Savior who has solved away the problem of eternal death for us.

Our Lord said, *"He who loves his life will lose it, and he who hates his life in this world will keep it for eternal life."* It is because people do not believe in the truth of life and remain unable to solve the problem of their eternal death that they are all facing the condemnation of their sins. Their life of flesh will end up dead while not being able to solve their own problem of sin. We all received this first life, the life of the flesh, from our parents. It is God's providence that this first life is appointed to pass away once. However, because people love this first life so much, they cannot avoid but end up losing the second life that would have enabled them to live forever. But those who believe in the gospel of the water and the Spirit, that Jesus Christ has saved us from sin and solved the problem of death and eternal life, love everlasting life. They will receive eternal life afterwards, which is more precious than the first life that is to die and disappear.

All must believe in Jesus the Savior as their own Savior. When they acknowledge by faith that they are bound to hell and believe in the gospel of the water and the Spirit, by this faith they will be able to get the clear answers to all the problems of sin, death, and eternal life. It is because some people love themselves too much even as they are inevitably bound to die that they cannot receive by faith the remission of sin given by Jesus. They therefore reject the gospel that has resolved everyone's problem of death and eternal life through the baptism that Jesus received and the blood of the Cross. Because they raise themselves up too high, they cannot receive the salvation that God has given them. Representative of such people is Buddha, who said, "Holy am I alone throughout heavens and earth." Such people never give up their endeavor to solve the problem of death by themselves. Put differently, each of them is trying to become his/her own savior. They will therefore end up being condemned to hell to be punished for their sins forever and lose their real life.

We all love ourselves more than others, for we are selfish by nature. However, there is someone whom we must love even more than ourselves. This someone that must be the object of our true love is Jesus Christ the Son of God. He has given new life to you and me by sacrificing His own life. We must believe in Jesus Christ who has solved all our problems of sin, death, and eternal life by giving us His own life. We must believe in our Lord who is greater than us. This is the right faith.

In these days, however, many people on this earth do not know and cannot believe that Jesus has solved their problem of sin and death, even as they wish eagerly to get this problem of death resolved. How many people actually know and believe that Jesus bore all the condemnation of their sins? Even such famous people of the ancient times as Genghis Khan, Alexander the Great, and Julius Caesar all failed to find the way to solve the problem of death and ended up dead. Though they wielded immense power and accomplished many great achievements on this earth, they all ended up dying in a relatively young age only to be buried in history. Like this, for everyone, the problem of death could not be solved by anyone. Countless philosophers have tried to resolve this problem of death, but none realized the truth.

Today, however, through the baptism that Jesus Christ received and His death on the Cross, you have realized the truth that these people had sought after so much, the truth that enabled one to be resolved of the problem of death. What an amazing truth this is? What a truthful way of faith? What an eternal life? If we know that our problem of death has been resolved by believing in Jesus Christ's righteous acts for our salvation, we can then follow the Lord freely, without worrying over the problem of our death. Is this not the case? Through His baptism and resurrection, Jesus Christ has solved our problem of sin and death. What else is this but a truly amazing blessing?

When Jesus was praying to the Father in the Gethsemane Garden, He said, "Father, save Me from this hour." Jesus Christ knew very well just how painful His death on the Cross would be. Imagine yourselves that you yourselves are to be crucified to death for your sins. Just how painful it would be?

Would you not try to avoid this, if possible at all? Jesus had to die on the Cross because He had shouldered our sins through His baptism, but because He also was in the weak flesh of a man, He wanted to avoid the punishment of Cross if possible. Being treated like some worm below a human being, ridiculed, and dying in great suffering were what this punishment of Cross entailed. Our Lord bore such a punishment for us.

It was to resolve our problem of sin and death that the Lord died on the Cross. Our Lord knew very well that He had to be crucified because of our problem of sin and death. This is why the Lord said, *"Unless a grain of wheat falls into the ground and dies, it remains alone; but if it dies, it produces much grain."* Do you believe that Jesus Christ has solved our problem of sin and death by being crucified, and that just as He rose from the dead again, He has also raised us from the dead through the gospel of the water and the Spirit? The Lord has given us the blessing of eternal life. The truth that Jesus has solved our problem of death is the truth that everyone, young and old, must all believe in. Human beings are mortal beings: Once they are born as sinners, they inevitably grow old, fall ill and eventually die once. And after that, they cannot but face God's eternal judgment for their sins. That's why all sinners must believe in the gospel of the water and the Spirit.

When I was at the cemetery today, I saw how the funeral business is booming. Before, there used to be some desolated fields all around the cemetery, but these were all overturned and tidied up as nice tombs now. But regardless of how the tombs were nicely arranged and their surroundings were beautifully adorned, how many of them do you think really had solved their problem of death by faith before passing away? How many of them, in other words, would receive new life, live again, and ascend to God when the Lord returns to this earth? How many would have carved out the word "a righteous person" before his or her name in the tombstones that stand before all those countless tombs? But in the epitaph of Deacon Myungchan Kim, who had believed in the gospel of the water and the Spirit, it was written, "Deacon Myungchan Kim, a righteous man, sleeps here waiting for the return of the Lord." Brothers and sisters, if I die before you while serving the gospel, I, too, want my epitaph to be written in this way: "Rev. Paul C. Jong, a righteous man, sleeps here waiting for the return of the Lord and his resurrection." Behind my tombstone, I would like it to be written, "Waiting for the people and servants of God to do their works and return soon," and on its sides, "Everyone, believe in the gospel of the water and the Spirit, and you will then be washed from your sins."

I thank the Lord with my faith for allowing my name to be written in the Book of Life in the Kingdom of God, and for resolving the problem of death and sin. All must now get the problem of their death resolved by believing in the baptism and death of Jesus. As I write this, it is April, with the Passion Week about to pass and the Easter to come. There are many Christians who fast during the Passion Week. Would you also like to fast, so that you yourselves may experience some aspects of the suffering that Jesus endured? However, what is more important than this is to believe that the Lord died to resolve the problem of our death. It is because we believe in this that we have thankful hearts.

Now, no matter when we die, we will go to the Lord. We who believe in the gospel of the water and the Spirit do not care exactly when we will go to the Lord. Why? Because the problem of death has already been resolved by faith. All that we have to do is just go to the Lord whenever He calls us, for we have already received eternal life by faith. To us who believe in the life-giving gospel of the water and the Spirit, the Lord has given eternal life. Because our resurrection is already given to us, far from worrying or agonizing over the problem of sin and death, on the contrary we give instead thanks to God.

Our Lord said, *"If anyone serves Me, let him follow Me; and where I am, there My servant will be also. If anyone serves Me, him My Father will honor" (John 12:26).* Jesus said that His Father would honor those who serve Him. Moreover, as He said that those who serve the Lord would also be where He is, if we believe in the gospel of the water and the Spirit and serve it, we will all go to where the Lord is. This is why the righteous do not care when they die as long as they have spread the gospel of the water and the Spirit fully. If the righteous are too lazy and not faithful enough to bear many fruits, even as the Lord has enabled them to do the works of God, then His heart can only ache. When it comes to spreading the gospel of the water and the Spirit that we serve, if we only pay enough attention, we can all fulfill such works well. We only regret that we had not dedicated all our hearts and been faithful to them. I want to serve the Lord faithfully, but it is my regret that I have not been wholly faithful. Are you not like this also?

I know that many regrets can arise when we are doing the works of God. But whenever such regretful thoughts come to our minds, wondering how things might have turned out if we had done certain things differently, we are still determined to please God by boldly and vigorously spreading the gospel of the water and the Spirit to the end. If we want to have no more regrets later by not being faithful to the works of the Lord now, then we must serve the gospel even better, until the day the Lord no longer permits the gospel to be spread on this earth. I want you to do the works of God now, when you are able to serve the gospel of the water and the Spirit to your hearts' content, without any regret. It is my hope that you would not regret when the time set by the Lord comes and He tells us to stop spreading the gospel.

As for myself, I think I will end up regretting if I am not faithful right now at this very hour. Even if I regret when the time of tribulation comes, it would only hurt my heart, for all my regrets would be in vain, and I would be able to undo none of them. Though my heart is content for receiving the remission of sin, I want to spread the gospel as much as possible when the Lord has permitted me the opportunity, ability, and time to serve the works of God, or else I would end up regretting. I do acknowledge that I am somewhat insufficient, but I still do not want to live a regretful life. Having lived my life to meet the Lord and serve and follow Him, I have decided not to become someone who regrets. This is why I do the works of the Lord, though I may be insufficient. And there indeed are many insufficiencies in me. But because I really want to become someone who has no regret, I am trying to do what I have to do, regardless of my shortcomings.

The problem of death for you, for all the saints and servants of God, has now been resolved because of the Lord. Believing that the Lord has resolved our problem of death, I thank Him once again. I am so thankful that such precious meaning, glory, and blessed fruits are held in the fact that the Lord was crucified. Because Jesus Christ fell into the ground and became the fertilizer that resolved our problem of death, you and I who believe have born the fruits of having all the problems of death resolved.

I give my thanks to God. Our hearts are sometime saddened, they struggle, and they are at times even captured by carnal thoughts. But by believing in the Lord who has solved away our problem of death, we must overcome all these things.

With our faith in the Lord, we must overcome all the weaknesses that bind us. By believing that the Lord has completed His mission to resolve all the problems of sin and death, we can become victors. Though our flesh is insufficient, we can still triumph with the faith that believes in the gospel of the water and the Spirit. By believing in this gospel of the water and the Spirit, we have all become holy.

Now that we believe in the gospel of the water and the Spirit, we must live following the Lord. Believing that the Lord has resolved our problem of death by being baptized and bleeding to death on the Cross, it is only proper for us to never again be troubled by our problem of death, but to give thanks to God, on the contrary, for resolving the problem of sin and death and giving us eternal life. I hope that you would all believe in the gospel of the water and the Spirit and live the rest of your lives without having any regrets before God.

I pray that you would live your lives by believing in the gospel of the water and the Spirit until the day you stand before the Lord. To those who believe in the gospel of the water and the Spirit, I believe that God has given the remission of sin and eternal life. Amen! Hallelujah! ⊠

HAVE YOU TRULY BEEN BORN AGAIN OF WATER AND THE SPIRIT?

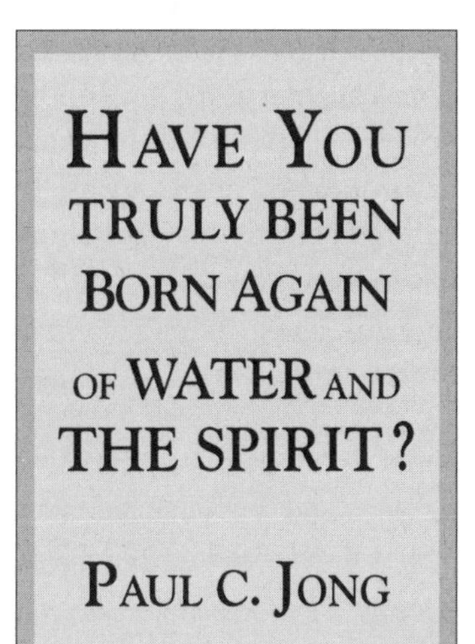

Among many Christian books written about being born again, this is the first book of our time to preach the gospel of the water and the Spirit in strict accordance with the Scriptures. Man can't enter the Kingdom of Heaven without being born again of water and the Spirit. To be born again means that a sinner is saved from all his lifelong sins by believing in the baptism of Jesus and His blood of the Cross. Let's believe in the gospel of the water and the Spirit and enter the Kingdom of Heaven as the righteous who have no sin.

RETURN TO THE GOSPEL OF THE WATER AND THE SPIRIT

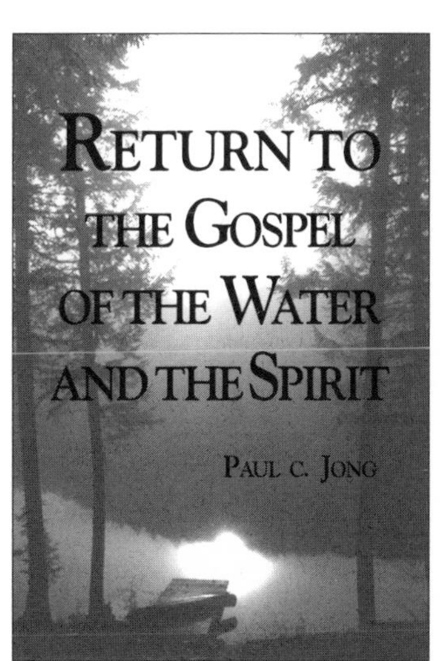

Let's return to the gospel of the water and the Spirit. Theology and doctrines themselves can't save us. However, many Christians still follow them, and consequently have not been born again yet. This book clearly tells us what mistakes theology and doctrines have made and how to believe in Jesus in the most proper way.

The Fail-safe Way for You to Receive the Holy Spirit

In Christianity, the most significantly discussed issue is salvation from sins and the indwelling of the Holy Spirit. However, few people have the exact knowledge of these two topics. Nevertheless, in reality people say that they believe in Jesus Christ while they are ignorant of true redemption and the Holy Spirit.

Do you know the true gospel that makes you receive the Holy Spirit? If you want to ask God for the indwelling of the Holy Spirit, then you must first know the gospel of the water and the Spirit and have faith in it. This book will certainly lead all Christians worldwide to receive the Holy Spirit through the remission of all their sins.

Our LORD Who Becomes the Righteousness of God (I) & (II)

The teachings in these books will satisfy the thirst in your heart. Today's Christians continue to live while not knowing the true solution to the personal sins that they are committing daily. Do you know what God's righteousness is? The author hopes that you will ask yourself this question and believe in God's righteousness, which is dealt in detail in these books.

The Doctrines of Predestination, Justification, and Incremental Sanctification are the major Christian doctrines, which brought only confusion and emptiness into the souls of believers. But, dear Christians, now is the time when you must continue in the Truth which you have learned and been assured of.

These books will provide your soul with a great understanding and lead it to peace. The author wants you to possess the blessing of knowing God's righteousness.

IS THE AGE OF THE ANTICHRIST, MARTYRDOM, RAPTURE AND THE MILLENNIAL KINGDOM COMING? (I)

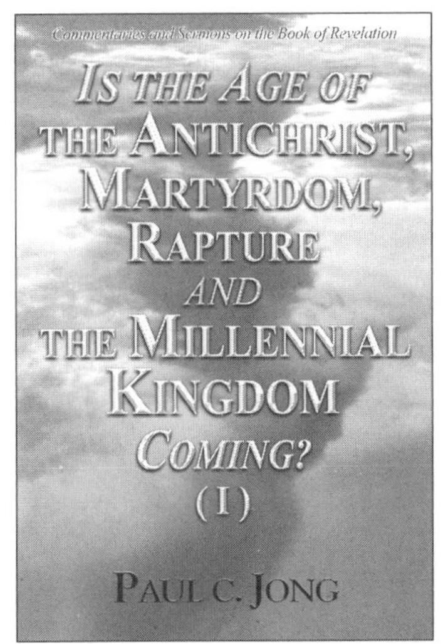

After the 9/11 terrorist attacks, traffic to "www.raptureready.com," an Internet site providing information on the end times, is reported to have increased to over 8 million hits, and according to a joint survey by CNN and TIME, over 59% of the Americans now believe in apocalyptic eschatology.

Responding to such demands of the time, the author provides a clear exposition of the key themes of the Book of Revelation, including the coming Antichrist, the martyrdom of the saints and their rapture, the Millennial Kingdom, and the New Heaven and Earth-all in the context of the whole Scripture and under the guidance of the Holy Spirit.

This book provides verse-by-verse commentaries on the Book of Revelation supplemented by the author's inspired sermons. Anyone who reads this book will come to grasp all the plans that God has in store for this world.

IS THE AGE OF THE ANTICHRIST, MARTYRDOM, RAPTURE AND THE MILLENNIAL KINGDOM COMING? (II)

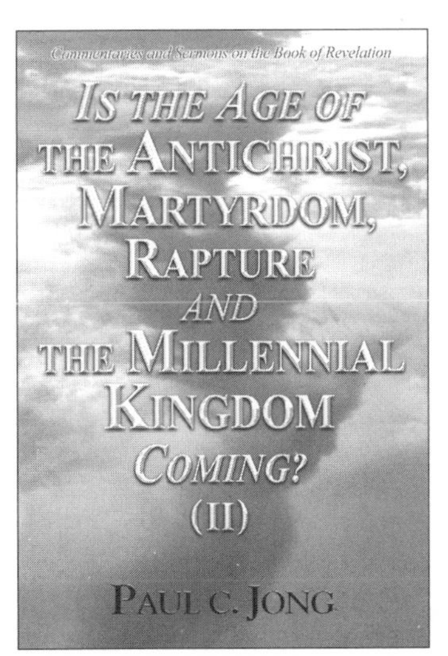

Most Christians today believe in the theory of pre-tribulation rapture. Because they believe in this false doctrine teaching them that they would be lifted before the coming of the Great Tribulation of seven years, they are leading idle religious lives steeped in complacency.

But the rapture of the saints will occur only after the plagues of the seven trumpets run their course until the sixth plague is all poured-that is, the rapture will happen after the Antichrist emerges amidst global chaos and the born-again saints are martyred, and when the seventh trumpet is blown. It is at this time that Jesus would descend from Heaven, and the resurrection and rapture of the born-again saints would occur (1 Thessalonians 4:16-17).

The righteous who were born again by believing in "the gospel of the water and the Spirit" will be resurrected and take part in the Rapture, and thus become heirs to the Millennial Kingdom and the eternal Kingdom of Heaven, but the sinners who were unable to participate in this first resurrection will face the great punishment of the seven bowls poured by God and be cast into the eternal fire of hell.

The TABERNACLE: A Detailed Portrait of Jesus Christ (I)

How can we find out the truth hidden in the Tabernacle? Only by knowing the gospel of the water and the Spirit, the real substance of the Tabernacle, can we correctly understand and know the answer to this question.

In fact, the blue, purple, and scarlet thread and the fine woven linen manifested in the gate of the Tabernacle's court show us the works of Jesus Christ in the New Testament's time that have saved the mankind. In this way, the Old Testament's Word of the Tabernacle and the Word of the New Testament are closely and definitely related to each other, like fine woven linen. But, unfortunately, this truth has been hidden for a long time to every truth seeker in Christianity.

Coming to this earth, Jesus Christ was baptized by John and shed His blood on the Cross. Without understanding and believing in the gospel of the water and the Spirit, none of us can ever find out the truth revealed in the Tabernacle. We must now learn this truth of the Tabernacle and believe in it. We all need to realize and believe in the truth manifested in the blue, purple, and scarlet thread and the fine woven linen of the gate of the Tabernacle's court.

The TABERNACLE: A Detailed Portrait of Jesus Christ (II)

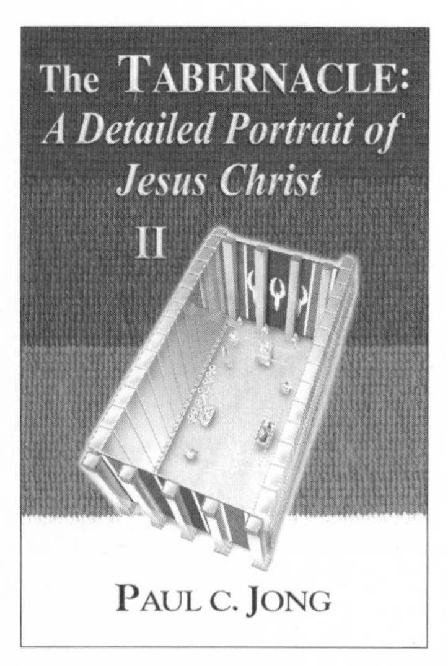

As God had commanded Moses to build the Tabernacle in the Old Testament, in the New Testament, God wants us to also build a Sanctuary in each of our hearts so that He may dwell in us. The material of faith with which we can build this Sanctuary in our hearts is the Word of the gospel of the water and the Spirit. With this gospel of the water and the Spirit, we must wash away all our sins and be cleansed. By telling us to build Him a Sanctuary, God is telling us to empty our hearts and believe in the gospel of the water and the Spirit. We must all cleanse our hearts by believing in the gospel of the water and the Spirit.

When we cleanse away all the sins of our hearts by believing in this gospel Truth, God then comes to dwell in them. It is by believing in this true gospel that you can build the holy Temples in your hearts. It is highly likely that until now, at least some of you have probably been offering your prayers of repentance to cleanse your hearts, trying to build the Temples by yourselves. But now is the time for you to abandon this false faith and be transformed by the renewing of your minds by believing in the gospel of the water and the Spirit.

The Elementary Principles of CHRIST

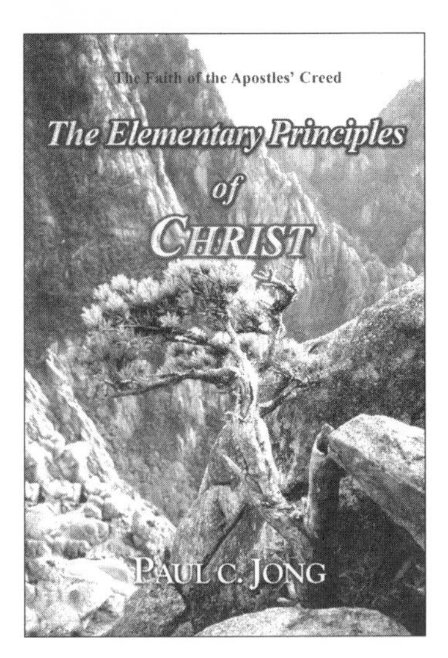

We must have the faith that the Apostles had and believe as they did, for their faith and beliefs came from the Holy Spirit. The Apostles believed in Jesus Christ, His Father, and the Holy Spirit as their God.

The Apostle Paul confessed that he died with Christ and was brought to new life with Him. He became an instrument of God by believing that he was baptized into Jesus Christ (Galatians 3:27). In God's gospel are found the baptism that Jesus received, the blood that He shed on the Cross, and the gift of the Holy Spirit that He has bestowed on everyone who believes in this true gospel of the water and the Spirit.

Do you know and believe in this original gospel? This is the very gospel that the Apostles had also believed. We, too, must therefore all believe in the gospel of the water and the Spirit.

The Gospel of Matthew (I), (II), (III), (IV), (V), (VI)

There are countless new Christians throughout the world, who have just been born again by believing in the gospel of the water and the Spirit that we have been spreading. We are indeed yearning to feed on the bread of life to them. But it is difficult for them to have fellowship with us in the true gospel, for they are all far away from us.

Therefore, to meet the spiritual needs of these people of Jesus Christ, the King of kings, The author proclaims that those who have received the remission of their sins by believing in the Word of Jesus Christ, must feed on His pure Word in order to defend their faith and sustain their spiritual lives. The sermons in these books have been prepared as new bread of life that will nourish the born-again to edify their spiritual growth.

Through His Church and servants, God will continue to provide you with this bread of life. May God's blessings be on all those who have been born again of water and the Spirit, who desires to have true spiritual fellowship with us in Jesus Christ.

The First Epistle of John (I) & (II)

He who believes that Jesus, who is God and the Savior, came by the gospel of the water and the Spirit to deliver all sinners from their sins, is saved from all his sins, and becomes a child of God the Father.

The First Epistle of John states that Jesus, who is God, came to us by the gospel of the water and the Spirit, and that He is the Son of God the Father. The Book, in other words, mostly emphasizes that Jesus is God (1 John 5:20), and concretely testifies the gospel of the water and the Spirit in chapter 5.

We must not hesitate to believe that Jesus Christ is God and to follow Him.

Sermons on Galatians: From Physical Circumcision to the Doctrine of Repentance (I) & (II)

Today's Christianity has turned into merely a world religion. Most Christians nowadays live in a situation of being sinners because they haven't been born again by spiritual faith. It is because they have only relied on Christian doctrines without being aware of the gospel of the water and the Spirit until now.

Therefore, now is the time for you to know the spiritual fallacies of the circumcisionists and keep distance from such faith. You have to know the contradictoriness of the prayers of repentance. Now is the time for you to stand firmer than ever on the gospel of the water and the Spirit.

If you haven't believed in this true gospel so far, you have to believe in our Savior who came to us by the gospel of the water and the Spirit even now. Now, you have to be complete Christians with the faith of believing in the gospel Truth of the water and the Spirit.

The Love of God Revealed through Jesus, The Only Begotten Son (I) & (II)

It is written, "No one has seen God at any time. The only begotten Son, who is in the bosom of the Father, He has declared Him" (John 1:18).

How perfectly did Jesus reveal the love of God to us! How perfectly did Jesus deliver us! What perfect Truth of salvation is the gospel of the water and the Spirit! We have never regretted receiving our salvation through our faith in Jesus, who came by water and blood (1 John 5:6).

Now, we have become His sinless people. Whoever believes in the gospel of the water and the Spirit can receive the eternal remission of sins and earn eternal life.

Eat My Flesh And Drink My Blood

Until now, most Christians have not known the Truth, but only inherited religious acts. From the gospel to Holy Communion, today's Christianity maintains its orthodoxy not through the knowledge of the Truth, but by emphasizing only formal procedures and consecrated rites.

As a result, when today's Christians come across the bread and wine that signify the flesh and blood of Jesus during Communion, they are thankful only for the sacrifice of His blood, and they can't help but remain completely ignorant of the fact that Christ took upon Himself all their sins once and for all by being baptized by John the Baptist.

Therefore, I admonish all Christians throughout the whole world to learn, even from now on, what the flesh and blood of Jesus mean within the gospel of the water and the Spirit, to believe in it, and to thereby receive their salvation and also partake in Holy Communion with the right faith.

The Relationship Between the Ministry of JESUS and That of JOHN the BAPTIST Recorded in the Four Gospels

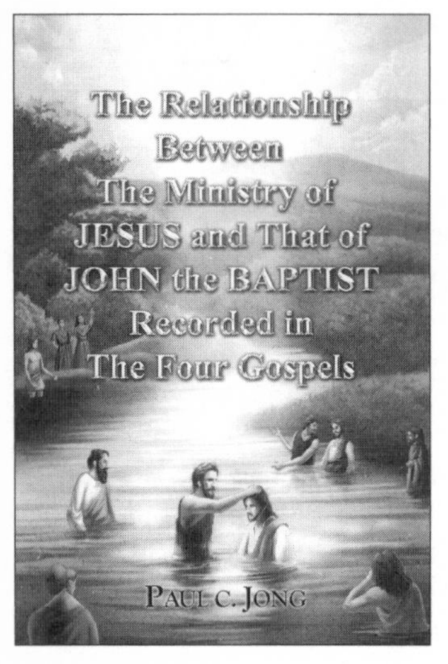

Do you perhaps think that it doesn't matter whether there needs to be the ministry of John the Baptist or not? You must believe according to the written Word of God. We must understand and believe in the ministry of John the Baptist within the frame of the ministry of Jesus Christ. John the Baptist in the New Testament was the prophet Elijah promised to be sent down to this earth according to the Book of Malachi chapter 4, verses 4-5. As the prophet Elijah to come, John the Baptist was born six months before Jesus, and he was the one who had pass on the sins of this world at once by giving Jesus the baptism at the Jordan River at the age of thirty. Thus, we must become the recipients of God's blessing by knowing the ministry of John the Baptist and accepting the ministry of Jesus Christ.

THE WILL OF THE HOLY TRINITY FOR HUMAN BEINGS

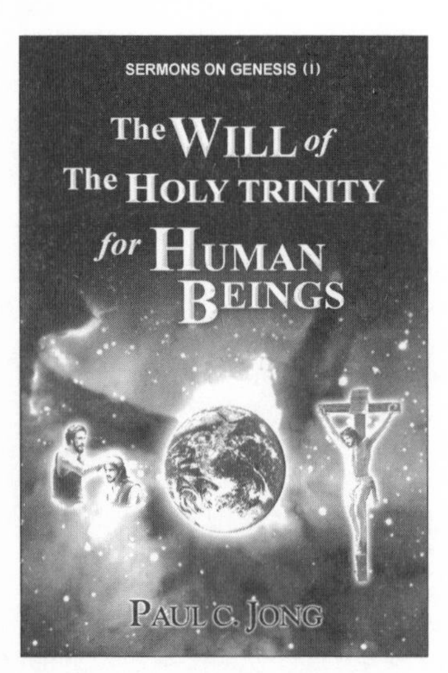

Through the Book of Genesis, God wants us to realize His good intentions toward us. Where is God's will for us revealed? It is revealed in the gospel Truth of the water and the Spirit that God accomplished through Jesus Christ. We must come into this good intention of God by faith, manifested in the gospel of the water and the Spirit. To do so, when we consider God's Word, we need to cast aside our existing carnal thoughts we have had, and believe in God's Word exactly as it is. All of us must throw away our mistaken knowledge accumulated until now, and open our spiritual eyes by placing our faith in the righteousness of God.

The Fall of Man and the Perfect Salvation of God

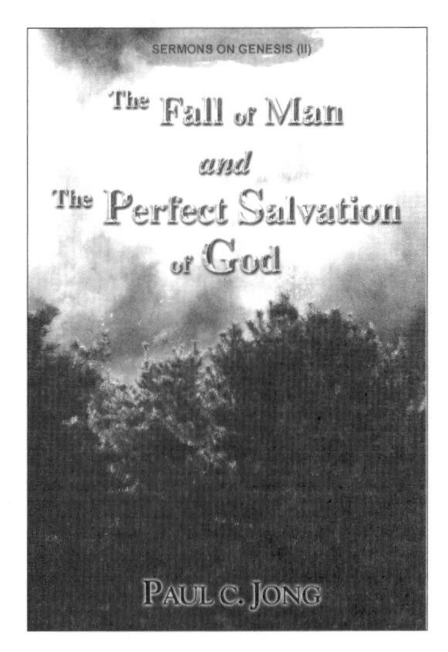

In the Book of Genesis, the purpose for which God created us is contained. When architects design a building or artists draw a painting, they first conceive the work that would be completed in their minds before they actually begin working on their project. Just like this, our God also had our salvation of mankind in His mind even before He created the heavens and the earth, and He made Adam and Eve with this purpose in mind. And God needed to explain to us the domain of Heaven, which is not seen by our eyes of the flesh, by drawing an analogy to the domain of the earth that we can all see and understand.

Even before the foundation of the world, God wanted to save mankind perfectly by giving the gospel of the water and the Spirit to everyone's heart. So although all human beings were made out of dust, they must learn and know the gospel Truth of the water and the Spirit to benefit their own souls. If people continue to live without knowing the dominion of Heaven, they will lose not only the things of the earth, but also everything that belongs to Heaven.

Heretics, Who Followed the Sins of Jeroboam (I) & (II)

Christians today do not know what the gospel Truth of the water and the Spirit that the Lord has made and given us is. Thus, they continue to believe in the doctrines of Christianity and not the gospel of the water and the Spirit. For that reason, the fact of the matter is that despite their claim of having faith in Jesus, they continue to believe in and follow golden calves.

We must discern those that worship golden calves as God within Christianity. And by coming back before God of the Truth, we must offer the sacrifices of righteousness to God. The sacrifice that God receives with rejoice is the sacrifice of righteousness that people offer by faith after having received the remission of sin by having faith in the gospel of the water and the Spirit. Before God, you must seriously think about whether or not you are offering the sacrifice of God-given righteousness by the faith of believing in the gospel of the water and the Spirit.

The Lord's Prayer : Misinterpretations and Truth

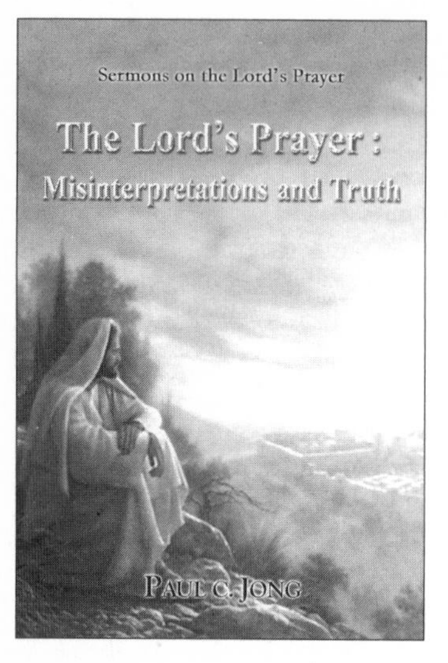

In order to interpret the Lord's Prayer correctly, we must first correctly understand the gospel of the water and the Spirit, which was spoken to us by the Lord. We have Truth in us when we not only know and understand the gospel of the water and the Spirit but also believe it with our hearts. The true gospel, which we believe in, has led us so far, so that we can lead truly faithful lives that the Lord wants from us in the Lord's Prayer.

Exegesis on the Book of ROMANS (I)

The righteousness of God is transparent. God's righteousness cannot be substituted by anything. That is because His righteousness is different from the righteousness of man. We need to know what God's righteousness is, and we need to believe in it.

God's righteousness is fundamentally different from human righteousness. The righteousness of mankind is like a filthy rag, but the righteousness of God is like a brilliant pearl shining forever. God's righteousness is the Truth that is absolutely needed by every sinner, transcending all ages.

HAVE YOU MET JESUS WITH THE GOSPEL OF THE WATER AND THE SPIRIT?

It is written, "No one has seen God at any time. The only begotten Son, who is in the bosom of the Father, He has declared Him" (John 1:18).

How perfectly did Jesus reveal the love of God to us! How perfectly did Jesus deliver us! What perfect Truth of salvation is the gospel of the water and the Spirit! We have never regretted receiving our salvation through our faith in Jesus, who came by water and blood (1 John 5:6).

Now, we have become His sinless people. Whoever believes in the gospel of the water and the Spirit can receive the eternal remission of sins and earn eternal life.

Sermons on the Gospel of Luke (I), (II), (III), (IV), (V), (VI), (VII)

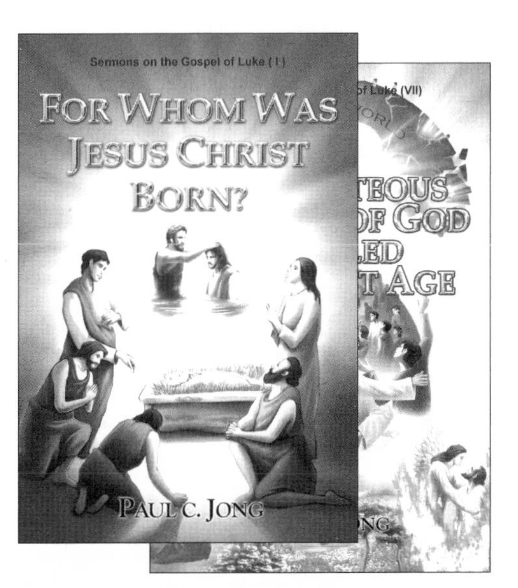

It is Jesus Christ who moves the entire history of this world. Our Lord came to this earth to save all humans from the sins of the world, and He has become the bread of new life for those of us who believe in the gospel of the water and the Spirit. In fact, it was to give this new life to us, who were all destined to hell for our sins that our Lord came looking for you and me.

Paul C. Jong's Christian books have been translated into 64 major languages at this point: Afrikaans, Albanian, Arabic, Bengali, Bulgarian, Burmese, Cebuano, Chichewa, Chin, Chinese, Croatian, Czech, Danish, Dioula, Dutch, English, French, Georgian, German, Greek, Gujarati, Hebrew, Hindi, Hungarian, Indonesian, Iranian, Italian, Japanese, Javanese, Kannada, Khmer, Kirghiz, Kirundi, Latvian, Luganda, Luo, Madi, Malagasy, Malayalam, Marathi, Mindat, Mizo, Mongolian, Nepali, Polish, Portuguese, Romanian, Russian, Serbian, Shona, Slovak, Slovene, Spanish, Swahili, Swedish, Tagalog, Taiwanese, Tamil, Telugu, Thai, Turkish, Ukrainian, Urdu, Vietnamese, and Zou. They are also available now through our free e-book service.

E-book is digital book designed for you to feel a printed book on screen. You can read it easily on your PC monitor in your native language after downloading the viewer software and a text file. Feel free to visit our web site at http://www.nlmission.com or http://www.bjnewlife.org to download our e-books, and you will get the most remarkable Christian e-books absolutely for free.

And, would you like to take part in having our free Christian books known to more people worldwide? We would be very thankful if you link your website to ours so that many people get an opportunity to meet Jesus Christ through our inspired Christian books. Please visit our site at http://www.bjnewlife.org/english/about/take_banners.php to take our banners to your website. In addition, we would be also very thankful if you introduce our website to the webmasters around you for adding our link.

The New Life Mission
Contact: John Shin, General Secretary
E-mail: newlife@bjnewlife.org

Memo